ON PHILOSOPHY AND PHl

CH00731564

On Philosophy and Philosophers is a volume of unpublished philosophical papers by Richard Rorty, a central figure in late twentieth-century intellectual debates and primary force behind the resurgence of American pragmatism. The first collection of new work to appear since his death in 2007, these previously unseen papers advance novel views on metaphysics, ethics, epistemology, philosophical semantics, and the social role of philosophy, critically engaging canonical and contemporary figures from Plato and Kant to Kripke and Brandom. This book's diverse offerings, which include technical essays written for specialists and popular lectures, refine our understanding of Rorty's perspective and demonstrate the ongoing relevance of the iconoclastic American philosopher's ground-breaking thought. An introduction by the editors highlights the papers' original insights and contributions to contemporary debates.

RICHARD RORTY (1931–2007) was Professor of Philosophy and Comparative Literature at Stanford University.

WOJCIECH "W. P." MAŁECKI is Assistant Professor of Literary Theory at the University of Wrocław, Poland.

CHRIS VOPARIL teaches philosophy and political theory at the Graduate College of Union Institute & University, Ohio.

ON PHILOSOPHY AND PHILOSOPHERS

Unpublished Papers, 1960–2000

RICHARD RORTY

W. P. MAŁECKI
University of Wrocław, Poland

CHRIS VOPARIL
Union Institute & University, Ohio

CAMBRIDGE
UNIVERSITY PRESS

CAMBRIDGE
UNIVERSITY PRESS

University Printing House, Cambridge CB2 8BS, United Kingdom

One Liberty Plaza, 20th Floor, New York, NY 10006, USA

477 Williamstown Road, Port Melbourne, VIC 3207, Australia

314–321, 3rd Floor, Plot 3, Splendor Forum, Jasola District Centre, New Delhi – 110025, India

79 Anson Road, #06–04/06, Singapore 079906

Cambridge University Press is part of the University of Cambridge.

It furthers the University's mission by disseminating knowledge in the pursuit of education, learning, and research at the highest international levels of excellence.

www.cambridge.org
Information on this title: www.cambridge.org/9781108488457
DOI: 10.1017/9781108763967

© Richard Rorty, W. P. Małecki and Chris Voparil 2020

This publication is in copyright. Subject to statutory exception and to the provisions of relevant collective licensing agreements, no reproduction of any part may take place without the written permission of Cambridge University Press.

First published 2020

Printed in the United Kingdom by TJ International Ltd, Padstow Cornwall

A catalogue record for this publication is available from the British Library.

Library of Congress Cataloging-in-Publication Data
NAMES: Rorty, Richard, author. | Voparil, Christopher J., 1969– editor. | Malecki, Wojciech, editor.
TITLE: On philosophy and philosophers : unpublished papers, 1960–2000 / Richard Rorty ; Christopher Voparil, Union Institute and University, Ohio, Wojciech Malecki, University of Wroclaw, Poland, [editors].
DESCRIPTION: Cambridge, United Kingdom ; New York, NY, USA : Cambridge University Press, 2020. | Includes index.
IDENTIFIERS: LCCN 2019042271 (print) | LCCN 2019042272 (ebook) | ISBN 9781108488457 (hardback) | ISBN 9781108763967 (ebook)
SUBJECTS: LCSH: Philosophy. | Philosophers.
CLASSIFICATION: LCC B945.R521 V67 2020 (print) | LCC B945.R521 (ebook) | DDC 191–dc23
LC record available at https://lccn.loc.gov/2019042271
LC ebook record available at https://lccn.loc.gov/2019042272

ISBN 978-1-108-48845-7 Hardback
ISBN 978-1-108-72636-8 Paperback

Cambridge University Press has no responsibility for the persistence or accuracy of URLs for external or third-party internet websites referred to in this publication and does not guarantee that any content on such websites is, or will remain, accurate or appropriate.

Contents

Acknowledgments

The editors would like to thank several individuals who helped us during the seven-year period of this volume's gestation. First of all, we would like to thank Mary Varney Rorty, who supported the project from the very beginning and saw it through its various stages. Second, we would like to thank the staff of the UC Irvine Special Collections and Archives, Critical Theory Archive, where the Richard Rorty Papers are located, in particular, Steven McLeod and Audra Eagle Yun. A word of thanks is also due to our colleague and friend, Colin Koopman, who was part of the initial editorial team when we first visited the archive. We owe a lot to his advice and critical insights over the years. We are grateful to our editor at Cambridge, Hilary Gaskin, for her enthusiasm for the project, and the anonymous reviewers of our proposal for their useful comments. Richard Bernstein, Rorty's lifelong friend, provided sound advice and generously responded to questions. Finally, we would like to acknowledge the help of Samuel Lelievre, Angel Lemke, Katarzyna Lisowska, Carlin Romano, Amie Thomasson, and Jarosław Woźniak in preparing the manuscript for publication.

Note on Sources

The essays collected in this volume are based on print or electronic documents from the Richard Rorty Papers, MS-C017, Special Collections and Archives, the UC Irvine Libraries, Irvine, California. As far as we have been able to determine, Rorty did not leave instructions regarding the future of these papers, nor any explanation for why they never left the drawer. In our judgment, considerations of quality alone fail to account for this fate. By and large, the papers match the general standard of work that appeared in print during his lifetime. Some are as good as his best published output. We think that the fate of most of these papers had to do with the fact that they were written for particular occasions – conferences and invited talks. In such cases, where no immediate arrangement for publication was in place, it is likely Rorty simply moved on to more urgent tasks and new invitations.

Independently of their scholarly quality, all of the essays demanded editorial work, to varying degrees. Our interventions were never substantive. Typically, they were limited to correcting obvious typographical errors and adding missing references for quotations. In these cases we did not mark such interventions in the manuscript.

The minimal editorial interventions we made in preparing the papers fell into two categories. First, for consistency with the volumes of Rorty's philosophical papers previously published by Cambridge, we removed obvious traces of the papers' original contexts of presentation. For instance, in some manuscripts Rorty refers to various authors as Professor X or Y (e.g., "Professor Ricoeur"), apparently because he expected them to be present in the audience. In another manuscript, Rorty refers to Alvin Goldman's paper, "The Relation between Epistemology and Psychology," as "today's paper" since it was part of a conference at which Rorty's remarks were given. "Professor Ricoeur" was changed to "Ricoeur," "the paper given today" to "The Relation between Epistemology and Psychology," etc. In many manuscripts, Rorty used contractions characteristic of spoken English ("I'm," "isn't," etc.), which he normally did not use in print. These were modified to make them consistent with his published work. These editorial interventions were limited to *obvious* traces of oral presentation that could be changed without affecting the content and tone of the text. We did not intervene in the style or syntax, which are sometimes rather casual.

The second type of intervention that demands a word of explanation relates to Rorty's famous habit of name-dropping, where he would simply say that a given thinker (e.g., Derrida, Foucault, or Quine) claims *p* or *q* without giving any reference to the relevant work by that author or even his or her first name. Normally, an editor's job would be to locate the relevant source and add the first name of a given author when he or she is cited the first time. However, since Rorty's practice of name-dropping was a characteristic element of his style, we usually chose not to do so. The exceptions were authors such as, for example, Wolfgang Stegmüller, who, while quite possibly familiar to Rorty's audience at the time, would be obscure to most of today's readers. In those cases we decided to add their first names and references to the works Rorty most likely had in mind, distinguishing our footnotes from Rorty's with "– *Eds.*" Where the typescripts contain Rorty's handwritten corrections or additions, we treated these as expressing his intentions for the final version and have incorporated them into the text.

A word is also due on our dating of the papers. In some cases, dates were given by Rorty himself directly in the manuscripts. In others, dates could be surmised from events where a paper was presented or from other circumstantial evidence. In several cases, a time frame could be narrowed but not precisely determined. For instance, we were unable to establish exactly when Rorty wrote his "Reductionism" paper, but since he focuses there on J. O. Urmson's 1956 book, *Philosophical Analysis,* treating it as a recent publication, and refers to "what Bergmann calls the 'linguistic turn'," a phrase first used by Bergmann in print in a 1960 book review, it was likely written in the early 1960s. Below we provide what we have been able to gather about dates and occasions of the papers. For physical copies, we indicate the box and folder location in the Richard Rorty Papers (e.g., "B44, F12"); for digital files, we note availability in the "born-digital" online collection ("b.d."), which begins in 1988. Several born-digital texts also appear in hard copy. Five papers bore no title in the original. For these, titles were added using Rorty's own phrases from each piece. These are "Philosophy as Ethics"; "Philosophy as Spectatorship and Participation"; "Phenomenology, Linguistic Analysis, and Cartesianism"; "Philosophy as Epistemology"; and "Brandom's Conversationalism."

1. "Philosophy as Ethics" (B44, F12) is an undated manuscript from a manual typewriter that we have narrowed to the early 1960s or, possibly, the late 1950s. The version reproduced here includes two pages of Rorty's handwritten text we found appended to the typescript.[1]

2. "Philosophy as Spectatorship and Participation" (B44, F12) is an untitled, undated manuscript typed on loose-leaf paper with heavy handwritten edits throughout. Since Rorty alludes to the "excitement over existentialism at the present time," and we know he was interested in existentialism already in the 1950s, we conjecture that this paper is most likely from the early 1960s, maybe the late 1950s.[2]

3. "Kant as a Critical Philosopher" (B44, F12; B8, F17), an undated, typed manuscript, was initially prepared as a talk, with significant editing in Rorty's own hand, from the same period as the first two papers. We encountered an additional, also undated, partial version of the first six pages in a different folder that had been retyped to incorporate the handwritten edits on the original copy.

4. "The Paradox of Definitism" (B10, F4), a similar typed manuscript, dates either from the late 1950s or early 1960s.[3] This manuscript contains typed subscript numbers that indicate footnotes, but unfortunately we were unable to locate the content of the notes. We kept the footnotes attached to quotations and used them to provide a reference for the quote; the rest have been removed from the published version.

5. "Reductionism" (B12, F1) is a typed manuscript with minor handwritten edits, likely from the early 1960s, as we explain above.[4]

6. "Phenomenology, Linguistic Analysis, and Cartesianism: Comments on Ricoeur" (B13, F14) is Rorty's typed remarks on Paul Ricoeur's paper, "Husserl and Wittgenstein on Language," delivered at the

---

[1] According to archive notes, the first three papers in this volume originally were in an undated folder of Rorty's labeled "Popular Lectures." See *Guide to the Richard Rorty Papers MS.C.017*: www .oac.cdlib.org/findaid/ark:/13030/kt9p3038mq/dsc/, accessed June 19, 2019.

[2] Rorty indicated his interest in existentialism in a draft of his application letter to Yale's PhD program, which he entered in 1952. See Neil Gross, *Richard Rorty: The Making of an American Philosopher* (Chicago: University of Chicago Press, 2008), 137.

[3] In the paper, Rorty treats the debate in the early fifties over the so-called prediction paradox as a live topic, calls an argument made by P. F. Strawson in a 1956 paper "recent," and does not cite any publication later than 1956.

[4] Cf. Rorty's 1961 paper, "The Limits of Reductionism," recently republished in Richard Rorty, *Mind, Language, and Metaphilosophy: Early Philosophical Papers*, ed. Stephen Leach and James Tartaglia (New York: Cambridge University Press, 2014), 39–54.

Society for Phenomenology and Existential Philosophy meeting on October 22, 1966.[5]

7. "The Incommunicability of 'Felt Qualities'" (B8, F8) was given at the Pacific Division of the American Philosophical Association meeting in 1968.[6]

8. "Kripke on Mind-Body Identity" (B8, F18) is mimeographed text of a lecture given at the State University of New York at Binghamton in April 1973, with minor handwritten edits.[7]

9. "Philosophy as Epistemology: Reply to Hacking and Kim" (B12, F12) was prepared for an APA Eastern Division symposium on *Philosophy and the Mirror of Nature* that took place on December 30, 1980. Wilfrid Sellars chaired the panel, and Ian Hacking and Jaegwon Kim presented papers, which were later published.[8] Rorty's in-depth reply has never appeared in print.

10. "Naturalized Epistemology and Norms: Replies to Goldman and Fodor" (B13, F13) was delivered at a conference on "Cognitive Psychology and the New Epistemology" held at Loyola University of Chicago on March 6, 1982. Rorty's lecture includes responses to papers by Jerry Fodor and Alvin Goldman that preceded his on the program.

11. "The Objectivity of Values" (b.d.) is a curious case in that it exists only as a born-digital file tagged with the date January 25, 2000. However, internal textual evidence suggests a much earlier provenance; we believe it dates to 1981.[9]

12. "What Is Dead in Plato" (b.d.; B12, F11) is an address prepared for a February 1988 event featuring political theorist Dante Germino.

13. "The Current State of Philosophy in the U.S." (B7, F9) is a lecture that Rorty dated September 22, 1994. Handwritten notes at the top suggest that it was given on more than one occasion.

---

[5] For the program of the symposium on "The Philosophy of Language: Husserl and Wittgenstein," see *The Journal of Philosophy* 63, no. 15 (1966), 452.

[6] See "News and Notes," *Philosophy East and West* 19, no. 1 (1969), 113–114. The reading of Wittgenstein Rorty develops here is marshaled to evaluate the perspectives of Pitcher and Cook in Rorty's 1970 article, "Wittgenstein, Privileged Access, and Incommunicability," reprinted in *Mind, Language, and Metaphilosophy.*

[7] Correspondence indicates that Rorty was invited by Theodore Mischel (see B8, F18).

[8] See Ian Hacking, "Is the End in Sight for Epistemology?," *The Journal of Philosophy* 77, no. 10 (1980): 579–588; and Jaegwon Kim, "Rorty on the Possibility of Philosophy," *The Journal of Philosophy* 77, no. 10 (1980): 588–597.

[9] At the end of the text, Rorty lists his affiliation as "Princeton University," where he taught from 1961 to 1982, and refers to "the late J. L. Mackie of Oxford," who passed away in 1981.

14. "Brandom's Conversationalism: Davidson and *Making It Explicit*" (b.d.; B13, F9) was prepared for an Author Meets Critics session on Robert Brandom's book at the APA Pacific Division meeting on March 31, 1995.

15. "Bald Naturalism and McDowell's Hylomorphism" (b.d.) was given at Columbia University on August 3, 1995.[10]

16. "Reductionist vs. Neo-Wittgensteinian Semantics" (b.d.) is a paper prepared in 2000.

17. "Remarks on Nishida and Nishitani" (b.d.; B13, F21) is the text, dated September 1, 1999, of the introductory lecture delivered the same year at Otani University in Japan.

---

[10] See Lance P. Hickey, *Hilary Putnam* (London: Continuum, 2009), 187.

Introduction: Rorty as a Critical Philosopher

W. P. Małecki and Chris Voparil

Among influential philosophers there are those who publish little and those who publish a lot. If Ludwig Wittgenstein and Edmund Gettier belong to the first group, the second includes, for instance, Jacques Derrida, Jürgen Habermas, and the provocative and prolific gadfly of American philosophy, Richard Rorty. In his lifetime, Rorty published hundreds of articles and more than a dozen books – so much that it is hard to imagine that he might have had the time to pen anything of philosophical value of which we are unaware. Yet, stacked in the Richard Rorty Papers archive at the University of California, Irvine, are dozens of boxes of such material. Some of these boxes contain lecture notes or early sketches of ideas, but others enclose fully developed philosophical papers that with only minor edits are publication worthy. This volume presents the material in the latter category.

The unpublished papers collected here span four decades of Rorty's philosophy. In the eighteen essays that follow, the reader will encounter instances of Rorty's initial forays of the early 1960s into metaphilosophy and the sweeping sort of *Geistesgeschichte* he admired in Hegel and Whitehead; crisply argued technical tracts characteristic of his first dip into analytic philosophy of language and of mind in the mid-1960s[1]; recognizable anti-Cartesian and anti-Kantian critiques of traditional metaphysics and epistemology; reflections on the state of philosophy at particular historical moments; and, of course, spirited engagements with philosophical friends and foes over the years. Rorty was profoundly at home in the essay form, and it shows. The sparkling prose, with its sharp sarcasm, lively wit, fresh turns of phrase, and against-the-grain interpretations that rankled, informed, and entertained generations of readers are on

---

[1] For Rorty's less familiar early published work, see his *Mind, Language, and Metaphilosophy: Early Philosophical Papers*, ed. Stephen Leach and James Tartaglia (New York: Cambridge University Press, 2014).

full display here. Even when writing on topics or thinkers not encountered in his published oeuvre, the signature style of the revered and reviled authorial voice that made Rorty one of the most-read and written-about philosophers of his generation graces these pages.

These papers also are noteworthy for new and often more acute angles on philosophical issues that are treated less extensively, or merely touched on, in his published output. Among the essays included here are inquiries into philosophical topics such as existentialism, the incommunicability of felt qualities, the objectivity of values, and naturalized epistemology. They also feature what are, to our best knowledge, the only papers Rorty devoted entirely to certain philosophical figures such as Plato, Kant, Sartre, Kripke, and Ricoeur. A 1999 paper offers what may be Rorty's most in-depth engagement with non-Western philosophers: Nishida Kitarō and Nishitani Keiji of the Kyoto School. The opening essay, "Philosophy as Ethics," offers an overarching frame which establishes the continuity of concerns that seem to emerge only later in his published writings. Virtually all chapters provide important insights into Rorty's philosophy; many provide important insights of general philosophical interest, and some offer both at the same time.

Chief among the papers that both illuminate Rorty's own thinking and feature bona fide philosophical contributions is "Kant as a Critical Philosopher" (Chapter 3). This essay presents an original notion of critical philosophy that enables Rorty to shed new light on Kant, as well as on the wider history of Western philosophy. He achieves this by depicting interesting analogies among Kant, Aristotle, and Wittgenstein, all of whom he considers critical philosophers. Briefly put, a critical philosopher aims to present a vocabulary that will invalidate both skeptical attempts at undermining a given datum and foundationalist attempts at grounding it, where this datum can be anything from "the common moral consciousness" to "the science and the mathematics" of one's day. The central aim of Aristotle, Kant, and Wittgenstein was precisely to develop a vocabulary of this kind – a vocabulary targeting two kinds of opponents, foundationalists and skeptics – and it is for this reason their philosophies provoke similar reactions. It is "much easier to know what they were against than to know what they were for; further," Rorty continues, "it is very hard to formulate even their criticisms of either one of their respective opponents. Whenever one tries, one finds oneself saying things that cannot be reconciled with their criticisms of the other of their respective opponents."

Anyone familiar with the reception of Rorty's work will recognize in those kinds of reactions the retorts his own philosophy provoked over the decades. Here the category of critical philosopher allows us to better understand Rorty's philosophy itself. For one thing, it elucidates the positive remarks on Aristotle and Kant scattered throughout Rorty's later oeuvre, which might otherwise seem puzzling given his familiar negative attitudes toward those thinkers. More importantly, it brings into sharper relief both the common core of Rorty's work across his career and an important shift that begins in the late 1960s and culminates in *Philosophy and the Mirror of Nature*, dividing his work into two recognizably different phases.

There was a time when secondary literature on Rorty portrayed this shift in terms of an orthodox analytic philosopher losing the faith and suddenly turning pragmatist. That narrative was later shown to be inaccurate. Rorty, in fact, was interested and versed in pragmatism even before becoming an analytic philosopher. Even during the period when his analytic essays began to garner recognition, present in his work already were pragmatist premises that became his trademark only later.[2] Since then, specialists have been debating the exact nature of the shift.[3] The category of critical philosophy can usefully contribute to these debates. That is, one can explain the nature of Rorty's shift by saying that while both in his early and later periods Rorty was primarily a critical philosopher, in the former period he pursued a local version of critical philosophy while in the latter a global one.

What is meant by "local" here is that in his early period Rorty pursued critical philosophy *within* the bounds of philosophy as it had been traditionally practiced in the West. He was arguing for vocabularies that allowed for the dissolution of certain attempts to undermine or ground given data, and saw this is as a contribution to philosophical progress. This is the Rorty who wrote like a professional philosopher and thought that

---

[2] See, for example, Neil Gross, *Richard Rorty: The Making of an American Philosopher* (Chicago: University of Chicago Press, 2008). For a fuller account of Rorty's philosophical development than we can provide here, see *The Rorty Reader*, ed. Christopher J. Voparil and Richard J. Bernstein (Malden, MA: Wiley-Blackwell, 2010).

[3] The difficulty with pinpointing this shift more precisely is that it is not a sharp break but a development that unfolds over time. Already in his introduction to *The Linguistic Turn*, Rorty highlighted key "difficulties" inherent in the turn to linguistic methods in analytic philosophy, difficulties that were both metaphilosophical – outlined already in his essays of the early 1960s – and epistemological, stemming from the critique of the spectatorial account of knowledge common to "Dewey, Hampshire, Sartre, Heidegger, and Wittgenstein." See *The Linguistic Turn: Recent Essays in Philosophical Method*, ed. Richard Rorty (Chicago: University of Chicago Press, 1967), 39n75, and *passim*. As he developed a full account of this epistemological critique and its implications, eventually published as *Philosophy and the Mirror of Nature*, Rorty continued to publish in an analytic style roughly until the mid-1970s.

philosophy, as practiced in his day, was important. What then happened was that Rorty came to believe that undermining and grounding were all that traditional Western philosophy consisted in, and that these goals are not worth pursuing at all. He thought that they were most likely unrealizable, given that no philosopher had hitherto succeeded at grounding or undermining anything, and that even if they were realizable, they could not help solve important social and political problems.

Rorty's critical philosophy then went global. Instead of offering vocabularies that aimed at dissolving particular instances of foundationalism and skepticism, he started offering vocabularies aimed at dissolving foundationalism and skepticism in general, that is, *globally*, and therefore at dissolving what he perceived to be traditional philosophy as such. This is the Rorty who stopped arguing like a professional philosopher and who thought that philosophy, as traditionally practiced in the West, had outlived its usefulness. This is the Rorty who advocated for a new philosophy with a different goal and method. The goal was to assist with existing projects of strengthening democratic attachments and to offer new visions of what such communal projects might look like. The method would be that of cultural criticism, an amalgam of cultural anthropology, literary criticism, and history. This pattern of switching from one mode of critical philosophy to the other is visible throughout Rorty's published work, as well as in the papers collected in this volume.

I Early Papers

The volume's first two essays, in particular, evidence the nature of Rorty's philosophical interests prior to his concerted effort to get himself up to speed on the analytic debates in which his new Princeton colleagues were so deeply engaged.[4] Already we see the influence of pragmatism on his thinking. Also unmistakable is his preoccupation with the ineluctability of choice amid pluralistic alternative viewpoints. In "Philosophy as Ethics," perhaps the most accessible piece in the volume, Rorty traces the historical origins of philosophy and the initial spur to philosophizing to the desire to justify values. In a Jamesian spirit, he underscores the futility of the two-

---

[4] Rorty himself described this effort of professional self-education, following his arrival at Princeton in 1961, as "striving to make myself over into some sort of analytic philosopher." "If I was going to win my colleagues' respect," he explained, "I had to speak to some of the issues with which they were concerned and to write in somewhat the same vein as they did." See Richard Rorty, "Intellectual Autobiography," in *The Philosophy of Richard Rorty: Library of Living Philosophers*, ed. Randall E. Auxier and Lewis Edwin Hahn (Chicago: Open Court, 2010), 13;11.

thousand-year-long "pathetic history" of failed attempts to justify ethical imperatives. Still, Rorty finds a positive lesson here, arguing that "a bad reason may be a good story." He uses James's theory of truth to show that there is a pragmatic way to argue an "ought" to an "is" that avoids problems associated with positivism and foundationalism.

"Philosophy as Spectatorship and Participation" (Chapter 2), Rorty's only extensive engagement with existentialism, reveals the influence the movement had on his thought, which hitherto only could be conjectured from the existentialist themes and references scattered throughout his other writings.[5] Its account of philosophy's conflicted ideals of detachment and engagement is both of general metaphilosophical value and particularly timely now, when philosophy is chided, on the one hand, for failing to contribute sufficiently to struggles for social justice and, on the other, for daring to contribute to them in the first place. Rorty argues that "the tension between being relevant and being rational, between immediacy and mediation, between participation and spectatorship is . . . *the* philosophical problem," and highlights existentialism's "refusal to seek for security through the quest for objectivity" as a unique break in the history of philosophy.

"Kant as Critical Philosopher" (Chapter 3) constitutes Rorty's only paper devoted exclusively to Kant and his most probing, sympathetic, and original account of the thinker. As discussed above, Rorty's novel take on Kant is based on a distinctive understanding of critical philosophy, which allows Rorty to do three things: first, to provide an explanation for the diversity of interpretations of Kant's oeuvre; second, to show striking analogies between Kant and other figures in the history of philosophy whom Rorty also classifies as critical philosophers, such as Aristotle and Wittgenstein; and, third, to highlight the lasting value of Kant's thought, which for Rorty is to "make it impossible" to think that "the task of philosophy is to provide constitutive principles which will back up regulative principles."

In "The Paradox of Definitism" and "Reductionism," Rorty begins to apply his early metaphilosophical insights to then-prominent topics in linguistic philosophy.[6] "The Paradox of Definitism" (Chapter 4) critiques modern philosophy's pervasive privileging, in metaphysics and epistemology, of sharp-edged definiteness over fuzzy indefiniteness, where the latter

---

[5] See, for example, the discussion of Sartre and "the 'existentialist' view of objectivity" in part three of Rorty's *Philosophy and the Mirror of Nature* (Princeton, NJ: Princeton University Press, 1979).

[6] These views are developed further in his introduction to *The Linguistic Turn*, by which time he already perceives the limitations of the linguistic project.

is deemed a function of human "ignorance and confusion," rather than, with Aristotle, seen as something existing in nature. Dubbing this bias "definitism," he characterizes it as "the view that there is nothing which can reasonably be called a statement which is neither true nor false." "The resurrection of pragmatism," he argues, with its contextualism, "has been causing trouble for definitists." But he also invites definitists into the pragmatist camp to avoid the paradox they face by recognizing Dewey's insight that "every transaction will involve both fuzzy and non-fuzzy elements" and Peirce's view of logic "as a normative rather than a descriptive discipline."

"Reductionism" (Chapter 5) takes up the question, "Can we abandon reductive analysis as a method of philosophical discovery and still keep the intellectual gains which have accrued from its employment as a method of deciding what questions to discuss?" After presenting the twentieth-century program of reductive linguistic analysis as a mature form of the seventeenth century's "reductionist conception" of the goal of inquiry, he examines J. O. Urmson's arguments, ultimately concluding that he "fails to take account" of "the cases in which reductive analysis is applied to the technical vocabularies of philosophers." Even though he agrees with Urmson that most reductive analyses, judged by their own standards, are unsuccessful, Rorty nevertheless thinks a basis for distinguishing useful from useless analyses is possible. We also see here Rorty's early interest in eliminability, which shortly thereafter becomes the basis for a distinctive contribution.[7]

In "Phenomenology, Linguistic Analysis, and Cartesianism," Rorty explains why he remained uninterested in Paul Ricoeur's hermeneutics. This piece converges nicely with the Kant essay in presenting the "contest between phenomenology and linguistic analysis as a competition between two groups of opponents of a single enemy" – Cartesianism. Rorty judges the linguistic analysts to be the better candidate of the two to lead "the anti-Cartesian revolution," and distills their position to three central metaphilosophical claims: the Pragmatist thesis; the Naturalistic thesis; and the Conventionalist thesis. He uses this platform to critique Ricoeur's phenomenological approach to problems in the philosophy of language.

"The Incommunicability of 'Felt Qualities'" (Chapter 7) focuses on the claim that has been at the center of many debates generated by Wittgenstein's *Philosophical Investigations*: that "we cannot communicate certain qualities" – for example, the special felt qualities of toothache – to

---

[7] See his "In Defense of Eliminative Materialism," *Review of Metaphysics* 24, no. 1 (1970): 112–121.

others. Rorty suggests that philosophers have been making too much of that claim. Instead, he argues that it is true only in a "philosophically innocuous" sense – we can never be sure whether we mean or know the same thing in describing "X" – and false when it becomes philosophically interesting, since using the noun *toothache* correctly in relevant circumstances denotes knowledge of the term, even if the felt qualities of a toothache were never experienced. By focusing on language use, Rorty alleviates the philosophical controversy and the threat of epistemological skepticism, concluding that we need deny "neither the existence of a perfectly good sense of 'know' in which there can be prelinguistic or nonlinguistic knowledge (or 'awareness' or 'consciousness'), nor the existence of unshareable mental particulars to which we have privileged access."

Rorty offers his most extensive and systematic treatment of Saul Kripke's work in "Kripke on Mind-Body Identity" (Chapter 8). He puts Kripke's arguments back into an often overlooked historical and philosophical context that sheds new light on their viability and overall significance. Anyone interested in mind-brain identity theory, in particular, who think it was shown to be untenable by Kripke's criticisms and remain puzzled by it still being alive and well will profit from Rorty's explanations why those criticisms, in fact, must "leave the issue about mind-body identity where it stood." Rorty predicts that in the wake of Kripke's criticisms, "the old issues will go over into the new vocabulary – with less talk about meaning and more about reference, but without dialectical loss to either side."

II Later Papers

In the essays that comprise the second part of the volume, there appear similar figures, conceptions, and arguments, but the tone is remarkably different, reflecting Rorty's switch from a local to a global version of critical philosophy. Virtually all of these essays provide critiques of certain projects within the philosophy of Rorty's time, but do so mainly to show that philosophy, as then practiced, needs to be abandoned. The projects are both skeptical and foundational, and include the attempts at renewing epistemology by Hacking and Kim and by Goldman and Fodor (Chapters 9 and 10), J. L. Mackie's moral skepticism (Chapter 11), Crispin Wright's and Bernard Williams's brand of realism (Chapter 14), the bald naturalism of John McDowell (Chapter 15), the reductionist semantics of "David Lewis, Saul Kripke, David Kaplan, and John Perry" (Chapter 16), and

Nishida Kitarō and Nishitani Keiji's brands of absolute idealism (Chapter 17).

Rorty aims to show that all these projects, however clever and intricate, amount to wasting intellectual energy on something of no real practical value. This is because, Rorty reiterates, the problems that these projects tackle are, most likely, insoluble, and even if they could be solved, the solutions would have no bearing on social life. Consider questions such as whether the world can "exert rational control on the mind" or whether "moral values are 'out there' or are just 'in us'" (Chapters 11 and 14). These problems will only be important to those who believe in outdated doctrines such as Aristotelian hylomorphism or the "seventeenth-century notion that what science does not know about is not real," and so will their solutions. In this sense, these and other problems of mainstream philosophy are like the problems of alchemy or scholastic philosophy; they should simply be left behind. In "Naturalized Epistemology and Norms," for instance, Rorty admits that Goldman succeeds in demonstrating "the relevance of psychology to epistemology," but he sees this as something akin to having successfully demonstrated "the relevance of particle physics to alchemy." Similarly, in "The Current State of Philosophy in the United States" (Chapter 13), Rorty admits that many analytic philosophers are "skilled, hard-working, enthusiastic, professionals" but stresses that this in itself does not mean that the problems they tackle are important. After all, there were many such people among seventeenth-century physicists discussing "how to use terms like 'natural motion,' 'violent motion,' 'quantity of motion,'" and "'inertia'"; or among theologians discussing "how many sacraments Christ instituted." Yet the problems they focused on seem merely quaint today.

Instead of tackling such problems, Rorty would want contemporary philosophers to contribute to the "furtherance" of "the projects of social cooperation (building an egalitarian, classless, casteless, society, for example)" by pursuing cultural criticism. He tries to set an example by engaging in cultural criticism himself, in the form of "explaining to people why philosophy will not do some of the things sometimes expected of it." The explanations Rorty offers in the second part of the volume take the form of sweeping narratives on the history of philosophy in general and the history of analytic philosophy in particular. By Rorty's account, the reason why analytic philosophy is socially useless is not only that it is preoccupied with a set of hopeless problems it inherited from the philosophical tradition (see "What Is Dead in Plato"), but also because it was invented as a way to put philosophy on "the secure path of a science" ("The Current State of

Philosophy in the United States") and thereby to separate it from history, literature, and politics.

It needs to be stressed here, however, that the picture of analytic philosophy painted by Rorty is not entirely grim, as he thinks there are analytic philosophers who escape the aforementioned dynamic. Rorty focuses in particular on Donald Davidson and Robert Brandom, situating them within the tradition of philosophical pragmatism and reconstructing its history (see Chapters 13, 14, 15, 16, and 17). He sees its origin in the classical pragmatists' project of combining Hegel and Darwin in order to develop a "thoroughly secularized philosophy" that would "contribute to efforts to make this world better, rather than deferring human hope to another world" ("Remarks on Nishida and Nishitani"). And he sees its contemporary manifestations in Davidson's and Brandom's attempts at naturalizing the philosophy of mind and philosophy of language (Chapters 14, 15, 16). In "Brandom's Conversationalism" (Chapter 14), he argues that these attempts allow us to eschew "the Platonic/Aristotelian account of human beings as distinguished from the brutes by their ability to penetrate through appearance to reality," along with a whole gamut of pointless debates this account generated, such as those between realists and anti-realists or empiricists and rationalists. It is to the full sweep of the pragmatic tradition, then, that Rorty looks for the seeds of philosophy's much needed change.

Now, one might argue that this picture has in many ways become obsolete. These days, after all, there are quite a few analytic philosophers directly concerned with urgent social problems. But one might still say that the picture retains its accuracy in the sense of warning us against the uncritical belief that philosophers can significantly contribute to solving today's social problems by working on the philosophical problems of yesteryear, the problems bequeathed to us precisely by the philosophical tradition Rorty is after. In addressing X or Y social problem, it is always tempting for a philosopher to start out by addressing the epistemology or ontology of X or Y, and to then circle around a set of old ontological and epistemological conundrums. One lesson which flows from Rorty's papers is that philosophers should cease taking for granted that their inquiries into the ontology or epistemology of a social issue will yield concrete results in a timely fashion and that such results, if obtained, might have any bearing on how that issue can be solved in practice. They should be more cautious than that. This is, as we hope to have shown, but one of the many important lessons offered by the essays collected in this volume.

I

Early Papers

Philosophy as Ethics

Philosophers suffer from a peculiar occupational hazard; people are always coming up and asking them just what it is that they do and how they do it. This is not the sort of question that biologists or economists or musicians get asked; people know, pretty well, what they do, and they may or may not be interested in the details. But a philosopher is different – it is very hard to imagine just what he does with his time.

In the first half of this paper, I want to give a very rough answer to the question of what philosophers do. This will, of necessity, be a historical answer. This is because there is no such thing as "philosophy" or "the philosopher" – there is simply what various people who were called philosophers have said or done at various times. In the course of trying to answer this question, some of the problems which philosophers face in justifying their existence will come to light. In the second half of the paper, I will try to indicate how I think one can avoid some of these problems.

Philosophy as opposed to science began, I think, when men began trying to justify their values. Thales, who became immortal by casually remarking that everything was water, is sometimes called the first philosopher. But, it seems to me that all Thales rates for this remark is the honor of founding science. It is Socrates, rather than Thales, who first asked philosophic questions – because it was Socrates who first asked, in full seriousness, how he could be sure that the values which he cherished were the right values. When Plato told us that there must be things called Forms, for if there were not we could never hope to know whether we were truly living well or not, he gave the first distinctively philosophic theory. It was philosophic because it was an answer to Socrates's question – a question about what we ought to do.

Not only is this where philosophy itself began but, I should suspect, it is also where every philosopher's interest in philosophy begins. Perhaps there are people who embark on the study of philosophy because they are worried about whether the external world really exists, or whether they can tell the difference between dreaming and being awake, or whether it is OK to argue in syllogisms, but I have never met any. Although one can, once one gets started, become thoroughly engrossed in any of these problems, one never starts with them. One starts with ethics; that is, one starts with the realization that not everyone has the same values as oneself and the hope that one will find some way to justify one's own values. This realization may occur in the toils of an actual moral dilemma, or in finding that a friend cannot see any point in a novel you admire, or in any other of an almost infinite variety of ways. Whatever there is in us that makes us want to fit every part of our experience together with every other part makes us also try to fit our values, our goals, our attitudes toward other people, into some larger scheme. The attempt to do this – to justify theses values and goals and attitudes is, I think, what starts people studying philosophy.

I would further want to suggest that the rest of the so-called branches of philosophy have evolved out of ethics. Simple curiosity and wonder have, of course, played their role in developing metaphysics, logic, and the theory of knowledge; but, although I cannot argue the point here, I would suggest that the ways in which these subjects have actually developed in the history of philosophy shows that the real motive behind them was the need to justify certain values. Although I cannot hope to show this, I can support it indirectly by noting that as soon as a set of problems ceases to be relevant to ethics, it ceases to be thought of as part of philosophy. I think that this can be seen in the history of what the word "philosophy" has meant. At the end of the Middle Ages, practically everything that we would now think of as "the sciences" – natural and social – was part of philosophy. Gradually, one by one, what we now call the sciences began to develop individual identities and to set up shop for themselves. This happened, I think, at the stage when it was realized that the subject matter of this science was not directly relevant to the choice between competing values. For example, physics became an independent field of inquiry in the seventeenth century not because it developed a brand-new method, or a sudden clarity and precision which philosophy had lacked, but because men came to see that the problem, for instance, of whether the earth went around the sun or vice versa was quite irrelevant to the problem of how they should conduct themselves. The controversy about the Copernican theory ceased to be a matter for the theologians and the philosophers and became a matter for the astronomers, when, and only when, the theologians and the philosophers realized that God's glory was reflected just as well by the Copernican as by the Ptolemaic theory and that the adoption of a model of the universe in which the earth moved around the sun need not really change our values. In other words, it ceased to be a philosophic question when it ceased to have ethical implications.

The evolution controversy in the last century is another example of this situation. As long as it seemed that from "Man is descended from monkeys" one could infer "Man has no reason not to act like a monkey," evolution was a philosophical issue, suitable for being discussed by bishops and professors of metaphysics. After it became clear that no such inference was possible or necessary, it became an issue for zoologists, and geology ceased once and for all to be a part of philosophy.

Even in our own century we have seen this process of disciplines falling away from philosophy as their irrelevance to ethics became obvious. What we now call psychology was taught in the philosophy departments as long as people thought that some new finding about the functioning of the brain could refute, or support, what Plato had said about knowledge or what St. Augustine said about freedom. When it became clear that men would face exactly the same problems about values on exactly the same terms, no matter what was discovered about their nervous system, psychology moved into the laboratories, and the philosophy departments had their appropriations cut in order to pay for those laboratories.

The very latest branch of philosophy to proclaim its independence is logic. Logic is still taught by philosophers, but in fifty years it will probably be taught exclusively by the mathematicians. As long as logic was supposed to be about the Laws of Thought, and these were supposed to somehow be cousins of the Laws of Being and the Moral Law, logic was naturally a philosophical matter. Now that formal logic has become largely a matter of arranging symbols in different way, and inventing new symbols in terms of which old symbols can be defined, the mathematicians, who are good at that sort of thing, have taken it over. What is interesting is that philosophers do not mind this very much. Once it becomes clear that formal logic is no more helpful than brain physiology in supporting what we want to say about right and wrong, philosophers tend to lose interest.

About all that the philosopher in our day can claim as his own proper subject matter is ethics itself, metaphysics, and the theory of knowledge. (Incidentally, when I speak of "ethics," I am using this term as an abbreviation for the larger subject, which includes aesthetics, political philosophy, and the philosophical parts of moral theology, as well as what is usually called ethics.) Unfortunately, even metaphysics is in danger – not because anybody else wants to take it away from the philosophers, but because its brother – the theory of knowledge – keeps trying to kill it off. The theory of knowledge asks, Just what is metaphysics, if it is something different from the sciences? We know how the scientist gets his knowledge – it is by induction from observable fact. We know how the mathematician gets his – it is by selecting some axioms and deducing theorems from them. But what does metaphysics do? It does not seem to use either induction or deduction. If there is some kind of knowledge about the world left over when all the special sciences have appropriated their subject matters, just what is it and how do you propose to get it?

In this paper I cannot, of course, go into all the answers that have been made to this question. Let me simply say that most contemporary philosophers find none of them very satisfactory. The problem they face is, What is left of philosophy, exactly, if metaphysics is as dubious a discipline as it seems? It is the leading characteristic of philosophers of the present day that, for the first time, they are seriously troubled by this question. They are no longer sure that they have any good answer when people ask them what they do all day. The suspicion among philosophers has gotten stronger and stronger in the last few decades that they have argued themselves out of a job.

Philosophers would like, I think, to retreat to the citadel of ethics, and reply that they are concerned with values, whereas all the special sciences are concerned with facts. But they cannot use this slogan without letting themselves in for the question, OK, so you are concerned with values, but just what do you do with values? Presumably you do not simply proclaim them – philosophers are supposed to argue, not just to preach. You certainly do not actualize them, as the statesman or the artist might. So what do you do with them?

Now at this point the philosopher would, I think, like to answer: "We justify them – that is, we show which are the right values and which the wrong, and we give arguments for this distinction." But if he says this, he is met by the same questions in the theory of knowledge which killed of metaphysics. Just how do you propose to perform this task? What special methods do you have to distinguish superior from inferior values? Just what are your arguments based on? And here, too, no generally acceptable answer has been forthcoming.

Now there are, roughly speaking, two possible reactions that one might have to this situation – what might be called a "negative" and a "positive" reaction. Negatively, one might say that this pathetic history shows simply that the emperor has no clothes on – that philosophy stands revealed as an absurd attempt to give justification to what cannot possibly be justified. The prima facie proof that ethical imperatives cannot be justified is just the historical fact that after two thousand years of trying, all we seem to have found out is that practically everything is irrelevant to their justification. If after all this time we still cannot answer Socrates's questions, presumably this shows that he was asking the wrong questions. This view of the nature of ethics is summed up in F. H. Bradley's definition of metaphysics: "Finding bad reasons for what we believe on instinct."[1]

This view of ethics is made precise and explicit by Kant's famous dictum that "the 'ought' cannot be inferred from the 'is'." In other words, a moral imperative cannot be supported or justified by any fact or any theory about facts scientific, metaphysical, or religious, or by anything except another moral imperative.

For example, an argument of the form

(1) "This is the best alternative, and therefore this ought to be desired by you"

is valid because an explicit "ought" is present in the phrase "this is the best alternative." Indeed, the premise and the conclusion are just different ways of saying the same thing. But an argument like

(2) "This will cause unnecessary pain to all concerned; therefore, you should not do it"

is not valid unless one includes the extra premise, which does express an imperative, that "One should maximize happiness." Similarly, an argument like

(3) "God wills this; therefore, you should do this"

is not valid unless one includes a premise which says, "You should do what God wills."

Thus it seems that we can add to our prima facie historical argument for the impossibility of ethics a purely logical, and quite conclusive, argument. On this view, then, to say that philosophy is the attempt to justify one's values is equivalent to saying that philosophy is impossible. This is the view which has been made popular by positivists like A. J. Ayer, who see no role for philosophers except that of using the theory of knowledge as a broom to sweep away all the confusions of previous philosophers.

However, one can also take a positive view of this history of philosophical attempts to justify ethical choices. One can say that ethics has been

---

[1] F. H. Bradley, *Appearance and Reality: A Metaphysical Essay*, 2nd ed. (New York: MacMillan, 1897), xiv. – *Eds.*

purified by showing the fruitlessness of saying that one should obey such and such a moral imperative because of such and such facts. One can suggest that ethics has now freed itself, at long last, from absurd attempts to show that one ought to accept certain moral values because the earth is the center of the universe or because science cannot understand the origin of life or because America has a high standard of living. This positive view can accept the Kantian dictum that imperatives cannot be derived from factual statements, but instead of assuming that this means that we can forget about ethics, it emphasizes and reiterates the fact that an ethical choice is a free act of decision, and that virtue lies in the authenticity of this decision. It welcomes the glad news that God is dead – both the God of religion and the million assorted substitutes for God, which philosophers since Plato have devised. This, in an oversimplified form, is the view held by existentialists like Sartre, who see the unjustifiability of ethics not as a disappointment but as a liberation, and who answer Socrates's question by saying like the positivists, but in a distinctly different tone of voice, that the question should never have been asked.

Philosophy at present is dividing into two camps, whose attitudes toward ethics and toward the future of philosophy are represented by these two reactions to the question of the justification of ethical imperatives. The hardest thing to find in the contemporary philosophic scene is a philosopher who attempts a straightforward answer to Socrates's straightforward question: "Why should I take these values as ultimate rather than those?"

But this is not for lack of wishing for such a philosopher. On all sides we are told that neither the positivists nor the existentialists offer us a satisfactory account of ethics. The positivists, we are told, shrug off Socrates's question too lightly and do not take moral issues seriously. On the other hand, the existentialists seem to open the way to utter arbitrariness and reckless irrationality. We must, people say, have a "return to reason" – in which philosophy will regain self-respect, resume business at the old stand, and, presumably, finally get around to telling us whether and why our chosen values are right or wrong.

Now my own position is roughly one of agreeing with all three sides in this dispute in their opinions of the other sides. I agree with the positivists that existentialists' deliberate and self-conscious irrationality is worse than useless, because it is potentially dangerous. I agree with the existentialists that the positivists have the moral sensitivity of a herd of cows. I agree with those who call for a "return to reason" that the justification of our moral beliefs is still something that should be attempted and that philosophy is still a worthwhile subject. But yet (and this is what I find most troubling) I agree with both the positivists and the existentialists that the "ought" cannot be derived from the "is." That is, I agree that the choice between alternative moral imperatives remains open no matter what facts are produced or what metaphysical theories are adopted. In the face of any conclusion that any philosopher will ever reach about the nature of reality or the nature and powers of the human mind, the question of what we should do will remain open. If it is proved to me once and for all that I am a sinner in the hands of an angry God, the question still remains open whether I should yield to the divine will or suffer a heroic martyrdom in defying it. If it is proved to me that I am a random assemblage of atoms thrown together by the indifferent laws of physics and doomed to dissolve without a trace when the sun blows up next Tuesday, I am still no further along in deciding what values I should live for in the remaining five days.

This tension – the feeling that ethics is both vitally necessary and utterly impossible – is a tension which has haunted philosophy since Kant and which has gotten stronger and stronger since his day. I obviously am not going to resolve it in this paper, but I do want to point toward what seems to me the only path which is still open. I turn now to the second, and perhaps more constructive, part of this paper.

***

Let us look more closely at the argument that the "is" does not imply the "ought." Suppose we ask, Does the converse also hold? That is, can we also never infer a statement of the form "There is a so-and-so" from one of the form "Such and such ought to be done"? At first glance, it would seem that we certainly cannot.

For example, the argument

(4)   "We ought to love one another; therefore, there must be a God whose will it is that we do so."

is obviously invalid. Similarly,

(5)   "We all should spend our lives in dialectical discussion, therefore there must be a Form of the Good for us to find through this dialectical search."

These arguments seem like obvious examples of wish fulfillment.

But suppose that instead of inferring from "there ought to be a such and such" we infer that "you ought to believe that there is a so-and-so." Notice that there is no logical error here. There is an "ought" in both premise and conclusion; we are inferring one imperative from another imperative. But such arguments have, nonetheless, usually been looked upon with suspicion. Consider the following argument:

(6) "There ought to be love among men; therefore, you should believe that there is a God who wills that this should happen."

This seems just as fishy as the first argument I mentioned. However, there are some arguments of this form which look a little better. Consider the argument that

(7) "You ought to accept what scientific research tells us; therefore, you ought to believe that man is descended from monkeys."

On the parallel argument that might be offered by an old-time fundamentalist:

(8) "You ought to have faith in Scripture, therefore you ought not to believe that man is descended from monkeys."

Now neither of these arguments is silly or logically objectionable, although perhaps neither is convincing. The reason they are not prima facie silly, whereas the argument that we ought to believe in God because we ought to love each other is silly, is that now the premise is an imperative about the conditions of belief.

Belief, after all, is one particular kind of action, and there can be, and in fact are, ethical imperatives about beliefs as well as about all other modes of acting. We constantly deduce consequences from a general imperative about the kinds of beliefs we ought to have, or the methods we should follow in choosing our beliefs, or the values we should look to in choosing between competing alternatives for our belief. There is nothing wrong with inferring from these, with the aid of additional, factual, premises, to a more particular imperative which says that we ought to have a certain particular belief.

Now it seems to me that this shows that there is a species of ethical imperative which does permit us to make inferences to statements about fact. In other words, I think we can and do and must argue from the "ought" to the "is." For I should hold that the phrase "there is, in fact, a so-and-so" and the phrase "we ought to believe that there is a so-and-so" are, for all the purposes which are relevant here, synonymous. This identification of the meanings of these two phrases may strike you as outrageous. If so, let me defend myself by invoking the authority of William James and the pragmatic definition of truth, in which "this sentence is true" means no more, and no less, than "this sentence expresses a proposition which you ought to accept." In the space of this paper, I obviously do not have time to meet the objections to which James's theory of truth is subject. Let me merely say that I think that all the developments in philosophy from James's time to our own serve to support both the positivists' inquiries into the nature of scientific method and the existentialists' development of Kierkegaard's slogan that "truth is subjectivity."

If you will for the moment suspend your disbelief in the pragmatic theory for the sake of argument, I should like to show why I think what I have been saying is relevant to the problem of justifying ethical imperatives. I have said that the point of ethics is justifying our action – or, more exactly, justifying the choice of imperatives by which we shall regulate our actions. The usual notion of justification is deductive. That is, philosophers have always tried to find an "is" statement from which they can deduce an ethical imperative. This is usually a metaphysical or a scientific or a religious theory about the nature of things or of man. Because the "ought" cannot come from the "is," they have always failed. But philosophers have despaired of any justification except a deductive one, because the only alternative seemed to be an inductive one, and it is obvious that this will not do. For the question of whether anybody obeys an imperative, or even wants to obey it, is irrelevant to the truth of the imperative. An imperative which tells us to "cast out all thought of self" is not falsified by the fact that nobody has ever succeeded in doing so, nor would it be falsified even if one showed that nobody ever even tried to do this. Values can still exist whether or not anybody follows them or notices them.

But if ethics cannot work deductively or inductively, what can it do? It seems to me that the fact that we can infer the "is" from the "ought," even though we cannot do the reverse, gives us the answer to this question. We can use in justifying ethical imperatives the same method that Milton used to justify the ways of God to man. We can tell a story – the story which has to be told if our imperative is the right one. Judged as argument, deductive or inductive, for the benevolence of God, *Paradise Lost* is a flop. Judged as a story, it is not bad. As a story which we ought to believe if we accept Milton's values, it is the best justification of those values which we can get.

But here you might say that Milton was, after all, only speaking symbolically, and what we are interested in is literal facts. But I say that a careful analysis of the methods of the sciences shows that in the realm of scientific fact, we also use ethical imperatives as necessary premises. Consider the following situation:

A: The earth goes around the sun.

B: Why ought I to believe that?

A: Why, just because it's a fact.

B: Surely not, it's a theory which accounts for the facts.

A: You're quibbling – a theory which accounts for the facts is a fact.

B: No, I'm not quibbling. The facts involved here – various optical phenomena, telescopic observations, and so forth – can be explained by, and will support, an almost infinite number of different theories.

A: But you have to admit that the Copernican model of the universe in which the earth does go round the sun – is by far the simplest and most elegant of these theories and harmonizes best with Newtonian physics.

B: Yes, I do admit this, but what's so good about simplicity and elegance and harmonizing with other theories? Are these ultimate values?

A: Well, they're certainly my ultimate values when it comes to deciding what I'm going to believe.

B: But they're not mine. The picture of the world which results from taking the earth – man's home – as the center of the universe is the one which satisfies values which I cherish much more than these.

Now the important point about this dialogue, the matter of which speaker you agree with, is that it starts out as an argument about literal fact; it ends up as an argument about ultimate values. More important still, this latter argument cannot be settled by "returning to the facts." The facts always leave room for interpretation, and it is an ought statement which determines which of the possible interpretations one is going to pick. This is an instance of the kind of inference from the "ought" to the "is" that I have been talking about. You take an ethical imperative as your premise, and from it you deduce the facts – that is, you deduce what story you ought to believe about the facts. There are in every case an infinite number of possible stories, from which we must pick one. The one we pick is determined by the purposes we want the story to fulfill, and our purposes are regulated by the ethical imperative under which we are working.

In the sense in which I am using the term "story," then the whole of modern science is a story – a story which satisfies the values of simplicity, elegance, and ability to produce practical technological consequences. Speaking for myself, I accept this story, because I think these values are ultimate. But if I were asked to justify these values, all that I could do would be to point to the fruits of accepting them. In other words, to point once again to the scientific world-picture. This mode of justification is not, and never can be, conclusive. Logically, in fact, it is circular. But I think that the lesson of the history of philosophy is that it is the only way we have got. To point to the set of theories which one's values oblige one to hold is all that one can do when one is asked to justify one's values.[2] This is the main point I wish to make in this paper. Let me conclude by drawing two corollaries.

The history of philosophy shows, I think, a long series of valid inferences from "ought" to "is" masquerading as inferences from "is" to "ought." I would suggest, for example, that what Plato's *Republic* really says is not: "There are Forms; therefore, we should live the Life of Reason." What it says is "We should live the Life of Reason; therefore, we should believe in Forms" – or, if you prefer a softer, but pragmatically equivalent, phrasing, "therefore, we should act as if there were Forms." Because we naturally look for deductive justification, we tend to think in terms of the Theory of Forms supplying "a metaphysical foundation for ethics"; but as soon as we speak in this way, we stand convicted of bad logic. To speak in this way is bad logic, and because it is bad logic, it is bad tactics if we are really interested in converting a Thrasymachus. It makes the more certain appear to depend on the less certain. What Plato was ultimately concerned about – what, I suspect, all systematic philosophers have been ultimately concerned about – was to commend a way of life. Part of a way of life is the set of things one says about what the world is like – one's science, or one's metaphysics, or both together. But this part is not the foundation for the whole.

Thus what has really happened in the history of ethics is not a gradual recognition of the need to pay attention to facts. It is not a process of distinguishing facts from values – putting them in separate compartments labeled "ought" and "is," compartments separated by the logical impossibility of going from one to the other. This is only what the history of ethics looks like when viewed from the perspective of a certain set of ethical values – those of Renaissance humanism and of the scientism of the Enlightenment. These are values which most of us share – and thus the world-picture which puts a wall between facts and values seems like the only possible one. But not everyone shares these values; for men as diverse as Lenin and St. Ignatius Loyola, there were values which were considerably more important. In Loyola's vision of the meaning of the Christian

---

[2] Bradley's remark, considered as a psychological observation, was correct when he said that metaphysics was finding bad reasons for what we believe on instinct and this remark, can, I think, be extended to all the rest of philosophy. But a bad reason may be a good story. The whole range of culture – including science as well as ethics, and poetry as well as metaphysics – is in my view, a series of stories – good ones and bad ones – which different people's different values have committed them to. Some of these stories serve other functions – science, for instance, lets us master our environment. But from a logical point of view in regard to their ultimate dependence on an implicit evaluation, they are on par with each other.

Church and in Lenin's vision of the liberated proletariat, we find the justification of values which assert the right to forbid us to accept the results of science as our beliefs about the world and about man. There are hierarchies of value in which "objectivism" – whether it be called "secular" or "bourgeois" – is a sin. The really important choices about right and wrong are choices which establish one of these hierarchies rather than another.

2

Philosophy as Spectatorship and Participation

I want to do two things in this paper. In the first part, I will make some general remarks about participation and spectatorship in philosophy; in the second part, I will give a fast, pedantic, spectatorial view of existentialism.

There is a certain feeling in the air these days that philosophy is too important to be left to the philosophers and that it needs to be rescued from them. This feeling is analogous to the feeling that literature is too important to be left to literary critics, that war is too important to be left to generals, and that religion is too important to be left to the clergy. It is difficult not to sympathize with this feeling. There are clearly certain choices for which it would be inhuman to abdicate responsibility by turning them over to specialists. The moral, aesthetic, intellectual, and spiritual choices involved in decisions about war, literature, religion, and philosophy seem clearly to be of this sort. Part of the excitement over existentialism at the present time is due to the impression that like previous philosophies, it is written for and by human beings rather than for and by specialists, and thus that existentialism has, somehow, rescued philosophy from the philosophers. There is a feeling, probably largely unconscious, but still fairly powerful, that philosophy from Aristotle through Hegel was a rather shady conspiracy to transform matters that are properly, and self-evidently, of immediate universal concern into the subject of an esoteric doctrine or of an esoteric competition among esoteric doctrines. The spirit of gamesmanship which Kierkegaard detected among the heirs of Hegel has been projected back into the past and forward into the present so that it has come to seem that the whole history of philosophy has been a kind of game. In the light of the Marxian interpretation of history, we have become accustomed to look back and see the history of theological controversy as pious humbug – a reflection of real struggles for social and economic power. Similarly, in the light of the existentialists' irony, we are now becoming accustomed to look upon the history of philosophy as the history of empty victories and empty defeats in a game which is either like theological controversies – a pallid reflection of real struggles in real life – or, still worse, a mere amusement for world-weary intellectuals.[1]

This feeling that professional philosophers have somehow put something over on the rest of us, and that they have made into a private amusement what is properly an essential concern of us all, can also be put in terms of the distinction between participation and spectatorship. We feel that a philosopher, like a poet or a warrior or a witness to a religious faith, should take risks – that what will set him apart from other men, if he is to be set apart, will be his willingness to adventure. When we say that professional philosophers have betrayed philosophy, we mean that they have taken up an attitude of detachment, of spectatorship, toward such adventures. It is as if the literary critics had begun to assume that only their critical writings were "really" literature and that the poems and the novels which they criticized were somehow not really literature but just a primitive form of such memoranda. The trick which is pulled in all these cases is to start with an obvious and self-evident contrast between participants and spectators, and then by a suitable and subtle redefinition of terms, have it to appear that being a spectator is really the most ultimate perfect form of participation. This gimmick annoyed the Greeks a good deal when it was used for the first time by Socrates. Socrates argued that by refraining from all participation in the political affairs of Athens (and simply standing around kibitzing), he was, in some weird fashion, actually participating in a higher and finer way than the men who actually ran the city. An aroused public opinion, as you know, eventually put Socrates to death. But by the time Hegel came around a couple thousand years later, people were sufficiently inured to this gimmick so that it sounded perfectly reasonable to hear Hegel saying that writing histories of philosophy was really the highest and finest form of philosophizing.[2] In Hegel's time, just before Kierkegaard came along and gave the game away, philosophers were doing very well for themselves. They had managed to convince the rest of the world that their specialist role of universalist spectator and their practice of certain mysterious techniques of inquiry were essential to the general welfare. They had, in fact, taken the place of the shamans and the priests as the people who were paid to keep an eye on what were vaguely

---

[1] This view of traditional philosophy as a game is not, of course, the exclusive possession of the existentialists. It is common ground for existentialists, Marxists, and analytic philosophers. But at the moment it is the existentialists who are making the most effective use of this polemical gambit.

[2] In fact, Hegel did so well with this line that he was, when he died, well on his way to becoming a powerful influence in political affairs.

referred to as "higher things," so that the rest of society could be spared to bother.[3]

Now, this way of looking at the contrast between existentialism and traditional philosophy, in terms of a reaction against philosophy as a spectator sport and a return to participation, is, I think, quite sound – as far as it goes. But my remarks about the disingenuous character of spectators state a thesis that needs to be balanced with an antithesis. It is quite true that philosophers betray their trust when they become mere spectators, but it is also quite true that they betray it by ceasing to be spectators. What makes philosophy such a tricky business is that the philosopher is supposed to be simultaneously an adventurer, risking his mind and his soul, and a dry and detached kibitzer who insists on objectivity, rigor, and critical analysis. Philosophers are viewed with suspicion as soon as they come out firmly in favor of something – because it is the philosopher's task to be "judicious," "impartial," and "objective." Philosophers are, after all, the spectators of all time and eternity, the people who can be depended upon to play it cool no matter what happens. Even the people who are delighted with existentialism (because what the existentialists say sounds so much more "relevant to their lives" than what traditional philosophers say) – even these people get a little nervous about existentialism sometimes and begin to murmur, "It may be exciting, but is it really philosophy?" In general, philosophers are damned if what they say is relevant to life and damned if it is not. If it is, they are criticized for being too "subjective," and if it is not, they are damned for being too "detached."

So we can see that the contrast between spectatorship and participation, which is highlighted by the contrast between existentialism and traditional philosophy, is not anything new – it is simply the current expression of a tension that has always existed and dilemma that every philosopher has always faced. The tension between being relevant and being rational, between immediacy and mediation, between participation and spectatorship, is the oldest problem in philosophy. In fact, it is *the* philosophical problem. The ultimate reason why philosophy really is adventurous is just that it is the attempt to solve the insoluble problem: the problem of being both adventurous and cautious, of being both sincere and clever, of being utterly convinced that the truth about a given subject is such and such while attending with genuine respect to all the people who say that it is not.

---

[3] Looked at from this angle, the present existentialist revolt against traditional philosophy is analogous to the revolt against the priesthood during the Reformation. In both revolts the individual tries to cut out the middleman and to conduct the necessary dealings with higher things on his own.

The attempt to straddle these opposites is a permanent dilemma in the life of everybody who thinks about philosophical problems, and it is the most familiar fact of life to the professional philosopher. In practice, its outcome is that every philosopher finds himself caught in a conflict of duty – on the one hand, he has a duty to his own humanity not to let himself become detached, and, on the other hand, he has a duty toward society to stay detached. Unless somebody stays detached, unless there is somebody to stand on the sidelines and sneer, historical sense will not be preserved. And where the historical sense is not preserved, society and culture become blind and inhuman. Knowing this, the philosopher finds himself playing two roles at once. He must be a philosopher, in the best sense of the term, the sense of a man who confronts human experience afresh at each moment and creates in language a new expression of this experience. But he must simultaneously be a mere philosopher – a philosopher in the worst sense of the term, a pedantic historian of philosophy, a man who strongly suspects that there is nothing new under the sun.

Thus the dictum that "philosophy is too important to be left to the philosophers" is echoed in each philosopher's soul. It corresponds to his sense that life is too short to be spent in a cynical weariness over the repetitiousness and apparent pointlessness of this history. In his terms, this dictum means: "Philosophizing is too important to be simply the history of philosophy." It is precisely because professional philosophers recognize this that existentialism is now rapidly becoming the fashion among professional philosophers as well as among amateurs. Nobody knows better than the philosophers themselves the point of the line which Kierkegaard quotes from Shakespeare: "We have our philosophical persons, to make modern and familiar, things supernatural and causeless."[4] Nobody knows better that anything a philosopher says will be discovered by the generation of philosophers that follows him, to have been a commonplace, and an old-fashioned one at that, worth at most a paragraph in a historical textbook. But besides this dismal awareness, the professional philosopher also knows that it is his job to sacrifice his own insights, his own creativity, his own glimpse of things supernatural and causeless, on the altar of that very textbook. As a philosopher, as opposed to a historian of philosophy – in his first role rather than his second – the philosopher is not different from anybody else, and it is ridiculous to speak of him as a professional. To confront human experience and express it is not a professional specialty – it is simply what humans – all human beings –

---

[4] William Shakespeare, *All's Well That Ends Well* (2.3.1–3) – *Eds.*

do, well or badly. As a participant in philosophy, the professional has, simply, the universal human responsibilities. But in his second role, as a historian of philosophy, as a spectator of philosophy, he has the special responsibility of being a good spectator. And this responsibility entails sacrificing his first role to his second – sacrificing himself to his special social function. He has the special responsibility leaving himself open to the same treatment which he, in his capacity as historian of philosophy, has handed to others.

What this last point comes down to is this: it is quite true that philosophy is too important to be left to the philosophers.[5] But what has to be left to "the philosophers," in this narrow sense of the term, is the opportunity to act as spectators, the opportunity to make modern and familiar things supernatural and causeless. This opportunity has to be left to them because they are the only ones who have the tools to do it – that is, they are the only ones who have the historical perspective which permits one to stay cool and detached no matter what happens. This opportunity is also an opportunity, and indeed an invitation, to turn oneself into a pedant, and, in the end, into a paragraph. But the ideal of a philosopher is the man who accepts this opportunity with his eyes open.

Let me try to make this point yet again by recurring to the analogy between the philosopher and the general. When we say wars are too important to be left to the generals, we tend to forget that generals are also human beings – human beings who are called upon to sacrifice their own sense of human decency when they give orders for the inhabitants of a city to be burned to death by incendiary bombs. They make this sacrifice in the name of their public function – they abandon what they share with other men in order to do what they think will, in the long run, serve their fellow men. Without trying to say that professional philosophers face the same sort of agonizing moral decisions as do generals (they quite obviously do not), I do want to suggest that their sacrifice is analogous. The general sacrifices his sense of human decency; the philosopher sacrifices his sense of purposiveness, his sense of seriousness. They both sacrifice something of themselves for the sake of a dimly envisioned goal which is social rather than individual in import. They both run the risk of losing their humanity altogether. The normal human condition is the condition of the participant, the exhaustion of one's forces in a purposeful endeavor, the unification of one's actions into a consistent ethical whole. It is the opportunity

---

[5] Indeed, this is trivially true, if by "the philosophers" one means those who spend their lives studying the history of the subject, since philosophizing never has been and never will be left to these people.

for this common human sanity which the philosopher sacrifices when he takes on his second role – his role as spectator of a historical drama. This sacrifice, insofar as it is radical and complete, prevents the philosopher from taking philosophy seriously, and thus prevents him from taking himself seriously. It throws him into an aesthetic rather than an ethical attitude toward philosophy, an attitude which encompasses himself in his first role. Now to see oneself as an aesthetic object is not pleasant; it is perhaps as close to insanity as one can get while still remaining capable of articulate communication. To see oneself as an actor in an unfinished drama, as a potential paragraph, is to abandon inwardness. And, as Kierkegaard said, the absence of inwardness is a kind of madness.

However, having now painted this immodest picture of the professional as a man of quite incredible gallantry and moral grandeur, I should repeat that I have been describing an ideal. There probably are not, in point of fact, any generals, nor any philosophers, who make such sacrifices in full self-consciousness. A general, by the time it gets to the point where he has the option of ordering the inhabitants of a city to be burned alive, will in self-protection have converted himself into an unthinking technician who simply does not see anything except the effect of firebombing on enemy production. He will make himself less than human by ceasing to be conscious of the need for choice. If he does this too often, however, he may never be able to unfree himself – he may never be human again. So it is, on a vastly diminished scale, with the professional philosopher, when he finds himself required, for the sake of a proper exposition of his point, to toss off a few dapper paragraphs which lump together and summarize the work of a dozen highly important and highly heterogeneous colleagues. He does it without a thought. He manages, usually, and mercifully, to forget what he is doing. He plays the game for the game's sake, trusting that the game has a point in the same unreflective way in which, for his own self-protection, the general blindly trusts the war has a point.

Having now said the general things I wanted to say about philosophers as participants and as spectators, I shall try to get down to business and talk about existentialism. My job is to take existentialism and reduce it to a few paragraphs in, as it were, a yet-to-be-written textbook of the history of philosophy. In other words, I shall try to put existentialism in some sort of historical context, thus, inevitably, taming it, and cutting it down to size. My remarks thus far have been simply an apology for trying to do this. Those who believe that existentialism has saved philosophy from the philosophers, often urge us to save existentialism from the philosophers. The danger they foresee is that the philosophers will magically change existentialism into, of all the dreary things, "just one more philosophy." Since I shall be doing my best to make it into just one more philosophy, I wanted to say something in defense of the attempt. My defense consists basically in saying that in the sense in which existentialism is not a spectator sport, neither has any other philosophy been a spectator sport. But in another sense, and looked at from the point of view of the historian of philosophy, it is as much a spectacle, and thus as much an object for speculation, as any other philosophy.

***

The most obvious thing to be said about existentialism is that it has something to do with subjectivity as opposed to objectivity. Not only does one find a lot of explicit talk in existentialist authors about subjectivity, and what a good thing it is, but one finds that the key terms they use are borrowed from the names of what one usually thinks of as subjective feelings. Where old-fashioned philosophers batted around cozy, familiar, time-tested problems about space and time, mind and matter, substance and causality, thought and being, the freedom of the will, the existence of God, and the like, existentialist philosophers ignore these fine old questions. Instead, they spend their time quibbling about things like the difference between fear and anxiety, the nature of stickiness as opposed to sliminess, and the relation between shame and disgust. Philosophical books used to have nice straightforward titles like "Process and Reality," "Experience and Nature," "Language, Truth, and Logic," and so on. But now they often have weird titles like "Death and Freedom" or "Shame and Self-Consciousness." The existentialist habit of using such terms as fundamental categories has led some people to try to debunk existentialism by explaining it away as simply a particularly pretentious brand of introspective psychology and not really philosophy at all. It has led other debunkers to say that existentialism is merely a disguised attempt to say in bad didactic prose what can be said, if at all, only in fiction or in poetry. Both such attempts at debunking are, I think, entirely wrongheaded. It is as silly to criticize existentialism for having gotten its categories from psychological introspection and from literature as it would be to criticize Plato for having gotten his categories from mathematics, or to criticize Aristotle and Whitehead for having gotten their categories from biology, or to criticize Hobbes for having gotten his from physics. It is true that philosophers do criticize each other for this sort of thing – Aristotle, e.g., accused Plato of not really being a philosopher but rather just a particularly pretentious mathematician. But they should not criticize each other in this way.

Philosophizing has traditionally consisted in taking aspects of experience as crucial, or as paradigmatic, and attempting to interpret the rest of experience in the light of these selected aspects. It is no criticism of a philosopher to say that he borrowed his categories from some extraphilosophic discipline; where else, after all, would he get them? Criticism can concern itself only with whether he made a good choice, and we only find out whether he did or not by inspecting his finished product – that is, by seeing how the whole of experience looks when seen in the light of the selected aspects which the philosopher has chosen as categoreal.

Nevertheless, it might seem that one could argue against the existentialists, even before examining their finished product, that terms like anxiety and shame are quite obviously the wrong choices. For it seems obvious that in philosophy what we want are categories which have as wide a range of application as possible. That was what was so suitable about categories like time and causality and substance. There is almost no item of experience which cannot be thought of as being in time, having a cause, and being either a substance or a property of a substance. But there are lots of items of experience which do not seem to have anything whatever to do with phenomena like anxiety, dizziness, and thrownness. Furthermore, the argument can proceed, one ought to choose one's categories in such a way that there will be a clear-cut way of telling what things are to be subsumed under what categories. An array of philosophical categories ought to be a well-designed set of desk pigeonholes, with no ambiguity about what goes where. If you pick space as one of your categories, for instance, you know right away that desks are spatial and ideas are not; no fuss, no muss. But with categories borrowed from introspection, there is no clear way of telling what goes in what. If you and I talk about the difference between God and the World, or between mind and matter, we feel certain that each of us knows pretty well what the other is talking about when he uses the words. But when we talk about the difference between anxiety and fear, there is no such certainty, and it is very hard to see how we could achieve any. Thus it is very hard to see how we could ever agree on what is supposed to go under which heading. More generally, if what we are after in philosophy is to get a way of thinking about everything that is acceptable to everybody, it seems obvious that we should not handicap ourselves from the start by choosing categories that mean different things to different people.

I have run this argument because I think that listening to the existentialist answer to it is an efficient way of seeing the basic insights that underlie the existentialists' revolt. The argument I have just outlined makes two crucial assumptions. It assumes, first, that the more items of experience a given term can be applied to, the likelier a candidate that term is for the status of being an ultimate philosophical category. The second assumption is that the more agreement there is between people about the meaning of a term, the more likely a candidate it is. These two assumptions might seem like self-evident truths. But they seem so only if one has a certain model in mind for what philosophy ought to be like. They will seem so if one thinks of philosophy as imitating the procedure of mathematics, as offering deductive arguments starting from unquestionable truths and proceeding to an infinity of more particular truths, a range of particular truths which is as wide as the range of items of experience itself. If this is what philosophical explanation is like, if philosophy is a kind of super-science in which we look for universal laws which explain particular cases, then, indeed, we shall need the kind of categories which are applicable everywhere and intelligible to anyone.

Now it is just this preconception about the nature of philosophical explanation which existentialists wish to challenge. In challenging it, they also challenge the two assumptions about how to choose categories which I just mentioned. Before trying to formulate the existentialist's challenge to them, however, I want to remark on how basic this preconception and its corollary assumptions are to the philosophical tradition and to suggest how deeply embedded they are in the way we usually think about philosophy.

To see this, we have to go back to the question, Why philosophize at all? If traditional philosophizing consists, as I have said, in isolating some aspects of experience and reducing other aspects to these, why do we want to do this? Why is it so important to reduce the Many to the One, or, at least, the Too Many to the Fewer? Now, the obvious answer to this would seem to be: things are easier to deal with in this reduced form. But what is meant by dealing with them? What kind of dealings are these? Just what is it that becomes easier if we have a reductive explanation? What profit do we get out of knowing the relations between universal categories as what dictates the relations between particular facts?

What becomes easier, clearly, is controlling experience. If we can reduce the teeming variety of experience to a series of instantiations of ultimate categories, we are in a better position to know how to make experience be what we want it to be. Philosophy as super-science has the same aim as science itself: control over the environment. The original motive behind the urge toward reductive explanation is the quest for security, for safety. If we can get an array of universal categories whose interrelations will shadow forth the behavior of all actual and possible facts, then we can be safe against surprises; we can, in fact, stop thinking, and, at long last, rest. Looked at this way, the whole history of traditional philosophy, from Plato to the pragmatists, is united by agreement on a single point – namely, that the aim of reasoning is to make reasoning unnecessary, and thus that the aim of philosophizing is to escape from the situation in which philosophizing is necessary.

Viewing philosophy in this light, we can see why the two assumptions I have mentioned are common to all traditional philosophers. There are two preeminent dangers which we face: the first is that things will do something we do not expect and cannot control, and the second is that some other human being will know something we do not know. Both fears contribute to our sense of insecurity, and philosophy must, if it is to do its job, eliminate both. It will eliminate the first if it can find categories which are not merely personal or regional, but rather ones which extend as far as the range of experience itself. It will eliminate the second, if it can formulate the relations between these categories in premises which no other human being can deny and which every other human being will be forced to grant. The ideal result of philosophic inquiry will be obtained when there is nobody left who can give us an argument, when we have an unshakable foundation for everything we say, and when we have something to say about everything. Thus we want categories which everybody can understand and whose meaning is clear to everyone; only thus can we be sure that everybody else realizes how unshakable the foundation which we stand on is; only thus can we feel secure.

Now another name for this kind of security is "objectivity." To say that the goal of philosophy is security and to say that its goal is objectivity are two ways of saying the same thing. The word "objectivity" wraps up, in its two senses, the twin goals of philosophizing. To have objective knowledge as opposed to subjective knowledge is to know the object as it is itself, rather than the way it appears; it is to get in command of things, rather than being at the mercy of their actions upon our senses and upon our other faculties. On the other hand, to be objective as opposed to being prejudiced or mystical or provincial is to be able and willing to give reasons for everything one says and to make anybody else understand what one thinks and why one thinks it. We think of the sciences as objective to the degree to which they fulfill both of these requirements. Thus we think of mathematics as being more objective than physics, physics as being more objective than biology, biology as more objective than economics, economics as more objective than sociology, and so on. When we come to philosophy, we think of it as being perfectly objective, as plugging all the gaps in our knowledge and providing the subordinate sciences with an unshakable metaphysical or methodological foundation. Philosophy as super-science is supposed either to lay down general principles from which scientific laws can be derived by instantiation, or at least to make perfectly clear what the methods, structure, and worth of the special sciences are, so that we may have no loose ends in the fabric of our thought. Philosophy's pursuit of perfect objectivity should, ideally, make our knowledge into a perfectly self-contained system and thus make us perfectly self-contained – perfectly secure.

This analysis of the meaning of objectivity puts us, at last, in a position to give some meaning to the cliché that existentialism emphasizes subjectivity rather than objectivity. The cliché comes down to saying that it emphasizes insecurity at the expense of security. This is true enough, but if that were all that existentialism did, it would be just one more attempt – one of many in the history of philosophy – to spur us on to making ourselves more secure by reminding us how awful it is to be insecure. What is important about existentialism is that it breaks with the conception of philosophy as a means toward security. It turns away from the notion of philosophy as super-science altogether. It simply does not see the force of the objection, which is constantly thrown at it, that it has nothing to tell us about nature or eternal values or God, and spends all its time talking about man. For existentialism, this is all that philosophy could or should talk about. As to nature, the sciences will give us what control over it we need, and philosophy can do nothing for them and take nothing from them. It is not the foundation of science, nor are the objects of science its objects. As for values, the existentialists suggest that the whole notion of the search for objective foundations for values is a fake, and that the history of this search has simply been a search for ways of defending values one had already adopted, rather than an attempt to find values to which one should adapt oneself. As for God, existentialists suggest that the only thing that is clear about God is that it is not by philosophical inquiry that one reaches him.

Similarly, existentialism does not see the force of the objection that the kinds of things it says about man are ambiguous, vague, hard to understand, and impossible to verify. For existentialism, there is no reason to expect that man should be such that one can say clear, unambiguous, and readily intelligible things about him. Indeed, there is every reason to expect the contrary. For existentialism, in fact, the important thing about man, the thing that needs to be said, is that man is insecure, vague, hard to understand, and impossible to keep track of. The problem which existentialist philosophers face is finding a way of saying this – saying it in a way that the audience will not go away saying to itself: "Ah yes, how true that is. Man is insecure and ambiguous. At least we know about man. How grateful we are to the philosophers for having solved this problem for us."

Thus what is most distinctive about existentialism is, I think, that it has managed to challenge a set of assumptions which philosophers, and their audiences, have accepted unconsciously ever since Plato. What distinguishes it from traditional philosophy is not just that it takes its categories from unexpected regions of experience or that it expresses itself in odd and paradoxical ways. All this has been done before. What is new is that it chooses these categories, and expresses itself in these ways, for the sake of a new goal. This goal – the preservation of subjectivity, the refusal to seek for security through the quest for objectivity – is genuinely foreign to the philosophical tradition. In place of the attempts to make man secure, existentialist philosophizing attempts to prevent man from buying security cheaply. In place of reductive explanation, the existentialist offers no more than simple description. His categories – shame, anxiety, and the rest – are not intended to serve as pigeonholes, but as pointers. They are not tools for getting control of the environment, but tools for keeping oneself open to the environment. For the existentialist, the goal of philosophizing is not to make thinking unnecessary but to overcome all temptations to stop thinking – and notably the temptation of "objectivity."

Let me now conclude this potted version of existentialism by returning to a question I dismissed as wrongheaded earlier: the question of whether existentialism is really a philosophy or not. It has been argued that when one abandons the quest for objectivity, one abandons philosophy itself, and that hence existentialism has no right to claim the title of a philosophy. The first thing to be said about this argument is that it is verbal, and in the form stated, not worth worrying about. If one wants to restrict the word "philosophy" to the activities of those people who accept the traditional ideal of objectivity, well and good. The use of one word rather than another does not change anything. But the second thing to be said is that this argument suggests a further problem, which cannot be dismissed as verbal. This problem centers around a point I made in the first part of this paper: the point that the philosopher must always play two roles and that in his role as historian of philosophy, he has a duty to maintain a historical sense. If this duty means anything, it means that he must not permit himself to lose communication with the past, that he must have sufficient respect for tradition so that he will never allow an absolute break in communication between the present and the past, that he must deliberately cultivate enough detachment from his own commitments to permit him to see the philosophy of the present as an answer to the same questions as were answered by the philosophy of the past. There is no disguising the fact that the existentialists call this assumption in question and thus throw doubt on the possibility of there being such a thing as a spectatorial history of philosophy. In doing so, they throw doubt on the legitimacy of any distinction between the philosopher as participant and the philosopher as spectator. Now I have no quick way of resolving this doubt. I have raised it only so that I may conclude with the following question, which seems to me to express, as it were, the existential predicament of existentialism as a philosophical movement. The question is, Can one revolt against the ideals of security and objectivity, in the name of insecurity which is fundamental to the human condition, without thereby losing whatever it is that makes the historical sense precious?

3

Kant as a Critical Philosopher

In this paper, I want this evening to present an interpretation of Kant. Kant is the sort of philosopher who demands to be interpreted. He cannot simply be studied. It is not simply that he wrote obscurely but that his works seem to point in two opposite directions at once. In this, he is like Aristotle. Most philosophers have just one opponent; Kant and Aristotle had two. Both Kant and Aristotle are reacting to a pair of extreme positions (dogmatism and skepticism): Plato and Democritus, in the one case, and Leibniz and Hume, on the other. Since they criticize both the dogmatic and the skeptical member of each pair, their works tend to divide up into two sets of passages, according to whom they are criticizing. The strength of their criticisms of each of their respective predecessors is such that, if one pays attention merely to the part of their works where they are criticizing one such predecessor, it is easy to think of them as just a modified version of the other predecessor. Thus, if you only read certain parts of Aristotle, he looks like a Platonist defending Plato against the heresies of atomists, physicalists, and sensationalists. If you read only other parts of Aristotle, he looks like a Democritean physicalist and phenomenalist debunking Plato. If you read all of Aristotle, it is terribly hard to find a single consistent picture. This is why there are as many Aristotles as there are Aristotelian scholars.

Similarly with Kant. If you read just the "Analytic"[1] or the first part of the *Prolegomena*, skipping a bit here and there, it is easy to see him as coming to the aid of the rationalists against Hume. If you read just the "Transcendental Dialectic" or just the last part of the *Prolegomena*, it is easy to think of him as a logical positivist born before his time, providing a verification theory of meaning with the aid of which one can debunk metaphysics. Depending on which part of the book you take to be the heart

---

[1] In what follows, Rorty's references to sections of Immanuel Kant's *Critique of Pure Reason* have been placed in quotation marks. – *Eds.*

of the *Critique of Pure Reason*, you can make Kant into a particularly successful rationalist or a particularly successful empiricist. But when you try to formulate distinctive and positive "Kantian doctrines" (doctrines which are his own positive contribution) you have a very hard time. This is why there are as many Kants as there are Kantians, whereas there are not as many Humes as there are Humeans or as many Leibnizs as there are Leibnizians.

To put this problem in other terms, when a philosopher is as profound and as original as Aristotle or Kant, it seems hard to conceive of him as doing a merely negative job – as merely exposing the errors of his extremist predecessors. Yet it is surprisingly difficult, in either Aristotle's *Metaphysics* or Kant's first *Critique*, to find anything except negative arguments. When one finds positive arguments, they seem the weakest part of the book. For instance, the one clearly positive and original section of the *Metaphysics* is the proof of the existence of the Unmoved Mover, and this is certainly the most dubious argument in the book. The one section of the *Critique* that looks most positive and original is the theory of the successive syntheses of the manifold, which we get in and around the "Deduction of the Categories," but that, too, seems the most dubious part of that book. Further, these positive sections are just the parts of the respective books which are most subject to divergent interpretation. Nobody quite knows how much to read into the notion of the Unmoved Mover in Aristotle, but everybody reads something in. Nobody feels quite sure how to describe what Kant is up to in the "Transcendental Deduction," but everybody feels that his own account of what he is doing will not do as it stands.

To sum up this first point, it is much easier to know what Kant and Aristotle were against than to know what they were for; further, it is very hard to formulate even their criticisms of either one of their respective opponents. Whenever one tries, one finds oneself saying things that cannot be reconciled with their criticisms of the *other* of their respective opponents.

I think that the explanation of the fact is that Kant and Aristotle occupy an almost unique position in the history of philosophy. They are *critical* philosophers. Their achievement does consist in their negations – not in any positive theses which they advance. Their greatness consists not in the importance of what they discovered but in the profundity of their criticisms of other philosophers. They are the great kibitzers of philosophy. Whereas Plato, Descartes, Spinoza, Hegel, and Whitehead are great dogmatic synthesizers, and Democritus, Hobbes, Hume, and Ayer are great skeptical analysts and debunkers, Aristotle and Kant present us with critical

philosophies. In this they resemble a third great philosopher –
Wittgenstein. Like Aristotle and Kant, Wittgenstein proves no theses and
makes no discoveries – all that he does is to show other philosophers where
they went wrong. For Wittgenstein, the object of philosophizing is not to
make discoveries, or to supply foundations for what we already know, but
simply to kibitz. Kibitzing here means kibitzing on what other philosophers
have done – showing them where they got themselves tied up in knots,
showing them how to say what they want to say without running off to
extremes, and showing them that the problems which they are concerned
to solve are not really very problematic. To show them, in Berkeley's
phrase, that they have been "kicking up the dust and then complaining
that they cannot see."

I want to sketch what Kant looks like if he is construed as doing
philosophy in the way in which Wittgenstein did it – as a *merely* critical
philosopher. I do not claim that the Kant whom I am going to present to
you is the Kant-in-himself: Kant as Kant looked to Kant. On the contrary,
I shall be constantly and shamelessly saying that Kant misinterpreted his
own work, misjudged his own achievement, and misdescribed his own
method. On the other hand, the Kant whom I am going to present to you
is, at least, an interesting philosopher. (At least, I think he is.)

Construed in the way in which I wish to construe it, "critical" philosophy
means the kind of philosophy which accepts certain data as simply given.
Critical philosophy neither casts doubts upon these data nor attempts to
justify them. For Kant, these data were the science and the mathematics of
his day, and the common moral consciousness of his day. A critical philosophy does not ask whether its data are real; it presupposes that they are real.
In this it differs from a skeptical philosophy. But neither does it attempt to
supply them with a *foundation*. In this it differs from a dogmatic philosophy.
Kant, on my view, simply has nothing to say in reply to someone who does
not believe that the synthetic a priori truths which he lists in the *Critique* (the
"Principles of Pure Understanding") are true – although he has a good deal
to say against skeptical arguments to the effect we could not know them to be
true. Similarly, Kant has no arguments to offer against philosophers who just
cannot find in themselves the sense of duty which, Kant says, is the content
of the common moral consciousness. Thus, Kant has no arguments to offer
against Thrasymachus or against Nietzsche or against Aristotle's ethics of the
gentleman. If you do not find the principle of causality true, or the categorical imperative true, Kant is not going to prove it for you. Kant, on my view,
thinks of the truth of the Principles of Pure Understanding (e.g., the
principle of causality) and of the categorical imperative as absolutely rock-

bottom data. There is no such thing as sticking a foundation underneath them nor as proving that they are false. Thus, philosophical problems for Kant do not have the form "Why are these principles true?" Rather, they have the form "Why has anybody (and, in particular, skeptical philosophers) ever thought them false?" or "Why has anybody thought that they needed a foundation (as dogmatic philosophers have)?"

Thus, it is a mistake to complain very much that Kant never really proves that his list of twelve categories is an exhaustive list of distinct ways of synthesizing the manifold of intuition. It is also a mistake to complain that his formulations of the categorical imperative are of no help in trying to resolve actual moral dilemmas. It is quite true that he does not show that the list of categories is the "right" list of categories, nor does he succeed in offering you a foolproof method for deciding cases of conflict of duties. But that fact is not very important – even if Kant would have thought it important, as he probably would have. What is important in Kant is the way in which he shows how it is possible for there to be synthetic a priori truths, not which particular truths he thought were synthetic a priori, and that it is possible for there to be a categorical imperative, not which statements properly formulate this imperative. Kant's interest and value as philosopher would remain even if we ceased to believe in any of the twelve Principles of Pure Understanding and even if we rejected entirely his description of the common moral consciousness. It would remain because the whole of his work can be taken as a hypothetical proposition: assuming that these data are given, how are they possible? In other words, assuming that these are the data which we find, why is it that philosophers cannot leave them alone? Why, in other words, are they continually bringing skeptical charges against this data and trying to undermine them (like Hume), or else trying to prevent them from being undermined and thus trying to stick foundations underneath them (like Leibniz)? As a *critical* philosopher, it is this question which Kant is answering. His problem is not what to believe or what to do – but merely why philosophers have said what they said. Whereas skeptical philosophers deny that the data are as they are, and dogmatic philosophers think that we need to discover new data in order to make sure of the original data, Kant just takes the data for granted and asks why these two kinds of philosophers say the silly things which they do say.

Let me now stop long enough to clear up a confusion. It might seem natural to suggest that the question "How is such and such a datum possible?" (e.g., "How are a priori synthetic judgments possible?" or "How is a categorical imperative possible?") is, as dogmatic philosophers have suggested, a request for a foundation – for a causal explanation. For instance, it might seem that the question "How is mathematical knowledge possible?" requires a causal answer – either one given by straightforward physical causes, in terms of the physiology of the brain, or given by metaphysical causes, as in Plato's doctrines of Ideas and/or Recollection. It might seem that the question "How is morality possible?" ought to be a request for a causal explanation of where the moral law comes from – so that we might resort either to psychological and anthropological explanations, on the one hand, or to metaphysical explanations in terms of a recollection of the Form of the Good or of the installation of a "moral sense" by a divine being. But in the sense in which Kant poses the question "How is the datum possible?" this question is not a request for a casual explanation. Indeed, the greatest single contribution which Kant made to philosophy was to help us see that the kind of explanations offered by philosophy as opposed to science, are not causal explanations. For a critical philosopher, to ask the question "How is the datum possible?" is simply a means of raising the further question "What makes you doubt that it is possible?" What he wants to do is to expose the reasons for doubting the possibility of the datum which philosophers have had. These reasons are usually first formulated by skeptical philosophers. But then they are taken up by dogmatic philosophers, who are so frightened of the skeptic that they feel that they have to provide a foundation for the datum. Clearing away the skeptic's reason for doubting or the dogmatist's reasons for attaining a "foundation" constitutes the main business of critical philosophy.

Specifically, in Kant, the main business of the *Critique of Pure Reason* is exposing the Humean skeptic's myth that we can analyze knowledge in terms of intuitions (what Hume called "impressions") without concepts, and exposing the Leibnizian rationalists' myth that we can analyze knowledge in terms of pure concepts without sensory intuitions. Once these myths are exposed, we can see that the possibility of the data at hand (namely, the various principles of pure understanding) is dubious only if one accepts one or the other of these myths. Once these myths are exposed, we lose our hankering after causal explanations of the grounds; we are able to accept them as the rock-bottom data which they are. This sort of exposure is what I have referred to above as the *kibitzing* which is the special sort of philosophy done by Aristotle, Kant, and Wittgenstein. It is also what I had in mind when I said that what was interesting and important in the works of these men were not their positive theses but their negative criticisms of their predecessors. The kinds of answers to the question "How is the datum possible?" which Kant gives are answers of the form "They only seem impossible or dubious if you look at them through the wrong set of spectacles." Take off the spectacles, and you will not find them impossible or dubious any longer. More precisely, they only seem impossible or dubious if you speak about them in the wrong language. Use a different language, and you will be able to take them at face value. In short, for a critical philosopher, philosophical problems are not solved; rather (to use the currently fashionable phrase), they are "dissolved." We do not answer the question "How is the datum possible?" in the traditional and straightforward way of providing a causal explanation of the datum, but rather in the oblique way of explaining why those who ask the question are asking it, and thus taking away their reason for asking it. Explaining how synthetic a priori knowledge is possible is not like explaining how the rainbow is possible (where we do give a causal explanation). It is more like explaining to a child how it is possible that the word "bear" should both be the name of a kind of animal and a verb meaning "to carry." In dealing with the child, we do not give an etymological explanation of the origins of the two words – and it would not satisfy him if we did. Instead we try clear away his mistaken assumption about the nature of language – namely, his assumption that the same sound can stand for one and only one word.

The notion of the methods and critical purpose of philosophy which I am recommending as an aid in the interpretation of Kant may be summed up by some quotations from Wittgenstein. These passages are pretty frequently quoted, but I think that what he says in them is important and bears repeating:

(1) We must do away with all *explanation*, and description alone must take its place. And this description gets its light, that is to say its purpose – from the philosophical problems. These are, of course, not empirical problems; they are solved, rather, by looking into the workings of our language, and that in such a way as to make us recognize those workings: *in despite of* an urge to misunderstand them. The problems are solved, not by giving new information, but by arranging what we have always known.[2]

(2) Philosophy simply puts everything before us, and neither explains nor deduces anything. Since everything lies open to view there is nothing

---

[2] Ludwig Wittgenstein, *Philosophical Investigations*, trans. G. E. M. Anscombe (New York: MacMillan, 1968), §109.

to explain ... The work of the philosopher consists in assembling reminders for a particular purpose.[3]

(3) My propositions are elucidatory in this way: he who understands me finally recognizes them as senseless, when he has climbed out through them, on them, over them. (He must so to speak throw away the ladder after he has climbed up on it.)[4]

In what follows, I want to apply this notion of what philosophy can and should be to Kant. I think I can at least show that if this notion is used to interpret what Kant is up to, then much of what is valuable in Kant can be preserved, and many difficulties which arise in interpreting Kant can be resolved. It may be that if one thinks of Kant's philosophical achievement in this way, one loses sight of important elements in Kant's thought. I do not, in fact, think one does, but this is one of the things which we can discuss later on.

Kant's Theory of Knowledge – The Copernican Revolution

I shall now stop talking in generalities about what kind of philosopher Kant was and try to say something specific about his central thesis in the theory of knowledge – the thesis that, since the assumption that all our knowledge must conform to objects leads to an inability to answer the question "How is synthetic a priori knowledge possible?" we must adopt the alternative assumption that "objects must conform to our knowledge." There are various ways to interpret the latter phrase, "objects must conform to our knowledge." In the first place, we can take it literally, in which case it is a hopeless and obvious falsehood. For if one thing is clear about human knowledge, it is that it does not change the things which we know. If one stands firm on this point, then the only question is why Kant ever thought it was necessary to say such an odd thing. The answer to that question seems fairly easy to give. The reason why Kant thought he had to say it was that he had accepted the Cartesian copy-theory of ideas, and he had found that this theory led only to skepticism or to dogmatism. Kant could not see any way in which to avoid skepticism or dogmatism except to say abandon the copy-theory of ideas – that is, to abandon the assumption that an idea is a sort of immaterial replica of a material object or part of such an object. He gave up the notion of our ideas copying the real and

---

[3] Ibid., §126–7.
[4] Ludwig Wittgenstein, *Tractatus Logico-Philosophicus*, trans. C. K. Ogden (New York: Routledge, 1988 [1922]), §6.54.

adopted the only alternative which occurred to him – namely, that our ideas *made* the world. Unfortunately, however, this alternative was absurd.

The position I have just outlined is one fairly widespread interpretation of Kant. Let me spell this interpretation out in a little more detail. The copy-theory of ideas is a theory which is common to all philosophers from Descartes through Hume. According to this theory, we know the truth only when our ideas accurately copy things. But, as Descartes and Berkeley made clear, we never are in a position to check our ideas against things. You cannot leap outside of your mind and see whether what is in your mind matches what is outside your mind. Therefore, it seems that we must choose between either Hume's skepticism or a metaphysical guarantee that some of our ideas really do copy things accurately. This kind of metaphysical guarantee was what was provided by Descartes's God, Spinoza's theory of the two parallel attributes, and Leibniz's preestablished harmony. Such guarantees are what Kant thinks of as typical products of dogmatic metaphysics. If you cannot stomach either Humean skepticism or dogmatic metaphysics, as Kant could not, then you have to give up the copy-theory of ideas. If you do give up this theory of ideas as copies, then you have to have something else to take its place. Since all that Kant could think of was a simple inversion – if ideas cannot conform to things, things must conform to ideas – he came up with the patent absurdity that our ideas have the power to affect, or even to produce, real physical things.

If one interprets the Copernican Revolution in the way in which I have just suggested, then one will have to conclude that although Hume, Leibniz and just about everybody else were hopelessly wrong about the nature of our ideas and how that Revolution was badly needed, Kant's Revolution is no help. If one follows out this line of thinking, one will reach the conclusions which Aristotelians, Thomists, and Heideggerians do reach – namely, that one has to give up both the copy-theory of ideas and Kant's absurd alternative to it. One therefore has to adopt a new theory about the nature of ideas. This new theory usually turns out to be an old theory – a theory attributed to Aristotle. This is the theory that ideas are entities that have a unique kind of existence called "intentional existence," which has the peculiar property that ideas can both be identical with things and yet different from things. This property is, I think, very peculiar indeed – and, in the end, too peculiar to serve as the foundation for a successful epistemological theory. However, I do not wish to discuss it here. I only wish to note that this the line of argument I have just been suggesting is what leads people to say that the net result of Kant's work is to make clear the bankruptcy of Cartesianism by exposing the absurdity of the copy-theory and thus that the moral of Kant's work is *Back to the Greeks!* (And, in particular, *Back to Aristotle!*)

For myself, I should heartily agree that Kant showed the bankruptcy of Cartesianism, but I should hold that the moral to be drawn is not *Back to the Greeks!* but, roughly speaking, *Forward to Wittgenstein and linguistic analysis!* Let me now suggest a second way in which one might interpret the phrase "objects must conform to our knowledge." Instead of thinking of Kant as saying (absurdly) that things are changed by our knowledge of them, let us interpret him as saying that knowledge is a product of two causal processes – one process working from the side of the self and the other from the side of the object. In other words, let us interpret him as saying that although, of course, the things-in-themselves are not changed by our knowing them, "objects" in the phrase "objects must confirm to our knowledge" does not mean "things-in-themselves." Rather, "objects" here means the products of the causal transaction between selves-in-themselves and things-in-themselves. These products are the ordinary spatiotemporal objects – tables and chairs – of daily life. On this view, we can interpret Kant as saying that tables and chairs and physical objects, generally, are made by taking some matter from the things-in-themselves (the "pure given") and some forms from the self-in-itself (space, time, the categories, and some empirical concepts) and putting them together in some complicated way. If we follow this interpretation, then it makes good sense to say that "objects must conform to our knowledge," since now all we are saying is that we only can be conscious of the thing-in-itself to the extent that it has already been given form by our ideas. Given this interpretation, we can now see that the answer to the question "How is synthetic a priori knowledge possible?" is simply that we can know in advance what things are going to be like, because if they were not like that, we would never be able to become conscious of them.

Now this interpretation of the Copernican Revolution is, I think, fairly close to what Kant himself had in mind. Further, I do not think that there is anything wrong with the Copernican Revolution, interpreted in this way, as long as one refrains from asking any question about the nature of the thing-in-itself and the nature of the self-in-itself. In other words, this interpretation works as long as you do not ask any embarrassing questions about how Kant knows so much about this process of constituting spatiotemporal objects out of nonspatiotemporal components. As soon as you do start asking such questions, this interpretation of what Kant is doing becomes incoherent. The reasons why it becomes incoherent are probably familiar to you, but let me rehearse them briefly.

The main point made in the "Transcendental Analytic" is that all our concepts are tools for grasping spatiotemporally presented intuitions. More specifically, what emerges from the "Transcendental Deduction of the Categories" is not just that "concepts without intuitions are empty and intuitions without concepts are blind."[5] What emerges is the stronger thesis that it is impossible to be conscious of a concept without using that concept to synthesize some intuitions; and it is not possible to be conscious of an intuition without having already synthesized that intuition with other intuitions with the aid of concepts. This means that any knowledge that we have must be an instance of the synthesis of a manifold of intuitions under concepts. Since all intuitions must be spatiotemporal, this means that any knowledge which we have *must be knowledge of spatiotemporal objects*. If Kant is right in what he says in the "Analytic," it is absolutely impossible to have knowledge of anything else. There are, if Kant is right, only three sorts of propositions that can be called true: analytic propositions, necessary propositions about spatiotemporal objects (the synthetic a priori truths), and contingent propositions about spatiotemporal objects (the synthetic a posteriori truths.).

But if this is so, then what is the status of the propositions which Kant asserts in the *Critique* – for instance, such propositions as that the thing-in-itself is the source of intuitions or that three syntheses are involved in the activity of the self-in-itself in unifying the manifold of intuitions? Are these activities which are conducted by spatiotemporal substance and which can be arranged in spatiotemporal causal sequences? Obviously not. Kant himself distinguishes firmly between the empirical self and the quasi-self, which he calls "the transcendental unity of apperception," or the "transcendental ego." The empirical self is temporal, and even in a sense spatial, and its activities can be observed and described in about the same way in which we observe and describe the behavior of tables, chairs, and rabbits. But the transcendental unity of apperception is not, and could not possibly be, a spatial substance or a causal agent. Even more obviously, anything said about the thing-in-itself is automatically a proposition about the nonspatiotemporal. It is therefore a proposition which we cannot possibly know to be true, on Kant's own grounds.

So it seems reasonable to conclude that if we interpret the phrase "objects must conform to our knowledge" in terms of a series of statements

---

[5] See Immanuel Kant, *Critique of Pure Reason*, trans. Norman Kemp Smith (New York: St. Martin's, 1965), A51/B75 – *Eds.*

about a causal transaction between the self-in-itself and the thing-in-itself, then Kant is flatly contradicting himself. Practically everything he says in the "Analytic" about the way in which our concepts constitute the objects which we know just *cannot be said*, if what he says about the limitations of our knowledge is true.

Having reached this conclusion, one can make various moves. One can say, first, that it is possible to reinterpret what Kant is saying in the "Transcendental Analytic" in such a way as to make everything he says a series of psychological propositions about the activities of the empirical self. In other words, one can try to interpret the discussion of the roles of intuitions and of concepts in our thought as a series of empirical discoveries about temporal sequences of mental occurrences which can be observed by introspection. This alternative is, I think, utterly hopeless, and I shall not discuss it further. It amounts to trying to transform Kant into just one more Humean empiricist. Even though I myself shall be trying to transform Kant into a kind of Wittgensteinian linguistic analyst, I think that the Humean transformation is going too far.

A second move one might make is to say that the "Analytic" is not telling us about empirically observable spatiotemporal entities, but rather about a special kind of a spatiotemporal entity. On this view, Kant is a peculiar kind of metaphysician. If one takes this line, one will say that the propositions which describe the activity of the self in forming matter provided by the thing-in-itself are a very special sort of proposition, exhibiting a very special sort of knowledge called "transcendental" knowledge. This "transcendental" knowledge will be something halfway in between our ordinary scientific knowledge of spatiotemporal entities and the "transcendent" metaphysical knowledge which Kant makes fun of (in the "Transcendental Dialectic") when it is claimed by dogmatic philosophers. In other words, one will have to say that Kant in the "Transcendental Analytic" is giving us a kind of knowledge which somehow does not fall under the restrictions on the range of human knowledge which he is offering, but which is necessary to establish these restrictions. This position may alternatively be described as thinking of Kant as offering us a "metaphysics of the transcendental ego." This alternative is also, I think, utterly unfruitful. It amounts to trying to get Kant out of a hole by postulating a brand-new subject for metaphysical inquiry, a brand-new kind of metaphysics, and a brand-new kind of metaphysical knowledge called "transcendental" knowledge. This tactic does not solve any problems. It just baptizes them.

I think that to get Kant out of this hole, one has to try another and quite different alternative. One needs to go back and ask once again about the meaning of the phrase "objects must conform to our knowledge." We need to see if any meaning can be salvaged from this phrase that will not land Kant either in absurdity or in self-contradiction. Let us consider this phrase in isolation for a moment. Kant is here speaking as if he agreed with the Cartesian tradition that there are two distinguishable sorts of entities – acts of human knowing on the one hand and the things that get known by men on the other. In other words, he is speaking as if there were two kinds of things, describable in the same terms, and the only problem is which has to conform to which? Now let us ask: in what terms can we describe both sets of entities? How shall we find a neutral way of describing both human knowledge and what human knowledge knows? I wish to suggest that the moral of the "Transcendental Analytic" is that we have no such way. That is, I wish to suggest that what Kant shows us in the "Analytic" is that the whole statement of the problem – do ideas conform to objects or do objects conform to ideas? – is totally misleading. Questions about what conforms to what make sense where we are talking about spatiotemporal objects. In such cases, we can sensibly ask whether they resemble each other, and we can ask, Which of them influenced which in what ways? It does not make any sense if we are asked to compare one spatiotemporal entity and one nonspatiotemporal entity and tell which influences which and whether and how they match. The "Analytic" shows us that all our concepts, and therefore also all our normal ways of speaking about objects of inquiry, are designed for speaking about spatiotemporal objects – substances which enter into causal interaction. But if, as the "Analytic" shows, concepts and intuitions are not spatiotemporal substances at all, then we need a new set of terms. Thus, I think that if we try to make sense of Kant's original statement of the problem, phrased as it is in traditional terms, we will inevitably fail – and that therefore we must look for some radically new way of stating the problem and of stating the so-called Copernican Revolution. Kant stated the problem of epistemology, "How are synthetic a priori judgments possible?," in terms which suggest that what is wanted is a causal explanation. His answer to the problem, "They are possible because objects must conform to our ideas," seems to supply such a causal explanation. The analogy with Copernicus confirms this suggestion that a causal explanation has been asked for and given. Copernicus's problem was "Why do the heavenly bodies move as they do?," and his answer was to suggest a new pattern of causal interaction between the sense organs of men on earth and these bodies. Kant's phrasing of his problem and his solution to it suggest that he, too, is suggesting a new pattern of causal interaction, between two entities of the sort that can engage in causal interaction – namely, spatio-temporal substances.

But, if what Kant says in the "Analytic" is sound, we can no longer ask for the answers to epistemological problems as if we were asking for the answers to scientific problems. And we can, therefore, no longer give epistemological explanations as if they were causal explanations. So we must conclude that Kant himself, in writing the preface to the second edition (where the passage about the Copernican Revolution occurs) did not see the impact of his own analysis upon his own description of the problem which his analysis was designed to solve. This means that we must find a new way of describing and stating epistemological problems. Suppose that we try the way I suggested earlier in this talk and construe the question "How are synthetic a priori judgments possible?" as "Why is it that philosophers have doubted their possibility?" Suppose we do this. How then can we construe Kant's answer? I suggest that we construe it this way: philosophers have doubted that synthetic a priori judgments are possible because they have described mental entities in a way which suggests that any given intuition can exist independently of any given concept, and conversely. That is, they have conceived of concepts and intuitions in such a way that each concept could be a content of consciousness without our necessarily being conscious of any intuition. Conversely, any intuition can be held in consciousness without our necessarily being conscious of any concept. The fundamental mistake involved here is that philosophers have described concepts and intuitions in the way in which we describe tables and chairs – as distinct quasi-substances, existing side by side in a mental quasi-space, interacting with one another in quasi-causal ways. Thus, they have thought that an intuition is as suitable a candidate for being "a content of consciousness" as a table or a chair. Given this picture of what the mind is like, it is no wonder that doubts about synthetic a priori propositions arise. For a synthetic a priori proposition is one which is phrased exclusively in terms of concepts and yet tells you something about intuitions. Since intuitions are clearly, on the traditional view, a quite different sort of entity than concepts, even though both are mental entities, it is difficult to see how concepts *could* necessarily and universally constrain intuitions. In fact, it is impossible to understand how they can do this – just as impossible, and for the same reasons, as to see how it is possible a certain kind of physical object must necessarily and universally bear certain relations to another kind of physical object. Once one thinks of the mind as an inner space filled up with self-subsistent interacting mental entities, then it is just as difficult to see how there could be *necessary* connections among these mental entities as it is to see how there could be *necessary* connections among interacting spatiotemporal substances.

So the answer to the question "How can we make people stop having doubts about there being synthetic a priori principles?" is as follows: we can do so if we can make them stop talking about mental entities in the way in which they talk about spatiotemporal entities. If they do stop this – specifically, if they stop talking about concepts as if they were one kind of object of introspective attention and of intuitions as if they were another kind of object of introspective attention – then maybe they will see how synthetic a priori truths are possible – or, in other words, maybe they will stop raising pseudoquestions about synthetic a priori truths. Still more specifically, if they see that a concept is not a kind of mental entity which can exist in consciousness apart from its use as a synthesizer of intuitions, and that an intuition is not a kind of mental entity which can exist in consciousness apart from their having been synthesized by concepts, then they will see that it is quite plausible that some concepts are used in the synthesis of all intuitions. (For instance, the concept of Substance is.) They will therefore cease to be unable to understand the possibility of synthetic a priori principles.

Now where does the Copernican Revolution come into all this? My answer to this question will probably strike you as pretty far-fetched and pretty remote from anything Kant had in mind. However, I shall give it anyway on the basis of my previous claim that any more conventional interpretation leads us to the conclusion that Kant was either being absurd or self-contradictory. I think that the true revolution in epistemology which Kant brought about was simply to make us see that the language in which we describe consciousness and knowledge need not be the same language as the language in which we describe the physical entities which we know and are conscious of. In other words, he made us see that our epistemological problems are not real problems to be answered by making scientific or metaphysical discoveries but rather verbal problems. They are problems arising from an attempt to talk about consciousness and knowledge of the physical world in the same way in which we talk about the physical world itself, and therefore problems which will disappear if we resist the temptation to talk about them in this way. When Kant tells us that a concept is not an entity in its own right but merely a particular way of unifying intuitions, and that an intuition is not an entity in its own right but always and only a mere analytic component of a synthesized manifold, he is taking the first step in the right direction. The second step, which he did not take, but which modern linguistic philosophy has taken, is to realize that this thesis itself – the thesis that concepts and intuitions *are not* the same sort of thing as physical entities and *cannot* be thought of as entering into causal relations with one another – does not express a discovery about the nature of mental entities but is merely a remark about our language and the pictures that are built into our language.

Let me put this second step in other words by asking and answering the following question: when we reinterpret the nature concepts and intuitions in the way Kant suggests in the "Transcendental Analytic," what kind of inquiry are we conducting? Certainly not a psychological inquiry. Certainly not a metaphysical inquiry. Certainly not a merely logical inquiry, in the sense in which Russell and Whitehead were conducting a logical inquiry. It is no help to say that we are concerned with epistemological inquiry or with transcendental inquiry. These names are just labels for problems. But if it is not a psychological inquiry or an empirical or a logical inquiry, what sort of inquiry is it? What are these things called concepts, intuitions, syntheses, judgments, and the like which Kant keeps talking about? What genus do they belong to? What are the faculties of Sensibility, Understanding, and Reason which he distinguishes? They are certainly not distinct portions of the empirical self. So what are we talking about? I suggest that what we are talking about are *words*. I suggest further that what Kant is doing in the *Critique* is just what linguistic philosophers hold that philosophy ought to do: namely, (in the first place) explaining how we use certain words and (in the second place) proposing new ways of using words which will avoid the verbal problems created by our old ways of using words. I do not suggest for a moment that this is what Kant thought he was doing – but I do suggest that it is the only way to describe what he did without becoming entangled in paradoxes.

I shall now take up the whole question of the Copernican Revolution again from the beginning and try to make this suggestion more plausible.

Kant's Theses as Analytic Propositions

I said previously that Kant, in the "Analytic," had shown that there were only three sorts of propositions which we could know to be true: analytic propositions, synthetic a priori propositions about spatiotemporal objects, and synthetic a posteriori propositions about spatiotemporal objects. If I may now take it for granted that whatever concepts, intuitions, judgments, syntheses, and the like are, they are not spatiotemporal objects, then it is clear that the propositions which make up Kant's remarks about human knowledge are not synthetic propositions. Synthetic propositions are propositions about experience; experience is only of spatiotemporal objects; therefore there are no synthetic propositions about intuitions, judgments, syntheses, concepts, and the like. The only possible conclusion is that all of Kant's remarks about human knowledge, must, on Kant's own grounds, be construed as analytic propositions. (This conclusion incidentally, seems in some passages to be accepted by Kant himself: for instance, he says explicitly that "the principle of the necessary unity of apperception" is an analytic proposition.[6])

If we construe the *Critique of Pure Reason* as a set of analytic propositions, we now need to inquire what analytic propositions are and how we discover them. Kant's own description of the process of discovering analytic propositions is metaphorical, misleading, and generally unhelpful: he says that we do it by "breaking up a concept into those constituent concepts that have all along been thought in it, although confusedly."[7] This suggests that there is a mental process of breaking up concepts analogous to the physical process of breaking up rocks or taking machines apart. Worse, it suggests that concepts are the kind of thing which one can introspect in isolation. That is, it suggests that they can be looked at independently of their function as synthesizers of intuitions, in the way in which one might take apart a milling machine even when the machine was not performing its function of milling things. If Kant's argument in the "Analytic" about the nature of intuitions and concepts is sound, however, we cannot do anything of the sort. For the point of this argument is that a concept is not a quasi-substance but, if you like, an activity. Further, on sheer commonsensical grounds, it is difficult to find any operation which one can actually conduct which would count as "breaking up a concept into its constituents." (Just try it.)

However, we clearly do perform some sort of operation on some sort of object when we discover and formulate analytic propositions. What is this operation, and what are these objects? The answer which has become current in contemporary philosophy, and which is (I think) the right answer, is that we examine *words*. One operation involved in such examination is that of observing how the words we use are used and discovering what we would say and what we would not say. In the process, for instance, we find that we would not call any bachelor married, any cube round, or any analytic proposition a posteriori. A second operation is that of coining new words, or giving new senses to old words. We do this in such a way

<hr/>

[6] See ibid., B135 – *Eds.*   [7] Ibid., B11 – *Eds.*

that the pattern of use of these new words, or old words used in new senses, will help us to avoid verbal problems which our old usage had led us into. By these two sorts of operations, we discover what propositions are analytic according to past usage, and we make new propositions analytic by devising future usage.

I should like to persuade you that the most useful characterization of what Kant is up to in the *Critique* is in terms of such operations. All I can really do is what I have been doing already – namely, pointing out the difficulties in any other interpretation of what he is doing. However, let me try to do a bit more by taking a sample of the sort of thing he does and showing how my interpretation of his discussion as a piece of linguistic analysis fits this case.

Consider the word "concept" and the word "intuition." As these words normally have been used by philosophers and as they are used by Kant himself most of the time, they functioned as names of quasi-substances. It made sense to speak, for instance, of breaking up concepts into other concepts, of concepts as tools, of intuitions as being presented in manifolds in the way in which grapes are presented in bunches, and so forth. The difference between the two kinds of things named by the word had thus been taken to be a difference analogous to, but in some vague way different from, the difference between two kinds of physical objects: say butter molds and lumps of butter, or cranberry rakes and cranberries. We thus accept such propositions as the following as analytic: "every concept which is different from other concepts is separable from every other concept," "no concept is inseparably conjoined with any other," and the like. Now let us consider another possibility: perhaps "concept" and "intuition" are more like words such as "north" and "south" or "left" and "right." These pairs of words have two interesting characteristics: (1) they are not, by any stretch of usage, names of kinds of things (they are primarily used as adjectives); (2) they are perfectly reciprocal, so that any occasion for applying one of them will automatically be an occasion for the use of the other. They are adjectival because we would have no occasion for talking about either north or south or left and right unless we had something other than leftness or rightness or northness or southness to talk about. In other words, we do not use them because there are such things as norths or souths or rights or lefts, but because there are spatial objects, whose spatial relations to one another we want to discuss. We can indeed speak of "the north" or "the south" or "the left" or "the right," thus converting words which were originally adjectives into nouns, but when we do so, we are always aware that we are speaking relatively. We always have in mind some specific reference point, and we are always prepared to admit that what is the north from one point of view is the south from another, and what is left from one point of view is right from another.

Now suppose we treat the words "concept" and "intuition" as simply hypostatized forms of the adjectives "conceptual" and "intuitional," and suppose we treat these two adjectives as reciprocal in the way in which north-south and right-left are reciprocal. It will then be analytically true not only that "concepts" and "intuitions" are not quasi-substances but that they are instead simply abbreviations for descriptions of pieces of knowledge – descriptions made from two different perspectives. We can look at our knowledge of the law of gravitation or of the color of this desk either from the side of unity or from the side of plurality. When we look at it from the side of its unity, we think of it merely as an arrangement of concepts. When we look at from the side of its plurality, we see it as referring to a cluster of past, present, and future sense impressions. If we look at it exclusively from the one side, we become rationalists; if we look at it exclusively from the other side, we become empiricists. If we look at it from both sides, and realize that the sides from which we look at it are not constituents of what we are looking at but simply perspectives upon it, then we can avoid both extremes. Rationalists insist that all intuitions are just confused versions of concepts; empiricists insist that all concepts are just confused versions of intuitions. But this is as silly as suggesting that all views from the left-hand side are merely confused versions of views of a table from the right-hand side or as insisting that all movements to the north of Philadelphia are merely confused versions of movements to the south. Kant's treatment of knowledge as a synthesis of intuitions by means of concepts makes us see that it is a mistake to use the words "concept" and "intuition" as if they were the parts of which a larger whole called "knowledge" or "consciousness" is made. They are no more parts of pieces of knowledge than rightness and leftness are parts of this table or than northness and southness are parts of Philadelphia. Every piece of knowledge can be looked at in either way – either as conceptual or intuitional – but the ways of looking at something are not parts of the thing being looked at. Every piece of knowledge can be described from either point of view – exclusively in terms of concepts or exclusively in terms of intuitions – but such descriptions will not be descriptions of two sorts of materials which go to make up knowledge, but rather descriptions of two functions which knowledge fulfills.

To summarize this point: what I am saying is that one of the chief lessons Kant taught us in the *Critique* is most clearly stated in terms of a thesis about the words "concept" and "intuition." Kant did not discover any new empirical facts about the nature of knowledge – only a psychologist can do that. Nor did he discover anything about the nature of his transcendental ego – only a metaphysician could do that, and Kant was no metaphysician. What he did do was to make us see that the vocabulary which had grown up among philosophers in their attempt to make new psychological and/or metaphysical discoveries had become an incubus. Philosophers had gradually saddled themselves with a vocabulary which was not only *not* helping them to make discoveries but was preventing them from seeing the plain facts. Starting out with certain obvious facts – for instance, our knowledge that this desk is brown, that everything that happens has a cause, that men are free agents, and the like – they had managed to build up a set of verbal puzzles which in the end prevented them from seeing these plain facts. By talking about concepts and intuitions in the same way in which we talk about cranberry rakes and cranberries, rather than in the way in which we talk about different perspectives or different directions, philosophers have constructed verbal problems for themselves. They have built themselves a picture of two sets of quasi-substances existing side by side in mental space; working within the limits of this picture, they worked themselves into two untenable and paradoxical positions – namely, rationalist dogmatism and empiricist skepticism. To quote Wittgenstein again: "A *picture* held us captive. And we could not get outside it, for it lay in our language, and language seemed to repeat it to us inexorably."[8] Kant's greatness was in making it possible for us to get rid of this picture.

I have presented this outline of a possible change in our use of the words "concept" and "intuition" as a suggestion of how one can interpret Kant's discovery. Let me now repeat that I do not claim that Kant thought of his discovery in this way. On the contrary, to the end of his days, he found no better alternative than to continue using the words "concepts" and "intuition" as names of quasi-substances; this fact, I think, explains why the things which he says about concepts and intuitions in the "Analytic" are, although clear at first, extraordinarily puzzling when studied closely. The reason is that Kant himself never drew the moral of his own discovery that we can have knowledge only of spatiotemporal objects. This moral, as I have said, is that mental entities, since they cannot be spatiotemporal, cannot be objects of knowledge. Because he did not draw this moral, he says such things as "It is just as necessary to make our concepts sensible,

---

[8] Wittgenstein, *Philosophical Investigations*, §115.

that is, to add the object to them in intuition, as to make our intuitions intelligible, that is, to bring them under concepts."[9] This passage, with its obvious suggestion that concepts can exist apart from their role as synthesizers and that intuitions can exist apart from their membership in a synthesized manifold, is a good sample of the sort of passage which has puzzled Kantians ever since. The trouble with such passages is that in them Kant continues to speak of consciousness in the old Cartesian way: as if the mind were a peculiar sort of replica of the physical world – a replica in which discrete mental entities capable of causal interaction exist in a sort of mental space. The puzzling thing is that these passages occur in the works of the very philosopher who showed us, once and for all, that consciousness of an object, is not, as the Cartesian tradition thought, the reduplication of this object through the construction of a replica of it. Kant's doctrine of the transcendental unity of apperception should have abolished, once and for all, the notion of the self as a peculiar kind of ghost in the machine which has or constructs ghostly replica of physical objects out of mental material called "concepts" and "intuitions." Given the theory of the transcendental unity of apperception which Kant presents in the "Transcendental Deduction," we should have been able to stop using the word "self" as if it were the name for a special kind of substance – namely, a mental substance – which entered into a peculiar sort of causal interaction with ordinary spatiotemporal substances. We should have been able to do this because in the "Transcendental Deduction" Kant gives us a substitute way of thinking of the meaning of the term "self" or "subject"; he there opens up the possibility of thinking of consciousness of an object as (in his phrase) simply the unity of our representations, not something over and above those representations. In other words, Kant showed us that the human self was not one more thing over and above all the other things which we are conscious of – but simply was the consciousness of those other things. Having shown this – or, to put it in the way I prefer, having suggested this abandonment of old ways of using the words "self," "subject," and "consciousness" and having suggested some new ways – Kant has no business talking about concepts and intuitions as if they were ghostly entities existing in mental space inspected by a ghostly self. But unfortunately, he does.

That he did so was, historically, a disaster. It was disastrous because it enabled Hegel and the nineteenth century, generally, to go around worrying about the problem of the relation between subject and object,

[9] Kant, *Critique of Pure Reason,* A51/B76.

without realizing that this problem had been dissolved in 1787, when Kant published the second version of the "Transcendental Deduction." But though disastrous, it was also quite natural. It is probably just too much to expect that a man should not only destroy the traditional picture of the way in which human knowledge works but should also realize what it is that he has done. Kant managed to destroy the picture of the human mind and of human knowing which was built into Cartesian language – which means commonsense language. What is miraculous about his achievement is that the language in which he carried out this destruction *was the very language into which this picture was built*. In reading the *Critique*, one can see Kant desperately battling against the limits of commonsense Cartesian language, and managing, at the cost of incredible obscurity, to overcome the picture which is built into it and shadow forth a new picture. But he *only* shadowed it forth. For the full impact of Kant's work to become apparent, I think, one has to wait until the rise of linguistic philosophy in the twentieth century. Linguistic philosophers like Wittgenstein are not more clever or more profound than Kant, but they do have one priceless advantage: they are self-conscious about the verbal snares which language sets. They realize explicitly (not merely implicitly, as Kant did) that epistemological problems are not solved by discoveries about the nature of concepts or the nature of subjectivity or the nature of reason, but are dissolved by changes in the use of words. Kant still thought of himself as making discoveries about knowledge in the old-fashioned way. Because he thought this, his way of describing the problems which he was dealing with is hopelessly inconsistent with the solutions to those problems which he himself offers. Even though much of what Wittgenstein later said is already present in Kant, it took Wittgenstein's methodological self-consciousness to get it said clearly.

If one does read Kant in the way I have suggested, one will take his statements about concepts, intuitions, judgments, consciousness, and the rest neither as empirical nor as metaphysical discoveries but as covert analytic statements. As analytic statements, they are dependent for their truth upon an inspection of the way we use the words in question or on proposals for using them in new and more enlightening ways. Thinking of Kant in this way permits one, I think, to see the relevance of the remark from Wittgenstein that I quoted earlier: the passage in which he says, of his own *Tractatus,* that his propositions will finally be recognized as senseless, once they are properly understood. Once they are understood, he says, they can be cast away like a ladder which one no longer needs. I think this remark can be applied to Kant as follows: once we have worked our way through Kant's solution of Cartesian epistemological problems stated in Cartesian language, we need to abandon the language in which these problems were stated and in which they were dissolved. In other words, we need to abandon the whole scaffolding of the *Critique of Pure Reason* – the distinctions between concept and intuition, between phenomena and noumena, between sensibility, Understanding and Reason, between manifold and synthesis, and all the rest of it. If we keep this scaffolding, we will simply be faced with the old Cartesian epistemological problems rigged out in slightly different guises. For now, instead of worrying about the relation between mind and matter, with Descartes, we shall be worrying about the relation between phenomena and noumena. Instead of worrying, with Descartes, about the relation between imagination and intellect, we shall be worrying about the relation between Understanding and Reason. Instead of worrying, like Descartes, about the relation between the Will and the Intellect, we shall be worrying about the distinction between Practical and Theoretical Reason. In other words, if we keep Kant's terminology, and interpret each of the various mental entities, mental faculties, and the rest, which he postulates as a really existent thing, whose nature requires exploration, instead of as a new way of speaking about the same old thing, then we might just as well have stuck with Descartes. (Descartes's terminology is at least a little simpler.) But if we throw his terminology away, we shall be free to interpret Kant not as having discovered something about the nature of consciousness which Descartes did not notice but rather as having described consciousness in a different way than the way in which Descartes described it – a way which frees us from Descartes's problems. If we interpret him in this way, we can see the *Critique of Pure Reason* in the way I suggested in the first part of this talk – as a purely negative work, a work whose sole value lies in replacing a misleading picture of human knowledge with a less misleading picture. But if we make the mistake of thinking the words which Kant has used to draw this less misleading picture are more than *just* words – if we take them as the names of real things which require philosophical investigation, then we shall simply need another Kant to do for Kantian language what Kant did for Cartesian language.

Constitutive and Regulative Principles

I should like to conclude with one more brief section. In this section I should like to show that in trying to interpret Kant's achievement with the aid of doctrines and methods of contemporary linguistic philosophers, I am simply following up a lead which Kant himself supplies. So far I have been talking primarily about what Kant accomplished in his discussion of the nature of knowing and of consciousness in the "Analytic." I should like now to turn to the "Dialectic," and to direct attention to a section which seems to me to represent the heart of what Kant has to say about the nature and purpose of philosophy. Kant's critique of metaphysical speculation is, of course, very rich and complex, but its essential upshot is, I think, summarized in his discussion of constitutive vs. regulative principles in the section called "The Regulative Employment of the Ideas of Pure Reason." In this section he tells us that regulative principles do not need constitutive backing. Since the traditional business of metaphysics has been to supply such backings, metaphysics is superfluous. In other words, the ultimate rules which tell us what to do do not require justification in terms of discoveries about the metaphysical nature of things. The point Kant has in mind here is illustrated by the case of the methodological principles used in scientific research. These principles tell us that we should pursue our empirical inquiries *as if* the universe had been arranged by a supreme intelligence. That is, we should never be satisfied unless we have found a scientific theory which explains the phenomena in a systematic, unified, economical way. Having stated that we ought to follow this principle, Kant raises the question of whether we do not need, as a foundation for this methodological principle, a metaphysical guarantee that we can always find such a theory – such a guarantee as would be provided by a proof of the existence of a wise and omnipotent author of the world. His answer, of course, is not only that we do not need this guarantee but that we could not have it if we wanted it – since the notion of such a deity is internally incoherent. But the main point to which I want to direct your attention is simply his claim that we do not need to. As long as we follow the regulative principle in question, whether we justify our adoption of this principle in terms of a muddled theology or not is quite irrelevant. What counts is the rules that you follow – not the reasons that you give for following them. Either the empirical sciences will find constantly more complete, unified, and systematic theories or they will not. All they can do is to keep trying. It is no help whatever to the scientist to be assured by the metaphysicians that the universe is arranged in an orderly and systematic way.

This point that it is what you do that counts, not your so-called metaphysical justification for doing it, is, I think, Kant's central insight about the nature and purpose of philosophical inquiry. Kant applies this insight not only in the case of the methodological rules followed in empirical inquiry but in the case of moral laws. The categorical imperative, for Kant, is an absolute rock-bottom datum. Nothing could show it to be false and nothing could show it to be true – for only descriptions are true or false, rules are neither. This means that the categorical imperative is not and does not need to be "justified" by or "grounded" upon any theory about the nature of man, the nature of the universe, or the nature of God. The imperative is obviously compatible with any and every empirical theory about these matters. It might seem, however (as it did seem to Kant) that it is in conflict with a certain metaphysical theory – namely, the theory of universal determinism. But Kant's answer to this metaphysical theory is not to offer a disproof of it, nor to offer an alternative metaphysical theory. Metaphysical theories cannot be disproved; they can only be shown to be pointless. The proper reply to a metaphysical theory which seems to interfere with a certain rock-bottom datum, such as the categorical imperative, is not a disproof, nor, God save the mark, a new metaphysical theory. Rather, the proper reply is simply a demonstration that the theory *is* pointless. (That is, a demonstration that the metaphysical theory in question is of no relevance to the datum in question and cannot possibly have any relevance to the datum.) All that the moral philosopher can do with a theory of universal determinism is to point out that though determinism does apply to all matters-of-empirical-fact, a moral rule is something quite different from an empirical fact, and that no empirical fact is capable of either supporting or weakening such a rule. In other words, all he can do is what Kant in fact did – namely, point out the difference between sentences containing the verb "is" and sentences containing the verb "ought." "Ought"-statements are rules; "is"-statements are descriptions. Determinism may be relevant to descriptions, but it is not relevant to rules. Determinism is true of the spatiotemporal world. But ought-statements are not about this spatiotemporal world nor about any other sort of world. Since they are rules (imperatives, rather than declarations), they are not about anything. That the empirical world, or even the world described by a metaphysician, is a world of causal regularities is utterly irrelevant to the fact that I ought to act in the way prescribed by the categorical imperative and that I am free to do so. For moral freedom is not an empirical or a metaphysical property of an empirical or a metaphysical self. Hence no empirical and no metaphysical theory could show me that I am free or tell me that I am not free. To be free is simply to follow rules. Freedom, Kant maintains, cannot be understood. But this is not to say that there is any mystery about it – it is merely to say that it is not the kind of thing which needs to be understood. Because freedom is not an empirical or a metaphysical property – because we can describe everything in the universe without ever mentioning freedom – we do not have to understand freedom. Indeed to ask for an explanation of freedom or an understanding of freedom is just to show that one has not grasped how the word "free" is properly used. If I understand what a rule is and follow it, then I have acted freely and done all that there is to be done – to ask me to give a description of my activity of following a rule is silly. It is as silly as asking me to isolate the property of leftness which this table contains which makes it to be the left of this chair.

At this point, however, one might object that Kant does seem to have some sort of a theory of the noumenal self and the noumenal causality which this self exerts. It is sometimes said, in fact, that Kant had to postulate a noumenal self in order to supply a foundation for morality. But this way of putting the matter is thoroughly misleading. What would it mean to postulate a "noumenal self"? What sort of thing would we be postulating? How, in the light of the analysis of the function of concepts which Kant gives us, could we postulate anything which was not a spatiotemporal substance or a property of such as substance? The notion of a noumenal self, taken as a positive notion, is nonsense. But taken in the way in which Kant himself tells us to take it – as a purely negative notion – it is a very useful notion indeed. As a negative notion, it merely says that the word "I" when used in sentences like, "I ought to do so-and-so" functions differently than when it is used in such sentences as "I am doing so-and-so" or "I was doing so-and-so." In the latter sentences, the word "I" is used as a name for my empirical self – in other words, for a certain pattern of spatiotemporal occurrences. In the first sentence – "I ought to do so-and-so" – it is not used as a name at all. There is nothing which is named by the word I in that sentence. If one likes, one can say that what is named is the noumenal self – but to say that is simply a picturesque way of saying that nothing is named. As Kant himself says, "What our understanding acquires through this concept of a noumena is a negative extension . . . The problematic thought which leaves open a place for noumena serves only, *like an empty space*, for the limitation of empirical principles."[10] Thus, when Kant talks about a noumenal self and the noumenal causality of the moral will, he is not providing a set of constitutive metaphysical principles which are supposed to provide foundations for the categorical imperative. Rather, he is simply saying: "Do not confuse empirical descriptions with *rules!*" This slogan is the cash value of his doctrine that

[10] Ibid., B312; A260.

regulative principles do not need constitutive principles to back them up, and his insistence that they can get along by themselves.

Now this maxim that we should not confuse empirical descriptions with rules is, I think, the common methodological principle which links Kant with contemporary linguistic philosophy. For philosophers like Wittgenstein, philosophic problems are problems which arise when we try to talk about something in terms which are inappropriate to it. In other words, philosophical problems are verbal, in that they result from using a certain way of speaking in situations in which another way of speaking is appropriate. The solution to philosophical problems is, therefore, to supply rules about how to speak. This means that the proper business of the philosopher is to discover and to create analytic propositions by discovering and creating uses of words. Verbal problems require verbal solutions. However, there is something strange about the suggestion that philosophical problems can be cleared up simply by laying down new rules for speaking. We instinctively suppose that there must be some justification for these new rules other than the fact that if we adopt them, then the philosophical questions which previously troubled us do not trouble us anymore. Even if we admit that philosophical problems can be diagnosed in terms of confused ways of speaking, it still may seem to us that there ought to be some criterion we could apply to philosophical theories other than the fact that they clear up linguistic confusions. Now in replying to this instinctive search for justification and for criteria, contemporary linguistic philosophy replies that this search is itself the product of a confusion between empirical descriptions and linguistic rules. In Kantian terms, it is a confusion between constitutive principles and regulative principles. What Kant showed was that all the constitutive principles that there were or could be would necessarily be the affair of the empirical sciences. If we grant that philosophy is not an empirical science, then we must grant that the principles which it provides are purely regulative. If we grant this, then it is hard to see what sort of regulative principles it could offer us except principles guiding our use of language. Thus, Kant and linguistic philosophy are in accord in repudiating the traditional conception of philosophy as a super-science. In this traditional conception, stemming from Plato, philosophy's mission is to find justifications and foundations for the regulative principles which we use, or would like to use, in scientific inquiry and in moral decisions. That is, the task of philosophy is to provide constitutive principles which will back up regulative principles. But after Kant it is (or should be) impossible for philosophy to think of itself as doing this. The point of Kant's struggle to make philosophy a *critical* enterprise, rather than a dogmatic or a skeptical one, was to abandon the traditional conception that philosophy could discover something new. It seems to me that contemporary linguistic philosophy may properly claim to be Kant's proper heir. For contemporary linguistic philosophy makes explicit what Kant discovered but left implicit: that in the case of such ultimate convictions as the point of causality and the moral law, we can hope for more justification than we have now.

4

The Paradox of Definitism

One way of describing what happened when, in the Renaissance, philosophers deserted Aristotle and became "modern" is to say that their notions of the location of indefiniteness changed. In Aristotelian thinking, the indefiniteness which we experience is in part a result of indefiniteness existing in rerum natura; after Descartes, indefiniteness, whenever encountered, is taken to be our fault, a sign of our ignorance and confusion. In particular, empiricism from Hobbes through Hume to Russell has taken for granted that what we encounter is sharp edged and that fuzziness occurs only in what we make. The history of empiricism has been, in large part, the history of attempts to draw the line between the found and the made by drawing the line between the definite and the indefinite. Orthodox empiricism has regarded as catastrophes precisely those philosophers who questioned whether these two lines were the same (e.g., Hegel, Bergson, Dewey).

When one tries to reflect on whether these distinctions do coincide, however, one becomes aware that there are many senses of "definite," and thus just as many of "indefinite." As the idiom of philosophic controversy changes, the senses of these terms change. At the present time, the struggle between orthodox empiricism and the heresy of objective indefiniteness is going on principally in the philosophy of logic, and the sense of "definite" involved is "susceptible to the unconditional application of the law of the excluded middle." What I shall be calling "definitism" is the view that there is nothing which can reasonably be called a statement which is neither true nor false. (As we shall see, the hedging involved in "can reasonably be called" is not easily eliminable from the definitist position.) The sense in which those who rally round this thesis are the intellectual heirs of earlier philosophers who phrased their fondness for the sharp edged in metaphysical or epistemological terms is, I think, clear enough. Donald Williams, who is the most explicit, consistent, and insistent exponent of definitism, makes this heritage explicit when he says,

> I believe that the universe consists, without residue, of the spread of events in space-time, and that if we accept realistically the four-dimensional fabric of juxtaposed actualities we can dispense with all those dim non-factual categories which have so bedevilled our race: the potential, the subsistential, and the influential, the noumenal, the numinous, and the non-natural.[1]

Most definitists are more skittish about making metaphysical remarks, but it is certainly a dislike of "dim non-factual categories" which provides their moral fervor. Even when the "made-vs.-found" distinction is dropped as too metaphysical or too vague, it is immediately replaced by the distinction between the reducible and the irreducible, and the same categories are singled out as the obvious choices for reduction. For definitism, "non-factual," "reducible," and "resistant to reconstruction in an extensional language" are pretty much synonyms.

In recent years, the resurrection of pragmatism, combined with the antireductionist tenor of ordinary language philosophy, has been causing trouble for definitists. This is not surprising, for the principal strand of thought common to both movements is contextualism, and contextualism in logical theory is the natural enemy of definitism, just as contextualism in epistemology is the natural enemy of sense-data empiricism and as organicism in metaphysics is the natural enemy of atomism. Definitists like to pretend that their opponents have the sort of dim and loose minds which project their own dimness and looseness out upon the world, just as their intellectual ancestors used to pretend this about idealists. Such a pretense results in attacking conclusions rather than arguments, and this in turn results in the issue about definitism being presented as a contrast between clear and dim views of an object, rather than (as it really is) a disagreement about how much one needs to know about surrounding objects before being able to view any given object properly.

The key word in the statement of the definitist thesis is "unconditionally." Contextualism says that there are conditions which must be fulfilled before excluded middle can be applied to certain statements. ("Indefinitism," if it existed except as a straw man for definitists to knock down, would presumably say that excluded middle is inapplicable to certain statements in *all* conditions.) Contextualists differ among themselves, however, as to what conditions are required for its application to which statements. Some would say that the coming of tomorrow is a condition for the applicability of truth-or-falsity to "There will be a sea battle tomorrow." Others would deny this, but would say that the truth of "I own some shirts" is required for the truth-

---

[1] Donald C. Williams, "The Myth of Passage," *The Journal of Philosophy* 48, no. 15 (1951): 458.

or-falsity of "All my shirts are at the laundry." Others might perhaps deny both and yet insist that the truth of "Alcibiades has reached the age of reason" is required for the truth of "Alcibiades is either a general or a non-general" and thus for the truth-or-falsity of "Alcibiades is a general." Still others might hold that the truth of "Epimenides is a non-Cretan" is required for the truth-or-falsity of the sentence "All Cretans are liars" when uttered by Epimenides.

To all such putative counterexamples to his thesis, the definitist will reply with one of the following strategies. He will either (1) claim that the purported statement is not really a statement (and that truth-or-falsity is thus unsurprisingly inapplicable to it); or (2) claim that the statement should be reformulated so as to contain, as a proper part, the assertion of the truth of the condition in question. The danger in using (1) is that the definitist may trivialize his thesis by simply restricting the term "statement" to things that satisfy it. If he does this, the argument simply shifts over to the question "What is an independent criterion for statementhood?" Once this (not easily answerable) question is raised, the definitist thesis begins to look more like a proposal for an alternative language than like a statement of fact. For this reason, definitists possessed of the *Sehnsucht* for an atomistic metaphysics illustrated by our quotation from Williams will usually adopt the second strategy and say that each putative counter-example S is simply a confused and elliptical form of a statement S' to which the solution given in (2) applies. This tactic restores the quasi-factual character of the definitist thesis by presenting the contrast between definit-ism and contextualism not as one of alternative practical proposals about efficient ways of talking but as the difference between noticing and not noticing the complexities of common parlance. The contextualist is pic-tured as one who snatches a casual ellipsis from the mouth of the man in the street and then sophistically confounds him by showing that the ellipsis violates elementary logical principles to which the man in the street had instinctively subscribed.

Now the weak point in this strategy is obviously the relation between S and S', and it is here that the contextualist's counterargument is brought to bear. In this article I want to formulate a generalized version of this counterargument and then show how this generalized version applies in two sample cases of the controversy about definitism: the so-called prag-matic paradoxes and the hassle about Strawson's notion of "presupposi-tion." I shall conclude by drawing the (perhaps obvious, but certainly neglected) moral that as long as the issues are taken to be factual ones, the contextualist is bound to win, but that if the definitist is willing to join

hands with the pragmatist, and convert his thesis into a regulative principle, he can find victory even in defeat.

I

I shall distinguish three replies to the claim that any counterexample
S which violates the definitist thesis can be replaced by an S' which does
not violate it. The first is a bad argument, the third (which states what I will
call "the paradox of definitism") is a good one, and the second is good only
insofar as it darkly shadows forth the third.

The first reply is that the possible replacement of S by S' does not get rid
of the existence of S and of the counterexample which it offers. That one
can construct a new language, or fragment of a language, in which S' occurs
and S doesn't is an artifice which proves nothing about S. Nor is the claim
that S' expresses the intent of utterers of S verifiable except by an appeal to
intuition (which a determined contextualist can always frustrate by saying,
"That is not what I meant at all; I meant S.")

This is a bad argument because if strictly applied (as it never is), it would
frustrate any explanation of anything – in science as well as in philosophy.
Unless we are willing to accept translations and use them, we are con-
demned either to faint under the load of dozens of different vocabularies
which lend no aid to each other's interpretation or else to be able to think
about things only in terms of whatever vocabulary we happened to pick up
first. The badness of this reply is that it argues from the difficulty of
checking translations to the claim that translation cannot solve any problems. An analysis of explanation which argues in this fashion will find
itself forced to agree with Cardinal Bellarmine that the Copernican theory
is not "really" an explanation. Not to insist on a decision-procedure for
checking translations but to rely on intuitive (and therefore fallible)
appreciation of the results of translating is an important aspect of the
virtue which Peirce called "logical self-control."

The second reply which the contextualist can make is a more sophisticated form of the first. It consists in raising the question "Would S' mean
anything to anybody who did not understand S in the first place?" The
most explicit recent use of this argument is perhaps Strawson's attack on
Quine's elimination of singular terms.[2] This reply makes more precise
what the first reply intended in calling a purported S' "artificial," or "ad
hoc." If we find we can use the language which embodies S' only by first

---

[2] P. F. Strawson, "Singular Terms, Ontology, and Identity," *Mind* 65, no. 1 (1956): 433–454.

passing through the language which embodies S, then we can plausibly argue that S has not been replaced in any sense other than the trivial one in which, for example, a Thomist might replace the usual mathematical formulation of quantum physics with a formulation in the vocabulary of Aristotle's physics. To rid the language containing S' of its apparent artificiality, it would have to be shown that it either can apply to the subject matter directly or can express within its own vocabulary the ways of achieving such application.

The force of this second reply will be seen when we take up the third. As it stands, however, this reply is inconclusive. Considering the question as an empirical one, there just is not any way of knowing whether we could have understood the S'-language if we had happened to hit on it first. Nor, because of the peculiar character of terms like "understand," is it easy to think of what experiment would count as confirming that we could have "understood" it. (Analogously, we can never be quite sure that an inspired Aristotelian could not have developed quantum physics without any of the mathematical apparatus which its actual development required.) In the case of singular terms, for instance, a definitist who wanted to defend Quine against Strawson might point to a digital computer as an instance of something whose language contains no referring expressions and yet deals with its assigned subject matter very well indeed. The contextualist who feels there is something fishy about the example can then appeal to the computer's programmer, who will say something like "Sure it thinks, but it is too dumb to know what it is thinking about." The contextualist can use this response to argue that the programmer-computer complex is able to solve problems only because the programmer *can* use referring expressions. But such a debate is not likely to settle anything.

What may settle the question is the third reply. This reply goes as follows: "We will accept S' as a replacement of S if, and only if, you can give us an analysis of the statement 'S' is a replacement of S' which satisfies your own definitist thesis." The force of the second reply (and, thus, indirectly, of the first) is here brought out by requiring that the definitist be consistent enough to apply to his own activity of explanation the standards which he applies to the subject matter of explanation. If the definitist turns out to be able to state the claim that "S' expresses the intent of S" only in a language which contains expressions having the flaw originally ascribed to S, then we may conclude that he is just reshuffling the old deck and not dealing out a new one. "Elimination" of indefiniteness, from the standpoint of this reply, would be like rubbing off a stain from one's right hand with one's left, thus getting it dirty, and then not letting the one hand know what the other is doing.

Now before starting to argue that the definitist cannot, in fact, satisfy the demand made by this third reply, and thus that definitism is indeed involved in paradox because it cannot, in any given case, make good its claim without simultaneously contradicting it, I want to answer an objection which might be made to the very form of such an argument. What difference would it make (one might ask) if the definitist could not explicate his own explication in the way in which he wishes to explicate his chosen explicandum? Does an inquirer's inability to describe his inquiry in the same terms in which he describes its subject matter cast a doubt on his results? This objection, I think, merely points up the difference between philosophy and science. Science is largely judged by its results, and if we get a bigger bang for a buck, or a unified field theory, we do not much care whether the research was done with a cyclotron or a Ouija board. We do not, that is, except insofar as we are philosophers and are interested in shaping method as well as matter into some sort of aesthetic unity. The definitist can, as I shall suggest below, avoid all contextualist objections by converting his thesis into some such imperative as "Note that the S'-language is, for certain purposes, a more efficient instrument of communication than the S-language." This is a remark with which no one could quarrel and which would force the definitist and the contextualist to ask themselves just who has had what trouble about communicating what. But as long as the definitist is dominated by an aesthetic impulse which leads him to present quasi-factual theses rather than imperatives, then he is subject to the self-referential line of criticism exemplified by this third reply.

II

The paradox of definitism (the thesis which is at the heart of what we have been calling "the third reply") runs as follows: "No statement which expresses the fact that a statement S to which excluded middle is conditionally inapplicable is replaceable by a statement S' to which excluded middle is unconditionally applicable will itself be susceptible to the unconditional application of excluded middle." This, like the original definitist thesis, is not the sort of thing which can be verified a priori. If it were, it would turn out to be a tautology whose force depended on assigning special meanings to "conditionally" and "replaceable" (just as the definitist thesis can be made into a tautology by using a special sense of "statement"). Rather, one can make it convincing only by running through sample cases of replacements of S's by S''s. This will be done (sketchily) for two such cases in the next two sections. But such theses as this can also be supported, or at least clarified, by pointing to their formal analogies with more familiar and more generally accepted theses. In this section I shall try to show that this thesis can fruitfully be thought of as a translation of various intertwined philosophical theses of a more familiar sort into a particular idiom.

Consider the original Cartesian relocation of indefiniteness – taking it out of nature and putting it into the mind – which I referred to in the opening paragraph of this article. In its rationalistic form, this relocation is perhaps best seen in Spinoza, whose monism requires that he eliminate external relations among temporal events in favor of internal relations among atemporal clear and distinct ideas. To do so, he has to put forward a radical appearance-reality dualism, and then relate appearance and reality by saying that "falsity consists solely in the privation which mutilated and confused ideas involve,"[3] and that the kind of language and thought which is built around appearance is replaceable by another which will "reconstruct" such confused "universal ideas" as evil, contingency, and thinghood by distinguishing the "common notions" which (when seen confusedly) go to make them up. Eventually an apprehension of appearance will yield to one of reality in the way in which a perceptual illusion is eliminated by a change of perspective. Now, just as the obvious objection to Spinoza's theodicy is that the appearance of evil is itself evil, so the fundamental criticism of his epistemology is that to explain away external relations as confusion is to admit that confusion is real and thus that certain external relations remain – namely, those between the confused and the unconfused modes of apprehending reality. One cannot say that temporality is mere appearance and still admit that the process of eliminating this appearance is itself temporal. The reason why philosophers have never remained satisfied with monisms is that even if all other phenomena can be saved consistently with monistic principles, the phenomenon of saving them cannot be.

When such reasoning as this began to make the appearance-reality distinction look silly, rationalism's habit of consigning indefiniteness to the realm of appearance got replaced by empiricism's habit of consigning it to the constructed as opposed to the given. Now, recent polemics against "reductionism" have made it clear that the question "Did you construct that distinction between the given and the constructed, or was it given to you?" is as embarrassing as the question "Is your distinction between the real and the apparent itself real or apparent?" The crucial question for

[3] Spinoza, *Ethics*, Part II, Prop. 35 – *Eds.*

somebody who wants to reduce one side of a distinction to the other, preferred side is "Can you tell us *in terms of your preferred side* just how the reduction was accomplished?" In asking all these questions, we are telling the philosopher that he cannot just throw away the ladder which he used to get to his explanations, because that ladder is one of the things we want explained.

These familiar paradoxes of the irrational element in reductionist rationalism and the unempirical character of reductionist empiricism have obvious family resemblances to our claim that definitism, in practice, is never able to rid itself of indefiniteness. The resemblances are so close that one is tempted to look for a comprehensive formulation of the dangers which confront people who erect dualisms and then want to derive one side of the dualism from the other. But most such formulations (e.g., those sprinkled through Dewey's writings) are so very comprehensive as to be merely picturesque. What we need are some methodological notions which are specific enough to help us cut at the joints of debate about particular definitist claims and yet neutral enough so that their application is not limited to debates conducted in some single jargon. The closest approach to such notions, I think, are those of "rule" and of "interpretation" as they are used in some of Wittgenstein's arguments in *Philosophical Investigations*.

In these arguments (stretching, roughly, from sec. 68 to sec. 111, and from sec. 198 to sec. 247), Wittgenstein is concerned to show, among other things, that if one sets oneself the project of eliminating the fuzzy borders of a concept, or of the range of application of a rule, one is liable to get caught in an infinite regress. The reason is that the same impetus which led you to ask for a rule is going to make you ask for a rule to interpret the first rule – and so on (86). The goal of the man who wants to eliminate fuzziness is a rule that somehow bears its own interpretation within it and thus ends the series. But this is not what rules (nor, a fortiori, concepts) are like. As Wittgenstein says, "Every interpretation, together with what is being interpreted, hangs in the air. Interpretations by themselves do not determine meaning."[4] Wittgenstein concludes that "there is a way of grasping a rule which is *not* an *interpretation*, but which is exhibited in what we call 'obeying the rule' and 'going against it' in actual cases."[5]

These remarks suggest a formulation of the dilemma which confronts all philosophers possessed of that reductionist spirit of which definitism is the

---

[4] Ludwig Wittgenstein, *Philosophical Investigations*, 2nd ed. (Oxford: Blackwell, 1967), §198.
[5] Ibid., §201.

current expression: either reduction will be infinitely long, involving first a rule which correlates S with S', then another rule which specifies the sense in which "correlation" is to be taken, another rule to interpret this last rule, and so on; or else this regress will be cut off at some point which will allow an opponent to say that the putatively objectionable fuzziness has been relocated, rather than eliminated. Now the reductionist, as we noted (for the special case of the definitist), can get out of this trap by becoming a pragmatist à la Dewey (admitting that every "transaction" will always involve both fuzzy and nonfuzzy elements) and à la Peirce (admitting that logic is a normative rather than a descriptive discipline). Spelling out the consequences of this pragmatism will lead him to the position which Wittgenstein sketches as follows:

> We can draw a boundary – for a special purpose. Does it take that to make the concept usable? Not at all! (Except for that special purpose.) No more than it took the definition 1 pace = 75 cm. to make the measure of length "one pace" usable. And if you want to say, "But still, before that it was not an exact measure," then I reply: very well, it was an inexact one. – Though you still owe me a definition of exactness.[6]

But, once again, if the reductionist is willing to go this far, he must ask himself who needs what sort of exactness about what, rather than offering a thesis about language or logic, or even a wholesale program for constructing a new "more exact" language.

III

Having tried to put our purported paradox of definitism in a larger context, we can now get down to cases. The first example of a debate about the definitist claim which I want to look at is the "prediction paradox," a problem which writers such as Paul Weiss have taken as showing that there is a "collective" sense of "or" (i.e., one in which "ϕ (p v q)" does not entail "ϕ (p) v ϕ (q)") which cannot be reduced to the usual "distributive" sense of "or" until, as Weiss says, "we do something to the range of items connected by the collective 'or'."[7] The paradox consists in our being tempted to argue from the announcement that an unexpected event will take place in the next *n* days, that the event cannot occur on the *n*th day (because it would then be expected), nor on day *n* – *1* (for the same reason, now that we have eliminated the *n*th), and thus that it cannot occur at all.

---

[6] Ibid., §69.   [7] Paul Weiss, "The Prediction Paradox," *Mind* 61, no. 242 (1952): 269.

We will avoid this temptation, Weiss says, if we remember that the dates on which the event can occur "are, on the date of an announcement made before the last day, not yet distinguished, and that we have already eliminated all other days when we treat the last day as a day distinct from all the rest."[8] Presumably the act of distinguishing these days is what we have to do in the range of the collective "or" of the announcement before we can make the inference.

Weiss's position is just the sort of thing which makes the definitist's hair stand on end. Not only does it offend his logical sensibilities by impugning the unconditional applicability of excluded middle, but it offends his metaphysical ones by attributing an objective indefiniteness to the future. Aristotle's claim that the coming of tomorrow is a condition for the truth-or-falsity of "There will be a sea battle tomorrow" is apparently being revived, and Donald Williams warns us that if we allow this claim, "we are abandoned of logic."[9] "We can assert confidently," Williams says, "that by whatever amount 'our' logic falls short of certainty, everything else falls much shorter, so that, generally speaking no argument can be cogent enough to warrant a deliberate breach of 'our' logic."[10] Thus, we find Quine saying that "this notion [that there is an actual paradox involved in the 'prediction paradox'] has even brought Professor Weiss to the desperate extremity of entertaining Aristotle's fantasy that 'It is true that p or q' is an insufficient condition for 'It is true that p or it is true that q.'"[11]

In the light of these remarks, it might perplex a naive reader (call him Jones), who has chortled of the "illogicality" of Aristotle and Weiss, when he reads, a bit later on in Williams's polemic against Aristotle, that Aristotle committed the blunder of inferring from "necessarily $(p \text{ v } {\sim}p)$" to "Necessarily (p) or Necessarily $({\sim}p)$." He may also be perplexed if he happens to run across Quine's compendium of instances of the failure of excluded middle in "Notes on Existence and Necessity."[12] Jones is bothered by the fact that it is quite all right for statements involving modal terms, quotation marks, and the like, to "violate logic," but that it is fantastic for statements about unexpected events and future sea battles to do so. He wants to know what the criterion is for when it is all right and

---

[8]   Ibid.

[9]   Donald C. Williams, "The Sea Fight Tomorrow," in *Structure, Method, and Meaning: Essays in Honor of Henry M. Sheffer*, ed. Paul Henle, Horace M. Kallen, and Susanne K. Langer (New York: Liberal Arts Press, 1951), 290.

[10]   Ibid., 285.   [11]   W. V. Quine, "On a So-Called Paradox," *Mind* 62, no. 245 (1953): 65.

[12]   Willard V. Quine, "Notes on Existence and Necessity," *Journal of Philosophy* 40, no. 5 (1943): 113–127.

when it is not. He may then have it explained to him that certain parts of ordinary discourse are "extensional" – in the sense that "logic" applies to them without any counterintuitive consequences – whereas other parts, where such consequences occur, are "intensional," but that Aristotle's and Weiss's examples, being plain statements of fact, are obviously extensional. Jones (noticing that he has not yet been given a criterion, but simply a restatement of the problem) now says, "Oh, I get it. You are not really quarreling about whether or not to abandon logic but about *where* to abandon it." He has then been told that we do not have to abandon it anywhere, because we can restate all the "intensional" parts of language in ways which make logic applicable to them without strain.

What has happened in the course of Jones's education is that he has been introduced to the fact that beside the rules ("logic") which tell him how to handle a subject matter, he has also got to know some other rules which tell him either (a) what the limits of this subject matter are, or (b) how to whip things into shape so that they can be included within this subject matter. He is now prepared to receive some training in the second set of rules by going through Quine's dissolution of the counterintuitive consequences which Weiss finds in the prediction paradox. If he finds the dissolution successful, he is prepared to regard Weiss, if not as illogical, at least as not having tried hard enough to bring language under the control of logic.

Que messieurs les assassins commencent. Quine epitomizes the paradox in question as follows:

> The plot, in each of its embodiments, is as follows: K knows at time *t* and thereafter that it is decreed that an event of a given kind will occur uniquely and within K's ken at time *t+i* for some integer *i* less than or equal to a specified number *n*, and that it is decreed further that K will not know the value of *i* until after (say) time *t+i-½*. Then K argues that $i \leq n\text{-}1$, for if *i* were *n*, K would know promptly after $t + n\text{-}1$ that *i* was *n*. Then, by the same reasoning with "*n-1*" for "*n*", he argues that $i \leq n\text{-}2$; and so on, finally concluding after *n* steps that $i \leq 0$ and hence that the event will not occur at all.[13]

K's mistake, Quine says, is the result of confusing

> (i) a hypothesis, by K at *t*, that the decree will be fulfilled, and (ii) a hypothesis, by K at *t*, that K will not know at $t + n\text{-}1$ that the decree will be fulfilled. Actually, hypothesis (i), even as a hypothesis made by K at *t*, admits to two subcases: K's hypothetical ignorance and K's hypothetical awareness of the hypothetical fact . . .

---

[13] Quine, "On a So-Called Paradox," 66.

... K's fallacy may be brought into sharper relief by taking *n* as 1 and restoring the hanging motif. The judge tells K on Sunday afternoon that he, K, will be hanged on the following noon and will remain ignorant of the fact until the intervening morning. It would be like K to protest at this point that the judge was contradicting himself. And it would be like the hangmen to intrude upon K's complacency at 11:55 next morning, thus showing that the judge had said nothing more contradictory than the simple truth.[14]

Our first reaction to this, I think, is that Quine has saved the judge from self-contradiction only by a "low redefinition" of "contradiction" and a "high redefinition" of "know." Our sympathy for K will be increased if we imagine the following dialogue:

JUDGE: I decree that (1) you'll be hanged tomorrow noon, and (2) that you won't know this fact until then. Do you have any last words?

K: What is this? Of course I know it. You just decreed it.

J: Sure I decreed it, but you don't know it. (Here the judge adds Quine's argument.)

K: You're just twisting the meaning of "know." It's true that a pardon might come through, or something, but if you stretch "knowledge" to mean "incorrigible knowledge," then the second part of your decree is trivial. In that sense, I'll *never* know I'll be hung.

J: That's your worry. You could only charge me with inconsistency if I'd specified that by "know" in (2) I meant "deducible from (1)."

K: On the contrary, to avoid inconsistency you'd have to specify that you *didn't* mean that, for the normal use of "know" and "decree" in contexts like this includes the presupposition that the auditor knows what the speaker decrees.

(At this point the dialogue goes off into a debate about whether one can properly speak of a "logic of ordinary usage"; when we tune in again, we hear:)

J: After all, look what such a presupposition would amount to. If I made it explicit, it would have to be a self-referring statement – like "You know that everything I say is true"–or else it would have to be an infinite series of supplementary decrees – so that for each decree *n* I'd have to add a decree *n+1* that said "You know *n* is true," and so forth.

K: Well, why *not* say something self-referential?

J: Because I can't without talking nonsense. Observe that "says," "decrees," and the like apply to sentences but "knows" applies to propositions. You don't expect me to confuse language levels just to save your neck, do you?

What has happened here is that K entered the courtroom with a set of presuppositions about the use of the word "know." He had heard predictions about his fate from his cellmates, phrased as "You don't know it, but

[14] Ibid.

you're going to hang," and had not found them paradoxical. In the context of the courtroom, however, he expected to hear ordainments rather than predictions. What he heard was a jumble of both, which did sound paradoxical. The judge could satisfy him by making explicit which presuppositions K should use to interpret which parts of the decree. But if the judge tries to do this, he has saddled himself with a tricky job.

Let K's presupposition, "hearing a court's decree licenses knowledge of what is said in the decree," be symbolized by (P). (P) is to the first part of the judge's decree as a rule of inference is to a premise. The dilemma of the judge, at the end of the dialogue, is the dilemma of someone who must either make a rule of inference (here, the denial of (P)) into a premise, or else make explicit the distinction between premises and rules of inferences. To put it another way, (P) can be considered a semantic rule of K's language, directing his use of "know," and the judge has to tell him to change these rules by substituting some rule (P') for (P). The judge's dilemma is thus the dilemma of someone who not only has to make a metalinguistic statement but has to explain what a metalinguistic statement *is*. This dilemma, however, may seem no great problem; for cannot the judge just read K the standard lecture on the theory of the distinctions between rules of inference and premises, or the one on the theory of metalanguages? This tactic will only work if K is willing to swallow some nondistributive "ors." For one cannot make these distinctions without using an intensional language. In particular, one cannot refer to the meaning of expressions, nor to rules for their use, without using quotation marks or some surrogate for them – nor, therefore, without creating contexts within which distributivity salva veritate will fail. Thus, if K has sense enough to play dumb and pretend only to understand extensional languages, he can drive the judge along an infinite horizontal regress of object-language statements, each of which is intended to provide an interpretation for the last. Even if he's willing to play along with the notion of metalanguages, he still has the option of asking the judge for a semantical rule by which to interpret the judge's last remark (which was phrased in metalanguage n), thus driving him to make a remark in metalanguage $n+1$, and so on.

The judge, however, may have heard that language levels are out of date, and this may encourage him to make some such self-referential statement as (P'') "No, you do not know that everything I say is true." K fires back: "OK, then how do I know that P'' is true?" The judge recalls (perhaps from reading Ryle and Lawrence on heterologicality[15]) that the way to get out of self-

---

[15] See Nathaniel Lawrence, "Heterology and Hierarchy," *Analysis* 10, no.4 (1950): 77–84; and Gilbert Ryle, "Heterologicality," *Analysis* 11, no. 3 (1951): 61–69.

referential paradoxes without invoking language levels is as follows: (a) divide
the universe of discourse into two or more classes; (b) say that the putatively
self-referential predicate can be affirmed or denied only of members of one of
these classes; and (c) show that it is misapplied in the putative paradox.
Therefore (having read Scriven[16]) he (a) distinguishes those of his statements
which are ordainments from those which are predictions; (b) explains that
the question "How do I know that what you say is true?" has a use only when
asked about predictions; and (c) classifies P" as an ordainment. This tactic,
like the language-level one, will only work if K will accept nondistributive
"ors." For the judge has now abandoned any claims to the sympathy of
definitists. He has admitted to using a sense of "true" in which statements of
the form "S is either true or false" are true only conditionally – the condition
being the truth of the statement "S is a statement of such and such a sort."

These two sets of tactics are not the only ways in which the judge might
try to reconstruct K's presuppositions and offer him new ones. There are
roughly (n x m) such ways, where n is the number of words occurring in his
initial bipartite decree and m is the number of distinctions which can be
invoked to solve what Carnap calls "the antinomy of the name-relation."
Pretty much any distinction will do (e.g., between propositions and
sentences, between ordinary and oblique nominata, between entities of
different logical type, between uses of "decree," or "know," or "true," – or,
for that matter, "that"), although probably none of them will give K any
greater enlightenment than his initial perception, in the course of the
dialogue, that the judge was, for some silly reason, using "know" so that
it did not mean "deducible from what I said." Our remarks on the two
distinctions which the judge does attempt to draw suggest, however, that
somewhere along the line a failure of distributivity salva veritate is going to
occur. If Jones (the man who got confused about when it was fantastic to
use nondistributive "ors" and when it was not) has followed all this, all he
will have learned is that you can always find a way, when confronted with
a counterexample to the definitist thesis, of making the counterexample an
affair of names rather than of what is being named or described. In
particular, if we restore the prediction motif in the judge's decree by setting
$n \geq 2$, we can tell Jones that we have replaced Weiss's nondistributive "or"
connecting nonlinguistic entities (days) by one which connects expressions, and his physical "condition" for eliminating indefiniteness (waiting
for days to pass) by the linguistic "condition" of assenting to a statement
which expresses some appropriate linguistic distinction. But unless Jones

---

[16] See Michael Scriven, "Paradoxical Announcements," *Mind* 60, no. 239 (1951): 403–407.

already has a parti pris in favor of attributing indefiniteness to thoughts and words rather than to things, he may not be much impressed. Nor should he be, for he undertook to study "logic," and it is now pretty clear that the choice of where one puts one's definiteness is, whatever else it is, not a matter of "logic."

5

Reductionism

Modern philosophy is usually dated from the seventeenth century. If one were asked to specify the most important feature of the shift in philosophical method and assumptions that occurred in the seventeenth century – the shift that made modern philosophy "modern" – a plausible reply would be that the seventeenth century witnessed the triumph of reductionism and that philosophy from then on has been dominated by reductionist ideals. By "reductionism" I mean the acceptance of the following doctrines: (1) many distinctions made by common sense and built into ordinary ways of speaking are merely verbal distinctions; (2) using these distinctions as guidelines of inquiry will lead one to miss certain important resemblances between the things distinguished; and (3) the aim of philosophy is to penetrate to these important underlying resemblances and to formulate new ways of speaking which will illuminate them and which will expose the old verbal distinctions as merely verbal. In the seventeenth century, both science and philosophy turned away from one conception of the goal of inquiry and adopted another, radically different, conception. The former was the Aristotelian conception, in which the purpose of inquiry was to discover the peculiar principles appropriate to each area of human activity and to discover the peculiar essences of each of a great number of distinct species. The new conception was of a world in which the commonsensical Aristotelian distinctions between theory, production, and practice, and between essence and accident, no longer applied. In this new conception, every feature of experience is capable of being rendered equally intelligible and rendered intelligible in the same way. The result of the successful exercise of thought is now taken to be, at best, a single scheme of propositions from which every occurrence of every such feature might be deduced, or, at the very least, a single vocabulary of descriptive terms in which every such feature might be described. The extent of the difference between this reductionist conception of inquiry and the Aristotelian "cartographic" conception may be crudely indicated by saying that before the seventeenth century, if a distinction was built into our ordinary ways of speaking, that was prima facie evidence of its *in*dispensability, whereas after the seventeenth century, it was prima facie evidence of its *dis*pensability.

In other words, the Aristotelian assumed that his job would be done if, for each of the major divisions between subject matters and between natural kinds within subject matters, he could formulate general characterizations. It was not for him either to subsume these various subject matters under broader headings, or to find a single vocabulary in which these distinctions could be reformulated, or to break down the distinctions between the various natural kinds by finding broader characterizations or more generally applicable descriptive terms. On the contrary, intellectual achievement was measured by the number of distinctions one could erect, not by the number one could break down. This conception of the purpose of inquiry rested comfortably upon an unselfconscious trust in the distinctions which ordinary ways of speaking had provided; given this trust, the purpose of reflection was naturally taken to be, primarily, making such distinctions explicit and clear, not eliminating them or bridging them over. The reductionist revolt of the seventeenth century was a revolt against this trust in the distinctions provided by common speech. It aimed at reducing the inconveniently large number of regional theories, vocabularies, and problems which, Aristotle and common sense taught, were required to deal with the various regions into which human inquiry, and the world, were naturally divided. Its hopes for such a reduction were reinforced by its scorn for verbalism – scorn resulting from disgust at the seeming fruitlessness of scholastic controversies combined with a general suspicion of anthropocentrism. This suspicion engendered the realization that ordinary speech was created by men for human purposes, and the consequent realization that its distinctions might reflect merely human interests, rather than what Spinoza called the "nature of anything in itself" and what Ryle was later to call "the form of the fact." This scorn for merely verbal distinctions, together with admiration for the unordinary ways of speaking used by mathematicians, and for the extraordinary successes of science in discovering theories whose range of application cut across the usual boundaries, convinced philosophers that the aim of philosophic reflection was synthesis. It convinced them further that one way in which synthesis might be achieved was through the development of simplified ways of speaking. These ways of speaking would replace the manifold regional distinctions embedded in ordinary language with the barest minimum of distinctions. Such a reduced vocabulary would, they thought, have two advantages. First, it would make impossible the formulation of the particular problems which the scholastics had debated and, generally, of all merely verbal problems; second, formulating a reduced vocabulary would lead to a recognition of those ultimate distinctions which really *did* belong to "the nature of things in themselves."

This reductionist conception of the nature of philosophical inquiry has been common to almost all modern philosophical movements (with the possible exception of Hegelianism). Its most recent manifestation has been in the context of what Bergmann calls "the linguistic turn" in philosophy. This has also been its most explicit manifestation, for the linguistic turn has enabled philosophers to achieve a degree of methodological self-consciousness which was previously impossible. In particular, the ideal-language method of philosophizing has, for the first time, enabled us to formulate relatively clear criteria for judging the success or failure of the attempts at synthesis-through-reduction which philosophers have under-taken. If one hears a claim that some metaphysical entities are reducible to others, or that some concepts are reducible to other concepts, it is hard to test the claim. But when philosophical problems are posed in the formal mode of speech, the vague notion of "reduction" can be made fairly precise.

One way to make it precise is as follows: we can define a *reductive analysis* as a demonstration of the *eliminability of a vocabulary for a given purpose*. The claim that vocabulary V – considered as a set of words defined by enumeration – is eliminable for a given purpose may in turn be analyzed in terms of the notion of the *translatability of a statement*. I shall leave this notion of translatability unanalyzed for the time being, but I shall be taking it up later on. Here I shall say only that I take equivalence to be the strongest form of translatability, but not the only form. I wish to leave room for such weaker senses of translatability as are, for instance, covered by the nonsymmetric relationship "says nothing more than," as illustrated by such remarks as that "Opium has a dormitive virtue" says nothing more than "Opium generally puts people to sleep," or that "Death is a way of being which takes over human existence as soon as it is" says nothing more than "People's choices are affected by their knowledge that they are going to die."

I shall say that a vocabulary V is eliminable for a given purpose if and only if for every statement S which is characteristically used for fulfilling the purpose in question, and in which a member of V is used, a statement S' can be formulated which meets the following conditions:

(1)   S' uses no words which are members of V (although it may, of course, mention such words).
(2)   S' is translatable into S.

This is the definition of "the eliminability of a vocabulary for a given purpose." If every S' into which an S is translated uses a member of a certain vocabulary V', then I shall say that V is eliminable for the purpose in question *in favor of the alternative vocabulary V'.*

To demonstrate the eliminability of a vocabulary, either simply or in favor of an alternative vocabulary, and thus to perform a reductive analysis, is thus to perform two operations about which controversy may arise. First, one has to determine what statements are characteristically used for the purpose in question. Second, one has to show that the projected translations can be carried out. Criteria for the success of a reductive analysis will therefore be of two sorts. First, there will be criteria for the identification of the purpose served by a given statement. Second, there will be criteria for the success of putative transitions.

Two points about this definition may be worth mentioning. First, this definition is designed to make clear that the unit of reductive analysis, unlike the unit of a nonreductive analysis, is always a vocabulary. No reductionist would feel that he had succeeded in reducing anything to anything else merely on the basis of having translated one statement into another statement which used none of the crucial terms occurring in the first statement. Such a translation might, if certain conditions were met, constitute an analysis of the first statement, but it would not contribute to a reductive analysis if the words used in S' were drawn from the same vocabulary as the words used in S. This is why the analyses produced by nonreductionist philosophers – Aristotelians, for instance, or ordinary-language philosophers – impress reductionist philosophers (like Descartes or Bergmann) as merely explicating the obscure in terms of the equally obscure.

Second, some reductive analyses are obviously trivial – as when one shows that the entire vocabulary of English is eliminable for all the purposes for which it is used since one can always speak Russian. Some are not trivial – as when one shows that number-words are dispensable for purposes of fulfilling the functions previously fulfilled by the statements of arithmetic. I shall mention various criteria of triviality for reductive analyses at various points in this paper, but I shall not try to formulate a criterion which will be applicable in all cases. One could not formulate one without giving a general criterion for choosing the members of the vocabulary which a reductive analysis claims to show is eliminable. In other words, one would need a general method for constructing the set of pigeonholes into which we shall put the various terms of the language. There can be no such general method. The criteria for what will count as a distinct vocabulary are as various as are the interests, aims, and prejudices of reductionist philosophers.

With this definition of "reductive analysis" in hand, I now return to tracing the fortunes of reductive analysis in modern philosophy. It was natural that the newfound clarity offered by the formal mode of speech should have led to a boom in reductionist philosophizing. This boom was the ideal-language movement. But the most striking fact about the linguistic turn in philosophy is not that it has enabled reductions to be performed more efficiently, elegantly, and securely, but that it has led many philosophers to repudiate reductionism altogether and has thus brought about a reversion to the cartographic conception of philosophy which the seventeenth century abandoned. The reasons for this switch, I think, are roughly as follows:

(1) The new clarity about the tests which reductive analyses performed by philosophers must meet only served to reveal that, to quote Urmson, "nobody was producing any satisfactory analyses."[1] In other words, nobody was passing the tests. In all the important and interesting cases (for instance, phenomenalistic reductions) it turned out that the statements proposed as translations of other statements just did not do the jobs done by the statements which they translated. In the sense of translatability which the reductionists themselves had adopted – namely, equivalence – translations between interestingly distinct vocabularies proved impossible to find.

(2) Reflection on (1) led philosophers to have second thoughts about the aims and methods of ideal-language analysis. Previously this sort of philosophizing had been seen as satisfying both the need to unify the language of science and the need to make philosophy scientific – needs which had been at the heart of philosophical inquiry since the seventeenth century. But now reductions performed by the construction of ideal languages began to look like merely the last, and the sneakiest, of the devices which philosophers had adopted in order to announce quasi-scientific discoveries while remaining in their armchairs. For it began to be clear that the prestige of reductive analyses was due to the success of analyses which were grounded on empirical discoveries – the sort exemplified by reductions in the natural sciences themselves. Philosophical suggestions about the desirability of using a single vocabulary to replace many diverse vocabularies began to

---

[1] J. O. Urmson, *Philosophical Analysis: Its Development between the Two World Wars* (Oxford: Clarendon, 1956), 149.

seem, in Ernest Nagel's words, "predictions, on what were often highly conjectural grounds, as to what would be the most fertile avenue of exploration in a given subject matter at a given stage of the development of several sciences."[2] The recurrence of the phrase "in principle" in the reductive analyses carried out by ideal-language philosophers began to seem suspicious. As a result of such suspicions, philosophers were put on their guard against confusing the sort of unification of vocabularies which is made possible by empirical discovery and the sort which is made possible by verbal maneuvering, and to wonder whether the latter sort could lead anywhere. In other words, it began to seem that the unification, not only of scientific theories but of the language of science, might have to be left to scientists. It thus began to seem that the need to unify the language of science and the need to make philosophy scientific were needs which might have to be satisfied quite independently of one another.

(3) Reflection on (1) and (2) gave rise to the suggestion that we should not really be surprised that reductive analyses performed by philosophers do not work out. For let us consider what sorts of translatability there are, the demonstration of which might supply support for a nontrivial reductive analysis. To say that certain S's are translatable into certain S-primes amounts to one of the following three claims: (1) certain S's can be translated into certain S-primes because, on empirical grounds, we know now that certain referring expressions in S refer to all and only the same things as certain referring expressions in S'; this may be called a claim to *empirical* translatability; (2) certain S's can be translated into certain S-primes because S is a theorem of a formal system whose axioms are translatable, with the aid of stipulative definitions, into theorems of another formal system which contains S' as an axiom or a theorem; this may be called a claim to *formal* translatability; (3) although neither empirical discoveries nor proofs of the subsumability of formal systems are offered, the translatability of statements can be discovered by virtue of an inspection of the situations in which we employ them; this third sort of claim may be called a claim to *analytic* translatability.

Qua philosopher, it is presumably only the third sort of claim which the reductionist philosopher is making. He is saying that he can demonstrate translatability by an inspection of use. But then he is making a new sort of empirical claim, a claim which is often perfectly reasonable in the case of

---

[2] Ernest Nagel, "The Meaning of Reduction in Natural Sciences," in *Philosophy of Science*, ed. Arthur C. Danto and Sidney Morgenbesser (New York: Meridian, 1960), 308.

nonreductive analysis but which is prima facie implausible in the case of reductive analyses. For in the latter case, he is claiming that given the presence of two distinct vocabularies in our language, one of them is superfluous. In other words, he is claiming that our language contains two instruments for doing the same job. If all the statements used for a certain purpose can be replaced by statements phrased in a quite different vocabulary, while the state of our empirical knowledge and our knowledge of the subsumability of formal systems remains constant, then it seems quite strange that the superfluous vocabulary has survived as long as it has. Since it has survived, it seems quite likely that reductive analyses based upon analytic translatability will fail.

This series of considerations has led many philosophers to conclude that the reductionist conception of the goal of inquiry which the seventeenth century introduced is admirably suited to science and to logic but quite ill-suited to philosophy. Or, to put the matter another way, they have concluded that the abandonment of reductive analysis as a philosophical method will at last enable philosophy and science to get disentangled from each other. The same series of considerations has also, naturally enough, led these same philosophers to be more charitable toward Aristotelianism and toward the scholastics than philosophers have been for three hundred years. These considerations, and the resulting conclusions, are clearly and elegantly presented in the final chapters of Urmson's *Philosophical Analysis*. In this paper, I wish to take up certain of these considerations in the form in which Urmson presents them. In the second section of the paper, I shall argue that certain of Urmson's arguments fail to take into account an important area of application of the method of reductive analysis – namely, the cases in which reductive analysis is applied to the technical vocabularies of philosophers. In the third part of the paper, I shall argue that although Urmson is quite right in saying that by the reductionists' own standards, most important reductive analyses founded upon analytic translations simply fail to work, one can nevertheless formulate a looser set of standards for such analyses which will help us to distinguish between useful and useless reductive analyses.

Before going on to the second section, however, I should like to close this first section with some further general remarks about the role of reductive analysis in modern philosophy. I have expatiated on this subject because I think that it is important to realize how very radical a change in the presuppositions of philosophical inquiry would be entailed by the complete abandonment of reductive analysis as a method. I wish to expatiate on it a bit more in order to emphasize the importance of the particular class of reductive analyses which I shall be discussing in the second section – the cases in which reductive analysis is used as a weapon in controversy between philosophical schools.

It is obviously no light matter to say, as Urmson says, that "there is no such thing as reductive analysis" and that "the ancient doctrine of British empiricism that all non-simple concepts are complexes of simple concepts must finally go."[3] But if it were just a matter of abandoning British empiricism, there might be no cause for alarm. Even if it were simply a matter of abandoning the search for those few, ultimate, simple, and elegant distinctions which putatively suffice to grasp "the nature of things in themselves," we might still be well enough off. Resting content with the very large number of distinctions built into common speech, we might take on the job of mapping this multitude of distinctions with an even temper and a contrite heart. But, if we abandon reductive analysis, what will become of our repertoire of demonstrations that many of the problems which have exercised philosophers in the past – problems which still exercise some of our colleagues – are merely verbal? What in particular, is to take the place of our custom of translating the statements occurring in works of metaphysics into either falsehoods or trivialities? The popularity of reductive analysis among modern philosophers, after all, is due at least as much to its obvious usefulness as a weapon against opponents as to its presumed usefulness as an instrument for exhibiting the true form of facts. If we now find it unsuitable for the latter task, it does not follow that it is unsuitable for the former, nor, indeed, that it is not indispensable for it. If, for example, we abandon our reductive analyses of the Thomist's demands that we get our ontology straight before proceeding further – what shall we then say about the nature of being?

This series of rhetorical questions may be epitomized in the question: Can we abandon reductive analysis as a method of philosophical discovery and still keep the intellectual gains which have accrued from its employment as a method of deciding what questions to discuss? There are two reasons, I think, why this question demands attention.

The first reason is that it is hard to believe that at least some of the sweeping attempts at synthesis-through-reduction which philosophers have carried out during the last three hundred years do not have permanent and positive value. The moral indignation which ordinary-language analysis has aroused among reductionist philosophers is largely the result of a suspicion that we are being asked to abandon the hard-won victories

---

[3] Urmson, *Philosophical Analysis*, 183, 161.

which our predecessors have won over obscurantism. To put it crudely, these philosophers (of whom Bergmann is a good example) fear that if we go back to the point at which Aristotle started – namely, to a simple faith in the utility of saying what we normally would say – then we shall end where the scholastics ended. Even if such reductions as those attempted by the Cartesians in metaphysics, the phenomenalists in epistemology, and the utilitarians in morals now strike us as having been hasty and as too simple-minded, it seems obvious that they did succeed in sweeping away a great many ways of speaking which should have been swept away and which should not be swept back in again.

The second reason is that the contemporary philosophers who are most distrustful of reductive analysis nevertheless want to retain the right to say such things as (to quote Ziff) "what is said [in works of metaphysics] is likely to be false when interesting and platitudinous when true."[4] If we want to say this, we must have available a procedure for translating the sentences occurring in these works into sentences phrased either in ordinary language or in some alternative jargon. Without such a procedure, it is presumably impossible to tell a platitude or a falsehood when one sees one. To put this point in another way, the difference between ideal-language and ordinary-language philosophers in their attitude toward reductionism is merely a difference of degree. The ideal-language philosopher feels uncomfortable about, and thus tries to dispense with, all but a relatively small selection of the total number of vocabularies which the language contains. For instance, he may feel happy only about the vocabulary of logic and the vocabulary used for reporting sensations. The ordinary-language philosopher feels comfortable with all but a relatively small selection of the total number of available vocabularies – namely, all those except the technical jargons of philosophers. Even philosophers who are thoroughly sympathetic to the dictum that every statement has its own logic, and who would, at a pinch, grant that the statements in metaphysical works have their own logics, still want to be able to argue that some of these statements, and their logics with them, can safely be dispensed with. The only candidate for the position of a thoroughgoing and consistent philosophical antireductionist whom I can think of is Hegel. Only a faith as great as Hegel's in the necessity of all occurrences, linguistic and otherwise, and in the impossibility of separating achievement from genesis, could admit that all vocabularies ever used by anybody are equally irreplaceable – that no voice is wholly lost. If one lacks this faith, and thus wishes to shrug

---

[4] Paul Ziff, *Semantic Analysis* (Ithaca, NY: Cornell University Press, 1960), 197.

off some vocabularies, I do not see that any method other than reductive analysis is available to justify shrugging them off.

I

I shall begin by considering the following dictum of Urmson, quoted from a chapter called "The Impossibility of Reductive Analysis": "Nothing can be reduced to anything else by philosophers, and hence there can be no philosophical successes or failures in this field."[5] As the context from which this is quoted makes clear, Urmson does not wish to deny that at least one sort of reduction is possible – namely, a reduction in the number of distinct vocabularies which we employ. That is, he is not denying that reductive analysis – in the sense of the demonstration of the eliminability of a vocabulary for a given purpose – is possible. What he is objecting to, rather, is the suggestion that to show that a certain set of words is eliminable – in the sense that we can find another vocabulary in which to phrase the statements which we have previously phrased in the putatively eliminable vocabulary – is to show anything beyond this. Specifically, he is denying that it shows that a certain kind of thing does not exist – namely, the kind or kinds of thing referred to by some or all of the various referring expressions which are members of the eliminated vocabulary. In other words, Urmson is here protesting against the tendency to pass from the discovery that "We can say whatever we want about A without using the noun N" to the conclusion that "There are no Ns." Quoting Urmson again: "It is not that reductive analysis was successful in some few cases and not in others, so much as that there is no such thing as reductive analysis. Russell's success in analyzing numbers did not show that there were really no numbers, and the failure to analyze nations into people did not show that there were nations as well as people in a metaphysically significant sense."[6]

Now there is an obvious sense in which we must accept this conclusion. One cannot pass from a reduction in the number of words that we are able to get along with to a reduction in the contents of the world, if one thinks of "a reduction in the contents of the world" as the sort of thing which is achieved by blowing up a city or exterminating a species of bird. Changes in the way in which we speak are not causally relevant to the annihilation of nonlinguistic entities, except in the exceedingly indirect sense that a change in our way of speaking may lead to a change in our way of acting, and thus

---

[5] Urmson, *Philosophical Analysis*, 183.   [6] Ibid.

to a change in our environment. On the other hand, it does seem that in some sense of "reductive analysis," we do want to say that there is such a thing, that sometimes it has succeeded and sometimes it has failed, and that when it has succeeded its success has told us something more than that a certain vocabulary is eliminable. Let us take this last point first: What are we aiming at when we set out to show that a certain vocabulary is eliminable? Why would anyone ever bother to show this? A traditional (and, I think, correct) answer to this question is: To dissolve pseudoproblems which arise when the eliminable vocabulary is used for certain purposes, and thus to clear the road of inquiry. Urmson, however, does not give exactly this answer. He says instead that the utility of such demonstrations of eliminability is to "get clear about the way in which the vocabulary in question is used."[7] Is there any difference between those two answers? There is at least this difference: the traditional answer entails that in some cases we stop using the words contained in the eliminable vocabulary in certain sentences (roughly, those sentences which are used to ask and answer pseudoproblems), whereas Urmson's answer suggests that we shall, of course, go on using it just as we do now, but that we shall now be clearer about how we are using it. Urmson's answer, in other words, suggests the same picture of philosophy innocently holding a mirror up to language as does Wittgenstein's dictum that "philosophy leaves everything as it is." But the latter dictum makes sense only if "everything" is construed to mean "everything except philosophy," and such a construal, which amounts to the philosopher officially declaring himself unreal, surely exhibits an excess of modesty. But probably Urmson does not mean this, for presumably he would grant that one of the consequences which may legitimately follow upon our "getting clear" about how we have been using certain words is that we decide to stop using them in certain ways. If so, however, then it would seem that we had better distinguish between two sorts of demonstrations of the eliminability of vocabularies: one sort will be such as to bring about a change in our use of the words which are members of the vocabulary in question, and the other sort will not. The first sort of demonstration will be of the trivial sort which would consist in, for instance, showing that one can do mathematics in French as well as English. The second sort will include all the cases of any philosophical interest. It seems clear that unless one thought that at least some of the statements in which members of the vocabulary in question had previously been used would cease to have a use, or at least cease to have the same use,

---

[7] We were unable to locate this quote in Urmson's *Philosophical Analysis* or anywhere else. – *Eds.*

once the vocabulary had been shown to be eliminable, one would never bother to set about demonstrating eliminability. Indeed, if the process of "getting clear" about our use of a word did not produce any change in our use of that word, one might well wonder what clarification was good for. Thus, Urmson himself says that "Russell's analysis is very useful; it will, for example, prevent us thinking of them [numbers] as groups of invisible units."[8] But what counts as thinking of numbers as invisible units? I take it that no one would be said to be thinking of them in this way unless he sometimes used, or was prepared to use, or accepted other people's use of, statements in which the word "number" or words designating particular numbers, or other related words, were used in ways which would be appropriate for references to groups of invisible units. Further, no one would have been said to have been prevented from thinking of numbers as groups of invisible units unless he stops using, or is no longer prepared to use, or to accept the use of, number-words in such statements.

I conclude that to show that a vocabulary is eliminable is either trivial or else such as to change our linguistic habits. This fact is concealed by our tendency to exclude the use of a word in philosophical discussions from the data about its use which we consider when we speak of the "use" of a word and announce that we want to get clear about it. Normally we have in mind only its *primary* use. The distinction between the primary and the secondary use of a term or of a vocabulary is, I think, essential to an understanding of the effectiveness of reductive analysis in changing our use of terms. But it is a distinction which, though resting on a fairly firm intuitive base, is hard to make at all precise. Roughly, one can say that the primary use made of a vocabulary is the use of its members in statements which meet the following criterion: if we ceased to make these statements, we should gradually cease to use the members of the vocabulary in any other statements. In cases in which referring expressions compose all or most of the members of the vocabulary, we can make the criterion for these statements a bit more precise and say that these statements are those which tell us about the objects referred to by those expressions. In most cases, we should probably be safe in saying that the primary use of a vocabulary was exhibited in those statements containing its members which are in actual practice most frequently made. But this latter criterion may fail us for trivial reasons: For example, the technical vocabulary of a new theory in one of the sciences may be borrowed, for purposes of providing startling metaphors or examples, by nonscientists. None of these criteria are of any great help in deciding borderline cases, but I think that in the case of most

---

[8] Ibid. [The word in square brackets is Rorty's addition. – *Eds.*]

vocabularies, we would in fact have no difficulty in identifying its primary use. For what purposes are such words as "good," "just," "splendid," and "noble" used? Well, lots, but if they were no longer used to commend, we should be inclined to say either that there was no point in using them at all or that they had changed their meaning entirely. For what purposes are the words "lion," "unicorn" "tiger," and "python" used? Lots, but if they ceased to be used to refer to various real and fictitious animals, we should be inclined to say the same. For what purposes are "thousand," "sum," "multiply," "equals," and "fraction" used? Lots, but if they were no longer used to express arithmetical truths, we should be inclined to say the same.

We may now note that (as is perhaps obvious) most reductive analyses are demonstrations of the eliminability of a vocabulary for the purpose which dictates its primary use. When we speak of the use of a word and announce that we want to get clear about it, we usually have in mind only its primary use. When we show, in the manner of Russell, that the vocabulary of number-words is eliminable, we are showing that it is eliminable for its primary use. In other words, we are showing that it is eliminable *for the primary purpose for which is used.* We have not shown that it is eliminable for any other purposes, and therefore for at least some of its secondary uses. On the contrary. The whole philosophic point of Russell's analysis is to make us see that various philosophical questions about numbers can be asked and answered only by using sentences in which the words of the putatively eliminable vocabulary occur, and cannot be asked when these sentences are translated into the terms of the new vocabulary which Russell suggests. By showing the eliminability of number-words in their primary use, Russell is highlighting their ineliminability in certain of their secondary uses – namely, for asking and answering such philosophical questions.[9] He is thereby suggesting that these secondary uses are objectionable, because they are now seen to be uses which depend merely on using certain words rather than others. Russell's analysis, in short, has the effect of telling us that certain questions which are asked and answered by using sentences which use number-words are *merely verbal* questions.[10] Thus, Russell's argument for their being merely verbal is that there is a vocabulary which permits the formulation of statements which will do the

---

[9] If we retain the ordinary number-words, we can treat them as names of groups of invisible units and thus can discuss the mode of subsistence of numbers, their immateriality, their connection with the pure intuition of temporality, and the like. If we adopt the Russellian substitutes for number-words, however, discussion of these issues no longer makes sense.

[10] By a merely verbal question, I mean one which we feel free to answer simply on the basis of a decision about how to use terms in the future. We feel this free only when we have assured ourselves that the primary purpose served by the vocabulary in question will not be affected by any such decision which we might make.

same job as was done by the statements which exhibit the primary use of number-words, but which does not permit the formulation of statements which do the jobs done by statements which exhibit certain secondary uses of number-words. His argument thus has the same structure as one which concludes that the problems about the cabalistic significance of certain words – questions which arise in languages like Greek and Hebrew, in which the letters of the alphabet are used as numerals – are merely verbal. They are verbal because they cannot be stated in languages in which the numbers are designated by other devices – languages which are at least as efficient as Greek and Hebrew for the primary uses of number-words. We are therefore free to settle such cabbalistic questions in any way we choose by adjusting our use of words, for we make such adjustments without fear that our ability to do mathematics will thereby be affected.

At this point we may revert to the question with which we began: the question of in what sense, if any, philosophers can reduce the universe. Granted Urmson's point that philosophers cannot annihilate items of the furniture of the world by demonstrating the eliminability of vocabularies, it is nevertheless no accident that we often put the result of such a demonstration in statements which have the form "There really are not any X's." For one primary use of statements of this form is to offer assurance that we do not have to answer certain questions about X's. Thus, if I come back from Arabia and people pester me to tell them about the mating habits of the phoenix, the normal way in which I get rid of these questions is by saying that there is not any such bird. But the need to assure ourselves that we do not have to answer certain questions about X's is, as I have just been arguing, the chief reason why we attempt to demonstrate the eliminability of the vocabulary in which the word "X" occurs. Thus, if I come back from my epistemological researches and somebody asks me what I have learned about the powers of the active intellect, I get rid of his questions by saying that I have discovered that there is not any such thing. Similarly, if I am asked what my views about the operation of final causality are, I get rid of the question by saying that I have learned that there just are not any such causes. In neither of these cases, unlike the phoenix case, would one be reporting an empirical discovery, but one would never-theless normally use an expression like "There are no X's" or "There is no such thing as X" to report the result of one's analysis. In both cases, we might, Urmson to the contrary, properly say that something has been reduced to something else by philosophers. For in both cases, there was, prior to the analysis, not simply a way of speaking but a certain subject matter to be spoken about – namely, the active intellect and the final causes of natural phenomena, respectively. After appropriate reductive analyses, these are no longer subject matters for inquiry. In other words, in some cases of demonstrations of the eliminability of vocabularies, we are led to conclude not simply that we can talk about topic A in vocabulary V_B as well as vocabulary V_A, but further that there is no topic A to be talked about, only topic B. It is such conclusions as this which have, in point of fact, been the chief contributions which philosophers have made to intellectual progress, for it is such conclusions which change the questions which men ask, rather than simply the answers which they give to them.

One way in which philosophers have expressed such conclusions is to say that they have reduced A's to B's or A-hood to B-hood. This mode of expression is, I think, quite unobjectionable in cases in which the reducer wants to say that a vocabulary is eliminable for all purposes, because he thinks that all the uses of the words which make up the eliminable vocabulary are objectionable. Let us call such cases *radical reductions*. Whereas an ordinary reductive analysis is, as I have said above, aimed simply at showing that a vocabulary's employment for a certain purpose is objectionable – for instance, the purpose illustrated by its secondary use by philosophers – a *radical* reduction is designed to show that it is objectionable in *all* its uses. To show that vocabulary is objectionable in a given use is to show either that the questions and statements which exhibit this use are all merely verbal questions or answers to such questions, or else to show that these questions and statements are advantageously translatable, because there is some other vocabulary in which they may be more efficiently stated. In the case of radical reduction, the reductionist wants to show that all the sentences in which these words appear are used in asking and answering questions which are merely verbal or are advantageously translatable. If this latter claim can be backed up, then I see no reason why one should not summarize the results of one's reductionist researches by saying, among other things, that there are no X's, where 'X' is some noun which occurs in the vocabulary which one has shown to be eliminable. One might, of course, suggest that such a remark would be misleading, because the expression "There are no so and so's" is reserved for cases in which "so and so" names a species of physical object; but I do not think that it is, in actual practice, so reserved, and I doubt that anyone is in fact so misled.

However, despite what I have been saying, Urmson's denunciation of reductionists nevertheless expresses a legitimate gripe. There are, obviously, cases in which remarks by the reductionists of the form "There are no X's" are very misleading indeed. These are the cases in which the reductionist does not aim at a radical reduction but nonetheless speaks as though he did. In such cases, the reductionist objects only to certain secondary uses of the word "X," and not to others or to its primary uses. Such cases are illustrated by "There are no physical objects," "There are no minds," "There are no numbers," and the like. Such expressions are misleading because they appear to commit the reductionist to a position which it may never have occurred to him to hold: the position, namely, that all the questions of the sort normally asked and answered about particular physical objects, minds, and numbers are either verbal or else better asked in other terms. The reductionist who goes around saying "There are no numbers," for example, is usually suggesting no more than that certain sensible questions which we ask about physical objects (such as "Where is it?") are verbal questions when asked about numbers; he is quite willing and eager that we should continue asking other questions (such as "Is 17 a prime number?") in the same old way.

Philosophers have caused a great deal of trouble by permitting themselves the use of expressions of the form "There are no X's" as dashing rhetorical tropes, even when they did not mean to suggest that all questions about X are either verbal or advantageously translatable. But this fact should not, I think, tempt us to outlaw such expressions or to allow them only when we want to announce empirical rather than philosophical discoveries. In other words, the mischief done by such silly overstatements as "There are no numbers," should not lead us to renounce in advance the possibility that some reductive analyses can lead to radical reductions and thus can show that there are no X's. They sometimes can, if this expression is taken as equivalent to the claim that there are no questions about X's which are worth asking. We need not rob philosophy of the laurels which it won in the reductionist triumphs of the seventeenth century merely in order to chasten a few exuberant materialists and nominalists.

The temptation to do so, however, is fairly common nowadays, and it seems, though it is not entirely clear, that Urmson succumbs to it. The temptation consists in supposing that any claim to the effect that all the questions asked and answered by the use of sentences using a given word are merely verbal or are advantageously translatable must inevitably be false. (Or, in other words, that every radical reduction must inevitably fail.) The usual argument for this supposition is, I think, what is in Urmson's mind when he says, in the same passage from which I have quoted previously: "We cannot turn the numerical into the non-numerical in any way that goes beyond the elimination of number-words; how otherwise could there be an equivalence?"[11] This remark, I take it, summarizes the following line of argument: Whenever we have analyzed the primary use of a given vocabulary

---

[11] Urmson, *Philosophical Analysis*, 183.

in such a way as to have shown the eliminability of that vocabulary by providing translations, we have thereby granted that the terms of the eliminable vocabulary do have primary uses; but if each such term has a primary use, then nothing could show that this use was not a proper use, for what could possibly count as showing that it was improper to use a term in the way in which it is, in fact, primarily used? Specifically, what could possibly count as showing that the primary use of a term was in sentences which were used to ask and answer merely verbal questions or questions better asked and answered in other ways? Granted that reductive analyses may show that some secondary uses of a term are objectionable, it would seem that there can be no criterion of impropriety of the secondary use of a term save conflict with, or irrelevance to, its primary use. As, for instance, Russell's treatment of arithmetic showed the irrelevance of questions about the mode of being of the immaterial to the primary use of number-words. But if this is so, then to speak of the impropriety of the primary use of a term is nonsense, and therefore to suggest that all the questions asked and answered by the use of sentences using the term are verbal or advantageously paraphrasable is also nonsense.

This line of argument, however, fails to take account of the case in which the primary use of a vocabulary is in sentences which pose questions. In other words, it fails to take account of the case of a class of terms which I shall call subject-matter terms, and of the vocabularies which grow up around such terms. The sort of terms which I have in mind are those whose primary use is to delimit a sphere of inquiry. These terms fill the blanks in such contexts as "the theory of ___ ", "the Smith theory of ___", "the nature of ___", "methods of investigating ___", "the importance of the study of ___", and the like. The triumphs of reductionist philosophizing have consisted largely in eliminating such terms and their associated vocabularies. Such eliminations have cured us of the habit of asking (what we now call) the "wrong" questions – questions which we now consider merely verbal, but which once were the very warp of inquiry. They thereby enable us to start asking what we now call the "right" questions.

Consider the following terms: "being," "contingency," "transcendence," "matter," "final causality," "the soul," "evil." There was a time when these all functioned as subject-matter terms, and there are philosophers – Thomists, for instance – for whom they still so function. However, thanks to three hundred years of reductionism, there are many philosophers who refuse to use them in this way. More important, they refuse to use them at all – although they may mention them, as I am mentioning them here. For their use as subject-matter terms was their primary use. The main job which they did was to fill the blanks in such contexts as those which I listed above, and thus to help delimit a sphere of inquiry. When we cease to use them for this purpose, we cease to use them at all.

To those who still use them, it seems a shame that nobody is interested in inquiring into these matters any longer. Such is the perversity of the modern ego that the real problems of philosophy, Thomists tell us, are no longer being investigated. It would be all very well, they continue, if analytic philosophers would explicitly state their own, probably false, theories about what being is, the nature of the soul, and the like. Then we could argue the matter out. But the perversity of analytic philosophers consists precisely in avoiding these subjects, but nevertheless saying things which implicitly presuppose theories about them. To such complaints, analytic philosophers reply that what they say cannot presuppose such theories, for there is nothing there for them to have theories about. They retort that the Thomists themselves are implicitly presupposing theories, probably false ones, about other subject matters – notably, about language. Now, if this sort of dialectical impasse is to be circumvented by "getting clear about how we use words," the process of getting clear cannot consist in appealing to the primary uses of the terms in question or the a priori assumption that these are automatically proper uses of them. For employing this criterion would always lead to the controversy being decided in favor of the Thomists. If I am right in saying that some terms have their primary use as subject-matter terms, and if we accept the line of argument which I have attributed to Urmson, then the philosopher who claims that all questions normally asked and answered in sentences using such terms are either verbally or advantageously translatable must always be wrong.

To see this, consider the sentence from Urmson which I quoted above: "We cannot turn the numerical into the non-numerical in any way that goes beyond the elimination of number-words; how otherwise could there be an equivalence?"[12] Suppose that for "numerical" we substitute "ontological" and for "number," "being." We then get "We cannot turn the ontological into the non-ontological in any way that goes beyond the elimination of 'being'-words; how otherwise could there be an equivalence?" Now this latter question expresses exactly the sort of argument which Thomists do in fact use to show that no matter how often the vocabulary of philosophy changes, we must still, in some sense or other, be offering or presupposing answers to the same questions which were asked and answered by Aristotle and Thomas. In other words, no matter how

[12] Ibid.

many analyses we offer of such questions and statements as "What is being?" and "Substance is the primary form of being," we can no more escape from ontology than Russell could escape from arithmetic. Either the statements produced by such analyses successfully translate their analysanda or not. If they do, then there must have been a primary, and therefore automatically a proper, use of such words as "being," "substance," and the like, for how otherwise could there be translatability? The Thomist, in other words, will not accept any translation of the statements which make up his syllabus of ontological problems unless the translation is such as to enable us to formulate a syllabus of ontological problems; how, he asks, could any other translation possibly be adequate?

I conclude, therefore, that unless we grant that some reductive analyses can succeed in showing that a given vocabulary is objectionable not only in some of its secondary uses but in its primary uses also, the dialectical impasse which I have mentioned cannot be resolved in favor of the analytic philosopher. If we wish to eliminate ontology by demonstrating the eliminability of the ontologist's vocabulary, our elimination must not merely propose a new way of doing the same job but must show that the original job need not and should not have been attempted. More generally, when we demonstrate the eliminability of a vocabulary whose members' primary use is as subject-matter terms, we are not proposing that there is a better way in which to talk about the same subject matter but that there was never any subject matter to talk about. I thus conclude that if we are to give a proper account of what happens when philosophers offer reductive analyses, we must explicate cases in which the effect of such analyses is to change the subject, as well as cases in which the effect is simply to offer a new way of speaking about the same subject. We must, Urmson to the contrary, allow for cases in which philosophers really do reduce things to other things – namely, some subject matter to some other subject matter. To do this, however, we need a general account of the criteria which decide whether or not a demonstration of the eliminability of a vocabulary is successful. Specifically, we need to distinguish various senses of translatability. In the third section of this paper, I shall try to sketch such an account.

Before beginning section III, however, I should like to take up two objections which can be made to what I have been saying so far.

First objection: "It is misleading to speak of such a term as 'being' as if it were *inherently* a subject-matter term, and thus to suggest that if it ceases to be used to delimit a subject of inquiry, it must thereby cease to have any use at all. For any term may, at some stage in the history of inquiry, play the role of filling the blanks in such phrases as 'the theory of ___', or 'theories of ___', and/or 'the nature of ____.' The normal result of our ceasing to speak of the 'theory of x' is not, however, that we stop using the term 'x', but rather that we move it into such contexts as 'the x theory of Y'. Thus, for a long time, one could properly speak of 'theories of the ether,' and this phrase was equivalent to the alternative phrase 'theories of the transmission of light.' But when it turned out that it was unnecessary to postulate a luminiferous ether, we began talking about the 'ether theory of light transmission.' Again, one used to speak of the 'nature of demonic posses-sion,' 'methods for investigating demonic possession,' and the like, but now we speak of 'demonic possession as a possible explanation of mental disorder.' Again, we might naturally speak before the Reformation, of 'theories of transubstantiation,' but afterwards we speak of the 'transub-stantiation theory of the nature of the Eucharist.' In other words, what happens to old subject-matter terms is not that they become useless but that they become used as names of hypotheses – usually, but not always, discarded hypotheses – about the proper answers to questions about a new subject matter designated by another, and often a new, vocabulary. Thus, it is misleading to say that a reductive analysis of such a vocabulary as that of Thomistic ontology, by depriving it of its primary use, deprives it of all use. We need not see ontology as a sheer mistake – an inquiry into a subject matter that turned out, oddly enough, not to be a subject matter at all. Rather, the parallels with the previous examples from science and theology require us to think of the vocabulary of ontology as having its use in permitting us to formulate an hypothesis (though perhaps a mistaken hypothesis) about a subject matter describable in some other vocabulary. Courtesy requires this also, for if we so describe it, then we can at least give the ontologist the credit due to a man who tried to do a job that needed to be done, but did not happen to hit upon the right tools for doing it."

So runs the first objection. Let me begin by granting the point that the sciences, and generally in disciplines in which, unlike philosophy, there is agreement among inquirers at any given stage in the history of inquiry on what it would take to solve a given question, the normal use made of old subject-matter terms is to convert them into terms which fill the first blank in expressions of the form "the ___ theory of ___." But this fact, I think, just underlines the difference between scientific inquiry and philosophical controversy. Reductive analyses in the sciences are conducted within a framework of common agreement about what questions are to be answered and about the criteria for answers to these questions; therefore, the result of reductive analysis is not, usually, the elimination of a vocabulary but the coordination of old and new vocabularies within the overarching framework of a third neutral and relatively permanent vocabulary. This third vocabulary is, in Carnap's terms, the "linguistic framework" within which the "internal questions" of the science or sciences in question are resolved; it provides the subject-matter vocabulary for that science. But philosophical controversy has no such agreed-upon linguistic framework within which to work. For, after all, what is Thomistic ontology a hypothesis about, if not about being qua being? What would fill the blanks in "the ontological theory of ___?" What questions shall we treat it as answering? Is it perhaps a series of mistaken hypotheses about the behavior of words? Or a primitive form of the philosophy of science? Perhaps it is, but it is no more obvious that it is that that, as has been claimed, *Language, Truth and Logic* is really just a series of answers to ontological questions. It is possible, of course, that a long sequence of dialectical interchanges with the ontologist might enable us to formulate some neutral third vocabulary, a characterization of the subject matter which both Thomistic ontology and linguistic analysis can describe themselves as investigating. This is possible, but it is certainly not imminent. I think that the search for such a neutral vocabulary is as important and urgent as it is difficult. For if the day comes when such a vocabulary is found, philosophers will be one slouch nearer its ever-retreating goal of "becoming a science." But until it is found, it is a mistake to discuss reductive analysis without taking into account the peculiar problems which its failure to be found presents. Describing the process of changing the questions which we ask is, to be sure, very much messier than describing the process of changing the answers to the questions which we ask. That is why metaphilosophy is, as compared with the philosophy of science, in a rather primitive state. But both processes occur, and they are quite different. There is no point in trying to pretend that the former is merely a special case of the latter.

Second Objection: "The objections which you offer to the view that every primary use must be a proper use (and thus that philosophy cannot presume to say that a job actually being done by a vocabulary is not a job worth doing) rest on lumping together ordinary and technical uses of language. No one would think of putting forward this view in regard to technical vocabularies, and especially not a philosopher's vocabularies. The principle which you attribute to Urmson – that a job done by a vocabulary is automatically a job worth doing – holds (if it holds at all), only for ordinary uses of nontechnical vocabularies. The criterion for whether a technical vocabulary, or a technical use of an ordinary vocabulary, performs a useful function is not, of course, whether it is used but whether it performs the function which it was invented to perform. A word like 'being' is, in the sense in which it is used by philosophers, a 'philosopher's word' and a philosopher's word has a proper use just in case they help us perform philosophical tasks."

So runs the second objection. My reply is based on the same fact as my reply to the first – the fact that we are not in a position to specify what task it is that a subject-matter vocabulary should perform. We cannot do so unless we have available an alternative subject-matter vocabulary which will permit us to see the statements which exhibit the primary use of the former vocabulary as expressing a theory about some subject. But this is just what, in the case of controversy between philosophical movements, is not available. If we could formulate what the problems which technical philosophic vocabularies were designed to help solve are, then we could indeed make a decision about whether to continue using any given philo-sophical vocabulary on relatively straightforward pragmatic grounds. But, once again, a distinguishing feature of philosophical controversy is that it involves controversy over what the subject matter being discussed is, and thus over what problems there are to discuss. As things stand, each philosophic caucus (for instance, the Thomists, the linguistic analysts, the Marxists, the Heideggerians) is in possession of a subject-matter vocabulary which enables them to offer translations of the statements made by each of their competitors and thus to perform reductive analyses of their competitors' technical vocabularies. Each such translation is designed to show that the subject-matter vocabulary used by the competi-tion does not, in fact, delimit a subject matter and thus that the problems which the competition discusses are, in fact, mere pseudoproblems. Each of the competitors so attacked replies that the inadequacy of the proposed translation is shown by, if nothing else, the very fact that the translation is made from statements which are used to formulate questions about a certain subject matter into statements which cannot be used for this purpose. In this situation, pragmatic criteria are no help. We cannot, as the objection suggests we can, simply inquire whether the "philosopher's word" in question performs the task for which it was designed. To do so, we should have to get clear about the nature of this task. I do not see that any method other than reductive analysis is available for discussing the question of whether such tasks are or are not mere pseudotasks. In the next section, I shall try to suggest that reductive analysis is, and should, be used to discuss such questions.

II

In this third, last, most conjectural, and (mercifully) shortest section of the paper, I shall try to make a first payment on the debt which I have contracted by leaning on employing the unanalyzed notion of *translatability* in the previous two sections. You may recall that I said that I would use the term "translatable" to name a generic relationship which holds between certain statements – a relationship one species of which is equivalence and another species of which is the nonsymmetric relation of "saying nothing more than." I now need to explicate this later relation and thus show that there is some interesting species of translatability, weaker than equivalence, which can be used in performing reductive analyses. I need to show this because I need to get around Urmson's argument that we should not hope for any interesting reductive analyses (nor, a fortiori, any radical reductions) in the absence of new empirical, logical, or mathematical discoveries. This argument is one that I have already sketched in section I. Very crudely, it is to the effect that if the vocabularies in which S and S' are phrased are sufficiently distinct so that a demonstration of the eliminability of the vocabulary of S in favor of the vocabulary of S' for some given purpose would be philosophically interesting, then S and S' will not be equivalent. Conversely, if they are equivalent, then the vocabularies in which they are stated will not be interestingly distinct. The crucial premises of this argument are the assumption that language does not normally contain superfluous vocabularies, and the corollary assumption that any vocabulary which is reasonably well entrenched in our language is probably serving to make possible the formation of statements which are not equivalent to any other statements formulable in the language. I think that this argument is sound. To get around it, therefore, I have to show that interesting reductive analyses may be achieved, or at least attempted by employing a weaker sense of "translatability" than "equivalence."

The shortest way of showing this will, I think, be to take up an example which Urmson uses to lend plausibility to the assumptions about the nature of language which I just mentioned. This is the example of the eliminability of the vocabulary which we use for talking about nations in favor of the vocabulary which we use for talking about people. Since it seems clear that there is, in some sense, nothing more to the behavior of a nation than the behavior of lots of individuals, it seems clear that reductive analysis will work here if it will work anywhere. But, Urmson points out, there is no statement about individuals which will do the work done by "England declared war on Germany in 1939." This is, roughly, because there are an indefinitely large number of actions by individual people which could have constituted such a declaration, and thus the only possible sentence about individuals which would be equivalent to the sentence in question would be an indefinitely long disjunction. Urmson suggest that this same situation will hold for all similar cases. The similar cases are those in which we have one vocabulary, V', in which we can report on matters of a certain kind K', and also have another vocabulary V in which we can, as it were, sum up such reports about K' matters in a way that does not say anything definite about K' matters but does say something definite about matters of another, "higher," kind – K. One such similar case is the relation between a sense-datum vocabulary and a physical-object vocabulary. In both this case and the case of nations, the fact that our grounds for statements about K matters always are, or at least always include, statements about K' matters, suggests that we could avoid talking about K matters entirely and talk only about K' matters. It suggests, in other words, that the vocabulary V is eliminable in favor of the vocabulary V'. But Urmson's point is that since the "higher" vocabulary V is designed not to say anything definite about *K'* matters, and would be pointless and super-fluous if it did, it will almost never be possible to find an equivalence between a statement using *V* terms and a finitely long statement using only V' terms. In other words, the reductionist is looking for equivalences between statements in vocabularies whose whole function consists in not permitting such equivalences.

This is a very abbreviated and crude version of what Urmson says, but I think that it shows the strength of his position; as I have said, I do not wish to quarrel with his conclusion that no equivalences can be found in the cases he discusses. On the contrary, I think he is quite right. I wish rather to ask whether there is any interesting sense in which it is true to say that "we could avoid talking about K matters entirely, and still not miss anything," even after we have granted that no statement which uses only members of V' is equivalent to a statement which uses members of V. I think that there is such a sense and that it can be expressed in the following way. I shall say that a statement S is evidentially translatable into another statement S' for a given user if and only if:

> For every statement X such that this user accepts X as adequate evidence for S and every statement Y such that this user accepts S as adequate evidence for Y, one can construct statements S', X', and Y' such that
>
> (1) the user would accept S' as adequate evidence for S, X' as adequate evidence for X, and Y' as adequate evidence for Y;

(2)   the user would accept X' as adequate evidence for S'; and
(3)   the user would accept S' as adequate evidence for Y'.

Let us now say that a statement S is *evidentially translatable* if and only if for every user of the language, there is some statement S' (not necessarily the same statement S' for each user) into which S is evidentially translatable for that user. Suppose that all the various statements S' into which S is evidentially translatable for various users contain no terms which are members of vocabulary V. Then we may say that vocabulary V is eliminable for the purpose of providing evidence about K' matters if and only if all the statements which use members of V and are used for this purpose are evidentially translatable. In other words, a demonstration of the eliminability of the vocabulary V will now depend not on discovering equivalences but on finding patterns of evidential connection between statements.

Let me now try to unpack, briefly, the notions which I have built into this definition. I have designed my definition of evidential translatability to fit the intuitive conviction of the reductionist that our habit of classifying the behavior of individual people in the ways provided by our nation-vocabulary is a convenience, but no more than a convenience. On this view, talk about nations is merely a handy device for rendering our inferences from pieces of individual behavior to other pieces of individual behavior more manageable. This being so, we could, at no greater cost than inefficiency, drop nation-terms out of our language and still not lose any knowledge which we might otherwise have gained. This notion is reproduced in the definition of evidential translatability because the definition insures that if evidential translatability does hold, then any chain of evidential relationships leading from one statement about nations to another statement about nations will be mirrored in a chain of evidential relationships leading from one statement about individual people to another such statement. In other words, it ensures that if all the statements which use nation-words and are used for the purpose of predicting the behavior of individuals are evidentially translatable into statements not using such words, then no knowledge about the behavior of individual people will be lost simply because we no longer use nation-words. For, starting with some S' which would serve as adequate evidence for some S, we shall be able to move along an evidential chain on the level of talk about individuals to some statement Y' – a statement which, in turn, would have been adequate evidence for any statement Y which we would have reached by starting with S and moving along an evidential chain of statements about nations. The only price paid for sticking to the primed statements and renouncing the original S's and Y's would thus be inefficiency. Obviously, however, this inefficiency would be very great, since the S-primes and Y-primes will, usually, be very long, although certainly finitely long, conjunctions.

Let me now briefly turn to the question of whether, in the sense of eliminability which is offered by this notion of evidential translatablity, our nation-vocabulary is eliminable for the purpose of predicting the behavior of individuals. Here I can only say that I do not know. I can think of no particular reason why a reductionists' demonstration of eliminability would not go through in this case, but I do not know whether it would or not. The question of whether it would is irrelevant to this paper, but mention of this question brings up another which is relevant. The weak notion of evidential translatability which I have developed must not be so weak as to permit all reductionist claims to succeed automatically. In other words, it must not be the case that every vocabulary V is eliminable for the purpose of predicting the behavior of K' matters. It might, at first glance, seem that all statements using V terms and used for predicting the behavior of K'-entities would naturally be evidentially translatable. However, I suspect, although I cannot prove, that this appearance is deceptive. I suspect this primarily because I suspect that, even using this weak notion of evidential translatability in place of the notion of equivalence, one would not be able to perform a successful reduction of statements about physical objects to statements about sense-data. That is, I doubt that even the rather narrow, and quite plausible, claim that statements using physical-object terms which are used for the purpose of predicting the behavior of sense-data are evidentially translatable. In other words, I doubt that it is possible to establish evidential chains linking sense-datum statements without the mediation of physical-object statements. But, as I have said, I am not able to offer you a satisfactory argument on this point.

***

This is all that I wish to say about evidential translatability. I think that formulating this sense of "translatability" helps us to formulate criteria for the success of a large number of reductionist claims: roughly, all those which involve claims that a given vocabulary is eliminable for the purpose of predicting the behavior of a certain kind of entity. The criterion will be, simply, whether the relevant evidential translations can be provided. Using this criterion, one can avoid discarding all reductive analyses not grounded on empirical or logical discoveries as trivial or unsuccessful – whereas one must so discard them if one insists that such analyses involve the discoveries of equivalences.

However, this notion of evidential translatability is not, in itself, enough to give us any help in developing criteria for the success of reductive analyses of *subject-matter* vocabularies. More specifically, it does not provide a sense of "translatability" which can be employed in radical reductions of technical philosophical vocabularies. There are two reasons for this. First, the primary use of subject-matter vocabularies is not to predict the behavior of a kind of entity. Rather, their primary use is in formulating questions and theories about a certain putative subject matter. In the second place, evidential translatability, like equivalence, is a relation which can only hold between statements; it cannot hold between questions. So if we are to have a plausible reductive analysis of a subject-matter vocabulary, we must have a sense of "translatability" which will apply to questions. We need to be able to say that a question Q asks nothing more than another question Q', just as we need to be able to say that a certain statement says nothing more than another statement.

These two considerations make clear why reductive analyses of subject-matter vocabularies are so much trickier than such relatively straightforward reductive analyses as those involved in reducing nations to individuals or physical objects to sense-data. In these more straightforward cases, it is relatively easy to get agreement about the various purposes served by the various sorts of statements in which the members of the vocabulary are used. For instance, the reductionist and the antireductionist can agree that one of the purposes served by nation-statements is to formulate evidence for statements about people. They may even agree on whether this purpose is primary – that, in other words, if this use were no longer made of them, all the other statements in which nation-words are used would also, eventually, cease to be made. Now in the case of subject-matter vocabularies, both the reductionist and the antireductionist do agree that the primary purpose of the vocabulary in question is to raise questions about a certain subject matter. But the reductionist wants to say that there is no such subject matter, and therefore he cannot say that the S-primes he offers as translations of the original S's will serve the same purpose as the original S's. Suppose, for example, that I want to get rid of the question "What is being?" as well as the jargonesque statements which Thomists use to answer this question. I obviously cannot claim that the statements into which I translate these latter statements will still answer the question "What is being?" But if I demonstrate the eliminability of the Thomist's vocabulary for any other purpose than its primary one of asking and answering just such questions, the Thomist will remain unperturbed. So if my reductive analysis is to have any force, I must find some way of arguing not, as in straightforward cases of reductive analysis, that I can do the same job without using certain terms, but that there is not any job to be done. In other words, I must propose translations of his questions, and find a criterion for the success of such translations.

I now wish to offer such a criterion for the translatability of questions into other questions. The intuitive basis for this criterion is our suspicion that if we have two sets of questions, both of which are answered by attending to the same sort of data, and if a change in an answer to a question of one set is always correlated with a change in the answer to a question of another set, then we may have one set of questions too many. This suspicion is perhaps best illustrated in our suspicion of ad hoc explanations. Consider the two questions: "Does opium put people to sleep?" and "Does opium have a dormitive virtue?" The same data will determine our answers to both questions, and if we change our answer to one we simultaneously change our answer to the other. Realizing that this is the case, we begin to suspect that one question asks no more than the other and that one of the two questions is superfluous.

Having outlined this intuitive basis, let me now propose the following criterion for what I shall call the *heuristic translatability* of questions. I shall say that a question Q is heuristically translatable into another question Q' for a given user if and only if:

For any statement S which is accepted by the user as an answer to Q, there is

(1) a statement S_e ("e" standing for "evidence") which he would accept as adequate evidence for S, and
(2) a statement S' for which S_e would also be accepted as adequate evidence by him and which he would accept as an answer to Q'.

This notion of "heuristic translatability of Q into Q' for a given user" can be generalized into a general notion of heuristic translatability in the same manner in which the notion of evidential translatability of S into S' for a given user was generalized. We can say that a question Q is heuristically translatable if and only if for every user of the language, there is some question Q' (not necessarily the same question for each user) into which Q is heuristically translatable for that user. If for all the relevant Q's, all the various questions Q' into which Q is heuristically translatable for various users contain no terms which are members of the vocabulary V, then we may say that vocabulary V, in its use as a subject-matter vocabulary, is eliminable. If its use as a subject-matter vocabulary was its primary use, then we may claim to have performed a radical reduction of this vocabulary and to have shown that there are no K's – where K is the kind of thing which this vocabulary purported to formulate questions about.

When such a claim is interpreted in the way suggested by this definition of heuristic translatability, it can be seen as a claim that we no longer need to have a theory of K, because all the pieces of evidence which might be used to support the statements making up a theory of K have already, so to speak, discharged their functions by contributing to answering the various questions Q' into which Q is heuristically translatable. Thus when we say that, if we have physics and semantics, we no longer need Thomistic ontology, or when we say that, if we have psychology and semantics, we do not need what Heidegger calls "fundamental ontology," our claim may best be interpreted as a claim that we could provide heuristic translations of all the questions which Thomistic ontology or Heideggerian fundamental ontology purport to answer. This claim, together, perhaps, with a claim that all the statements made in Thomas's or Heidegger's ontological theories are evidentially translatable is what is required to back up our claim that these questions are verbal questions and thus that we may safely stop asking them.

Such a reductive analysis of a technical philosophical vocabulary, basing itself upon the attempt to provide evidential and heuristic translations rather than equivalences, is, I think, what we in fact find ourselves producing when we argue with fellow philosophers whom we think are asking the wrong questions. In proposing these definitions, I have tried simply to describe the actual procedures which we employ in such arguments. I do not claim to have discovered any new, knock-down arguments which can be used in such situations. But I hope that what I have said is sufficient to justify my claim, in section II, that reductive analysis of subject-matter vocabularies is, despite its difficulty, a practicable method of arguing about what questions do and do not need to be answered.

6

Phenomenology, Linguistic Analysis, and Cartesianism: Comments on Ricoeur

The contest between phenomenology and linguistic analysis is a competition between two groups of opponents of a single enemy. The enemy is Cartesianism, and the two sides try to outdo each other in mining ever deeper for hidden Cartesian assumptions. Each accuses the other of being still in bondage to such assumptions. To the linguistic analysts, phenomenological descriptions of the *Lebenswelt* look like disguised versions of the sort of "revisionist metaphysics" practiced by, for example, Bradley and Whitehead. Such descriptions, the analysts say, would only be taken seriously by people who have not yet undergone the therapy necessary to realize that Cartesian problems are unreal. To phenomenologists, linguistic analysts look like the descendants of those "naturalists" whom the early Husserl attacked; they appear as the currently fashionable representatives of the "objectivism" which Merleau-Ponty wanted us to overcome. Naturalism and objectivism, phenomenologists say, can still be taken seriously only by those so deeply imbued with Cartesian dualism as not to understand the need for developing new, non-Cartesian, philosophical categories.

In what follows, I want to present a portion of the linguistic analysts' argument for the claim that they, rather than the phenomenologists, form the avant-garde of the anti-Cartesian revolution. I am not sure myself how good this argument is, but it seems useful to develop it in order to see what issues must be settled before we can agree about what, if anything, needs to be done in the philosophy of language. I shall begin by presenting three theses – planks of a possible metaphilosophical platform for the linguistic analyst. I shall then discuss to what extent these theses entail or are entailed by the adoption of Wittgensteinian views about language. Finally, I shall examine certain remarks of Paul Ricoeur's and criticize these on the basis of this platform.[1]

[1] This paper is a response to Ricoeur's "Husserl and Wittgenstein on Language," which was later published in *Phenomenology and Existentialism*, ed. Edward N. Lee and Maurice Mandelbaum

The first thesis is that the only justification for a philosopher's redescription of a phenomenon – for example, thinking, perceiving, or using language – is that such a redescription makes it impossible to formulate some traditional philosophical problems which have arisen concerning this phenomenon. By redescription I mean the use of a jargon (which may involve either coining technical terms or assigning technical senses to familiar terms) which is unfamiliar to the nonphilosopher. It will be noticed that this plank leaves wide open the issue between constructionalists like Carnap and ordinary-language analysts who follow Wittgenstein in thinking that philosophy "leaves everything as it is." It does not mean that philosophers are not to use jargon if they must, but only that the sole excuse for the jargon can be its utility in dissolving problems. I shall call this the Pragmatist thesis.

The second thesis is that the only interest which language has for the philosopher is that discovering, or inventing, uses of linguistic expressions permits him to dissolve traditional problems. Part of the thrust of this thesis is that there are no transcendental questions to be asked about language, or, to put it another way, that all questions about how language as such is possible are to be turned over to empirical disciplines (e.g., psychology, sociology, physiology). I shall call this the Naturalist thesis.

The third thesis is that if an appeal to linguistic usage will not decide whether a given proposition expresses a necessary truth, nothing will. This thesis is a sophisticated variant of the familiar positivistic claim that necessary truths are true by convention. Note that this thesis leaves open the issue between the friends and foes of the analytic-synthetic distinction. It merely says that if we can make any sense of the notion of necessary truth, this sense will have to be explicated solely by reference to concepts occurring in the metatheory of empirical linguistics – namely, syntactical and semantical concepts. I shall call this the Conventionalist thesis.

Wittgenstein, in the *Investigations*, adopts the Naturalist and Conventionalist theses fairly explicitly. He does not adopt the Pragmatist thesis, but rather a stronger thesis – one which says that there is *no* justification for the philosopher's redescribing phenomena. His argument for this, insofar as he has one, is that all the traditional philosophical problems can be dissolved simply by "bringing words back from their metaphysical to their everyday use."[2] I do not wish to defend or examine

---

(Baltimore, MD: Johns Hopkins University Press, 1967); and in *Analytic Philosophy and Phenomenology*, ed. Harold A. Durfee (The Hague: Nijhoff, 1976). – *Eds.*

[2] Ludwig Wittgenstein, *Philosophical Investigations*, 2nd ed. (Oxford: Blackwell, 1967), 48.

this latter thesis, since I do not think that Wittgenstein's own anti-Cartesian arguments are properly described by this phrase. More generally, I think that Wittgenstein's own metaphilosophical remarks in the *Investigations* are not in accord with his own philosophical practices and that they can safely be neglected. It seems more in point to focus attention on the relations between his anti-Cartesian view of the relations between language, thought, and reality, on the one hand, and the Naturalist and Conventionalist theses on the other.

Wittgenstein argues from the premise (accepted by Husserl as well) that there is no thought which is not in words, to the conclusion that there is no way in which we can answer questions about whether and how our language is an adequate representation of reality. Very roughly, the argument is that whenever we wish to compare language and reality, we always find ourselves comparing two linguistic representations of reality. One might think that we could at least compare our language with experience, but here Wittgenstein insists that the best we can do is to compare other bits of language with those bits which are reports of experience. Wittgenstein regards the notion of "experience unmediated by language" or of "prelinguistic experience" (where this term is construed as referring to experiences inadequately described by everyday language) as one more variant of the Kantian thing-in-itself – as a mythological entity generated by the use of a mistaken epistemological model.

It might seem, however, that one could grant all this and still insist that there are intentional structures to be examined – for instance, the structures which underlie our use of signs. Granted, one might say, that there is no such thing as a prelinguistic "Given," it would seem that problems remain about how we manage to bridge the gap between linguistic symbols and the nonlinguistic reality symbolized. Thus, we find Ricoeur saying that "we are forever separated from life by the very function of the sign."[3] From Wittgenstein's point of view, however, the notion that such a gap or separation exists is one more relic of Cartesian dualism. Further, the notion that there is a discipline whose job it is to discover the intentional structures which bridge the gap is either (a) just a jargonistic way of describing the practice of linguistic analysis – namely, the detection of rulish relationships which exist between linguistic usages, or (b) a vain hope of discovering features of a mythical prelinguistic experience. To enforce this dilemma, a Wittgensteinian will draw upon the Conventionalist thesis

---

[3] Paul Ricoeur, "Husserl and Wittgenstein on Language," in *Analytic Philosophy and Phenomenology*, ed. Harold A. Durfee (The Hague: Nijhoff, 1976), 95 – *Eds.*

and argue that the only necessary truths which we can hope to discover are those embedded in our linguistic practices. The Conventionalist thesis thus comes to the aid of the Naturalist thesis by helping the Wittgensteinian to debunk putative transcendental approaches to philosophical problems and, in particular, problems in the philosophy of language.

But at this point the phenomenologist might argue that the Wittgensteinian's reasoning is circular. No one, it might be said, would adopt the Conventionalist thesis who had not adopted the Naturalist thesis already. For if the Naturalist thesis is false – if there are necessary presuppositional relationships which hold between our linguistic practices and something else (call it the structure of the *Lebenswelt*) – then the Conventionalist thesis is also false. I think that this charge of circularity is well founded, but the story is not yet over. For now the Wittgensteinian can fall back on the Pragmatist thesis.

He can do so in the following way: let us grant, he may say, that there are philosophical problems about how we manage to use signs to represent. What we want to do is to find a way of describing signs and their uses which avoids these problems – a way of describing the phenomena of linguistic use in which no "gaps" or "separations" appear. If one chooses to call this description a description of the *Lebenswelt*, well and good. All that matters is that the problems are avoided. If, for example, we say with Merleau-Ponty that language does not "express thoughts" but rather "is the subject's taking up a position in the world of his meanings,"[4] this may help us dissolve the traditional pseudoproblems about the relation between a thought and its linguistic clothing. It may help us much more than, say, Wittgenstein's quasi-behavioristic attack on the notion of thoughts as inner, intuitable, episodes. I have already conceded that Wittgenstein's own work is more a redescription of the phenomena than a simple inspection of the language games actually played with, say, words like meaning and "sign." I am happy to concede further that a better redescription may be found.

But this concession still leaves the Wittgensteinian and the phenomenologist far apart. For the former, the aim of such redescriptions is not accuracy of description of something unfamiliar ("lived experience," "intentional structures") but purely and simply the dissolution of problems. It makes all the difference whether one says "I no longer have the

---

[4] Maurice Merleau-Ponty, *Phenomenology of Perception*, trans. Donald A. Landes (New York: Routledge, 2005), 225 – *Eds.*

traditional problems because I know that I have now, at last, accurately described the *Lebenswelt*" or rather "I know that I have accurately described the *Lebenswelt* because I no longer have the traditional problems." The Wittgensteinian, feeling that the phenomenologist has no criteria for successful phenomenological description other than success in dissolving problems, is inclined to shrug off these references to the *Lebenswelt* as merely empty compliments which the phenomenologist pays himself.

So much for the general confrontation between Wittgensteinian and phenomenological approaches to problems in the philosophy of language. I want to turn now to two things which Ricoeur says and show how they look when viewed from the perspective I have been developing.

I turn first to what Ricoeur says about Husserl's regressive questioning. We find him on guard against the accusation that Husserl falls back on Cartesian notions of "givenness." He cautions us against "any recourse to something like an 'impression' in the Humean sense."[5] Immediately after this caution, he goes on to say that it is "from within the world of signs and on the basis of *doxa* in the sense of the *Theaetetus* – i.e., of judgments of perception – that we 'inquire' regressively towards a primordial lived experience; but this so-called 'lived' experience, for us men who were born among words, will never be the naked presence of an absolute, but will remake that toward which this regressive questioning points."[6] I cannot stop here to quarrel with the dubious suggestion that for beings other than "men who were born among words" there might be such a thing as "the naked presence of an absolute." I wish rather to ask: if we really are remaking our lived experience as we do our regressive questioning (or, more generally, as Merleau-Ponty has said, if "the phenomenological world is not the bringing to explicit expression of a pre-existing being, but the laying down of being"[7]), then in what sense can regressive inquiry be thought of as discovery, rather than invention? How do we know whether a remade lived experience was ever lived at all? Is this notion of a prelinguistic lived experience any more than the latest disguise of the thing-in-itself – something which nothing can be said about, but which is invoked as a handy heuristic device to help explain what it is we do when we do phenomenology? To decide whether it is more than this, one has to ask whether we have criteria for choosing one set of answers to successive *Rückfrage* over another. I do not know the answer to this question.

---

[5] Ricoeur, "Husserl and Wittgenstein on Language," 92.   [6] Ibid.
[7] Merleau-Ponty, *Phenomenology of Perception*, xxii.

Second, I turn to Ricoeur's suggestion that Wittgenstein's conception of language is one dimensional. The suggestion is true enough if it means that Wittgenstein thinks that language-as-*lekton*, a *lekton* in which "the meaning is a term within a system of inner dependences,"[8] can be reduced to language as speech-act. Wittgensteinianism in philosophy does lead to the view that empirical inquiry about people's speech-acts is a sufficient basis, and the only possible evidence, for an account of those syntactical relations which form the "system of inner dependences." (This is true whether one's approach to linguistics is Chomskyan or Skinnerian.) Such a reduction may fail, and then so much the worse for Wittgenstein. But in the meantime it is no criticism of the suggested reductionist program to say that this conception of language is "undialectical." That is precisely what it was designed to be. Nor is it necessary, in order to justify the claim that "a critique of ordinary language is itself possible," to view language as "a mediation . . . between *Logos* and *Bios*."[9] We can adopt Wittgenstein's view that for human experience, insofar as philosophical inquiry can reach it and describe it, there is no gap between *Logos* and *Bios*, and nevertheless hope, *pace* Wittgenstein, to transform *Bios* through the transformation of *Logos*. There is no necessary connection between the notion that signs bridge mysterious Cartesian gaps and the notion that philosophy may become a critique of the multitude of interpretations which we place upon our life. If we wish to develop a hermeneutics of the sort envisaged in his *De l'interprétation*,[10] we can do so just as well from a Wittgensteinian starting point as from an Husserlian one.

---

[8] Ricoeur, "Husserl and Wittgenstein on Language," 94.   [9] Ibid., 95.
[10] Paul Ricoeur, *De l'interprétation*, Collection "L'ordre philosophique" (Paris: Éditions du Seuil, 1965).

7

The Incommunicability of "Felt Qualities"

Much of the discussion of the existence or nature of private mental episodes which has been generated by Wittgenstein's *Philosophical Investigations*[1] has centered around the claim that

(1) We cannot communicate certain qualities (the "special felt qualities") of our sensations to others.

Wittgenstein, or at least some Wittgensteinians, have used this thesis as a key premise in arguments for such conclusions as "'Toothache' is not the name of a sensation"; "It is senseless to say that I know that I am in pain, because I feel it"; and "If we construe the grammar of the expression of sensation on the model of 'object and name,' the object drops out of consideration as irrelevant."[2] I do not wish to trace these arguments in this paper, but instead to focus on the claim I just cited – a claim which I shall call the Thesis of Incommunicability. I want to argue that in one sense this thesis is true but philosophically innocuous while in another it is false. This disambiguation will turn on distinguishing two senses of "knowledge," and I shall end the paper by arguing that a neglect of this latter distinction is one of the roots of epistemological skepticism.

What reason is there to think that

> We cannot communicate certain qualities (the "special felt qualities") of our pains to others?

Obviously no argument for this thesis – the Thesis of Incommunicability – can consist in listing such qualities, for, ex hypothesi, no language is available for formulating such a list. Is there grounding in common sense for the idea that such qualities exist? Only, I think, the fact that we sometimes say such things as:

---

[1] Ludwig Wittgenstein, *Philosophical Investigations* (Oxford: Basil Blackwell, 1953).
[2] Ibid., para. 293.

(A) You cannot know what that experience is like if you have never
     had it.
(B) You (who are congenitally toothless) cannot know what it is like to
     have a toothache (or: . . . cannot know what a toothache feels like).
(C) I felt something at that moment which I can find no words to
     express, but I would know it again at once should it recur.

I want to suggest that "know" in these three sentences means "imagine,"
"imagine" in the sense of "being able to form an image of or have a memory
of." So construed, we can all think of situations in which these sentences
would be true. We can also, I think, see how these situations produce the
notion of "special felt qualities." There obviously are some features of some of
my experiences (e.g., that it occurred at high noon on a Wednesday, that it
had something to do with my teeth) which I *can* communicate, in the sense
that you can indeed imagine that you would have an experience which you
would want to say had the features I mention. But if, as (A), (B), and (C)
assert, there is (for some experiences, with respect to some interlocutors) an
incommunicable residuum, presumably these are features of the experience
which I *felt*. For how would I know that there was an incommunicable
residuum if I did not *in some sense* know what that residuum was? And how
could I know it save by having felt it? (Nobody, after all, could have told me
about it.) And what could I have felt save some qualities of the experience?

   I think that the right answer to "How would I know that there was an
incommunicable residuum?" is simply: because you have found that your
discourse is unable to instill the ability to *imagine* something, where (to
repeat) imagine means "have appropriate images or memories or responses
to occurrences of the thing in question." I only know that I have failed to
communicate what an experience is like if my audience does not respond in
the desired way. Experiences do not come labeled "incommunicable," nor
do any of their features. Incommunicability is something we attach to
them by virtue of failure to communicate. We test failure to communicate
by such questions as "Can you visualize it?" and "Have you ever had the
sort of experience which would make you do such and such (become
oblivious to your surroundings, be tempted to bow down before
Universal Nature)?" We know that we have had a unique experience, or
at least that our present audience is not "with" us, because of the replies we
get to such questions. We do not know in any sense what that residuum
was – we simply know that there was a residuum. Thus, the "special felt
qualities" are not objects of knowledge. They are ways of summarizing
failures to communicate.

But, it may be objected: what I am failing to communicate is some piece of knowledge I have. So I must know *something*. To answer this objection, we can begin by considering the following distinction between two senses of "know what X is." In the first sense of know,

> S knows₁ what X is iff S can have an image or a memory of X at will and can recognize X's on sight (or "immediately" through some other sense).

In the second sense,

> S knows₂ what X is iff S can use the word "X" in most normal ways (though not necessarily in reports of observations), and can offer adequate grounds for believing a large number of true and interesting propositions which he expresses by sentences containing "X."

The relevance of this quarrel to our present topic is that if "know" has the first sense, then it is indeed knowledge which I fail to be able to communicate in situations which call for statements like (A), (B), and (C). For if "can imagine what X is like" entails "is able to have an image or a memory of X at will," then of course my superior imaging and recognitional capacities count as showing that I know₁ something that you do not. But if "know" has the second sense, then it is not knowledge – for I can know₂ a great deal about things which I can neither recognize on sight (nor by the "unmediated" use of some other sense) nor form an image of nor have memories of. So now our question becomes: What counts as knowing what, for example, "redness" or "pain" means – knowing₁ what redness or pain is, or knowing₂ what redness or pain is? This, of course, boils down to such questions as: Does, for example, the congenitally blind man mean by "red" what we sighted people mean? Does, for example, the man who has never felt pain know what "pain" means?

If the answer to these latter questions is "yes," then we are in a fair way to blocking any paradoxical consequences of the conjunction of the Thesis of Incommunicability. For now (A), (B), and (C) are true only in the first sense of "know." All that the Thesis then comes to is the fact that I cannot, through the use of language, endow you with some appropriate recognitional or imaging capacities. But now the "special felt qualities" of the Thesis cease to even look like "objects of knowledge." For "I cannot communicate the special felt qualities of my sensations to you" turns out to mean no more than "I cannot, by the use of language, instill in you the ability to have the sort of images I have or perform the feats or recognition I perform." Further, *the criteria for your inability to have these images or perform these feats can themselves be phrased in our shared, public, language.*

Thus, if I tell a congenitally blind man that he cannot recognize red objects on sight, he knows exactly what I mean – as also when I tell him that he cannot form a visual image of red things. He knows exactly what it is that he cannot do, and may cheerfully admit that he cannot grasp or be aware of or know the special felt qualities of the experience of seeing red things.

But in making this latter admission, he will not be admitting that he does not know$_2$ what red is. If he is told that there is no assurance that he means by "red" what we do, he should challenge not (1) – the Thesis of Incommunicability – but

(2) I know what a given sort of sensation is only because I know about certain incommunicable "special felt qualities" which are characteristic of certain sensations I myself have.

and

(3) I do not know whether it would be appropriate to apply the name of a given sort of sensation – for example, "pain" – unless I know whether I am talking about something which has certain incommunicable "special felt qualities."

If we accept these theses, we have to grant that a man who does not have certain abilities does not know what "pain" means – and analogues of (2) and (3) would force us to draw a similarly negative conclusion about the blind man's grasp of "red." These latter theses express the view that if a class of things has special felt qualities – that is, if there are some capacities of the relevant sort (imaging, recognitional) which I cannot instill in others merely by using language (unaccompanied by ostension) – then the meaning of the name of that class of thing cannot be taught to those in whom those capacities cannot be so instilled. But this view is absurd. For any evidence which would be cited in its favor would be evidence based on the linguistic behavior of people who lacked these capabilities – linguistic behavior which would only count as evidence if these people did indeed know the meaning of the name in question. We cannot know whether a man perceives colored surfaces as colored unless we know whether he knows the color-predicates.

The point of the last few paragraphs may be summed up as follows: reference to incommunicable qualities of an experience is a way of referring to limitations on the abilities of those who lack that experience to do certain things, but we cannot say that among those things is "understanding the terms used for describing that experience." For if we said that, we would be in no position to know what experiences a man had or had not had. Put in terms of a criticism of Wittgenstein, it is not private sensations which "drop out" or which should not be construed on the model of "object having a designation" – it is simply those incommunicable qualities. They drop out of the question of language mastery as irrelevant. Indeed, saying that they do is merely saying that what counts as knowing what X is, where this is equivalent to knowing what "X" means, is knowing₂ what X is. And this in turn is merely a way of saying that knowing the meaning of "X" is guaranteed by being able to use "X" in some normal ways (though not necessarily in all the normal ways – for example, not necessarily in expressions of noninferential knowledge).

Thus the slogan "The meaning is the use" (toned down to "If you get a reasonable amount of the use right, you know the meaning") turns out to be the heart of the argument against the skeptic who suggests that we cannot know whether we both mean the same thing by "pain." This we might have expected, and if Wittgenstein had confined himself to invoking this principle, he would have been on firm ground. But, as far as I can make out, he did not. In the passages about private sensations in the *Investigations,* he protested against (1) while taking (2) and (3) for granted. He thus wound up attacking a set of propositions – for example, that "pain" is the name of a sensation; that "I sometimes know that I am in pain" – which are perfectly harmless. He thereby generated an attack on the whole notion of private objects – one which has persuaded his disciples to attack the notion of privileged access, and other equally respectable and harmless notions, to no good purpose.

The gist of what I have said so far is that as long as one does not have an oversimple notion of how terms get their meanings, the notion of incommunicable qualities will be philosophically innocuous. It can be argued that Wittgenstein himself held this view and that it was only certain of his followers who have made the errors I have suggested. However, I do not wish to pursue this exegetical question now. Having used certain interpretations of Wittgenstein as stalking horses to introduce the distinction between two senses of "knowing what X is," I now want to beef up this distinction by making some related distinctions between senses of related terms and showing the application of these distinctions. Consider the following theses:

(4)   We can have knowledge about something which is distinct from knowledge that certain propositions are true of it; thus, we can have "knowledge of" which is distinct from "knowledge that."

(5)   We can have knowledge of the truth of propositions which we have no means of expressing in our public language.

Debate has raged between proponents and opponents of what Sellars calls "psychological nominalism" (the view that "all awareness of anything is a linguistic affair")[3] concerning the truth of these theses. But I think that all that needs to be done about this issue is to invoke our previous distinction, this time in the following, more general form:

> S knows$_1$ about something iff he has some appropriate set of dispositions to nonlinguistic behavior toward that thing (or representations – mental and physical – of that thing)
>
> S knows$_2$ about something iff he is able to give adequate evidence for his beliefs about that thing – where the process of giving evidence entails sufficient linguistic ability to discourse intelligently about that thing.

All that needs to be done about (5) is to invoke the following form of the distinction:

> S knows$_1$ that p iff his nonlinguistic behavior is such as would be expected of people who would assent to "p," and p is true
>
> S knows$_2$ that p iff p is true, he understands and assents to "p," and he can provide adequate evidence for p.

Crude as these definitions are, they suffice to give us the senses in which animals and infants are said to know about things and to know that propositions are true. The vagueness of "appropriate set of dispositions" and of "such nonlinguistic behavior as would be expected" is matched by the vagueness of the grounds on which we conclude that dogs know about dangers confronting their masters, that birds know about north and south and about wind directions, that infants and amoebae know the truth of such propositions as "It is warmer on that side," and that a properly equipped robot could know all about everything and the truth of all true propositions. But since it is just such cases of "knowledge" which are cited (and are *all* that is cited) in favor of (4) and (5), our analysis of the senses in which these theses are true need be no more finely grained.

Since these theses are trivially true when "know" is construed as "know$_1$," and trivially false when it is construed as "know$_2$," why should there be an issue about (4) and (5)? Why has the equivocation on senses of "know" managed to engender philosophical perplexity? I think that such perplexity arises only when we assume that knowledge of what X's are in the second sense must be "based on" knowledge of what X's are in the first sense. If "based on" means "requires as a causal antecedent," this claim is normally true but occasionally false (as in the case of the congenitally blind

---

[3] Cf. Wilfrid Sellars, *Science, Perception, and Reality* (New York: Humanities Press, 1963), 160.

meteorologist who busily and accurately predicts the visual features of sunsets). "Based on," however, is often construed by philosophers as "inferred from." It is only when we conceive of an inference from what the prelinguistic infant has to what the meteorologist has that we run into problems about the private and the public. But of course there can be no such inference. Inference is from proposition to proposition. The notion of inference from a given pattern of dispositions to discriminative behavior, or a given pattern of associations of or abilities to have, certain memories or images, to propositions makes no sense. Nor can there be a problem about translation between what the infant or the animal knows and what the adult human knows. For translation is from language to language, and language is just what the infant and the animal do not have.

The principle which expresses this confused notion of inference, and which lies at the bottom of much of traditional epistemology, is the following:

(6) If "X" is a referring expression which is also an observation-term, then if there is no assurance that the pattern of capacities to recognize X's through observation, and to have images and memories of X's, are similar in two persons, there is no assurance that the term "X" has the same meaning for these two persons.

This principle generates the corollary that

(7) If "X" is a referring expression which is also an observation-term, then no one can have knowledge$_2$ of what X's are who does not have knowledge$_1$ of what X's are.

It is (7) which inspires epistemological skepticism about knowledge of the external world. For as long as one is convinced that the flow of images through our minds may count decisively in figuring out whether you and I mean the same things by what we say (and, a fortiori, know the same thing), one will wonder how one can be sure that this flow is the same. It will not count as deciding that it is the same that we both describe it in roughly the same terms – for anybody who doubts that we both mean the same when we apply "red" to a barn will have the same doubts when we both report a red mental image. The hostility of many recent philosophers (Gilbert Ryle, e.g.) to mental images – and even to Herbert Feigl's "raw feels"[4] – is, I think, largely due to the assumption that as long as we admit

---

[4] Herbert Feigl, *The Mental and the Physical: The Essay and a Postscript* (Minneapolis: University of Minnesota Press, 1967). – *Eds.*

that there are such things, we shall never be able to answer the epistemo-logical skeptic. But dismissing something as irrelevant is as good as denying its existence. One need deny neither the existence of a perfectly good sense of "know" in which there can be prelinguistic or nonlinguistic knowledge (or "awareness" or "consciousness") nor the existence of unshareable mental particulars to which we have privileged access, in order to be free of the worries about the incommunicability of our knowledge about these particulars.

8

Kripke on Mind-Body Identity

At the conclusion of a discussion of the notions of identity, necessity, and reference, Saul Kripke brings some of his conclusions to bear on the so-called contingent identification of sensations with brain states, which has become associated with some modern materialists.[1] He claims that

(a) We can distinguish between terms used as "rigid designators" (those which would pick out the same object in any possible world) and terms which are not so used;

(b) We can distinguish between essential properties of objects and accidental properties;

(c) If it is the case that the object picked out by two rigid designators "X" and "Y" is the same, then it is necessarily the case that X=Y, even though the identity may not be knowable a priori;

(c') Referents get picked out "by means of certain properties" – which may be either essential or accidental;

(d) But in the case in which two rigid designators – "X" and "Y" – both pick out their referent by a different essential property thereof, if we can imagine something having the one property but not the other, then it cannot be the case that X=Y, for this would violate (c); and

(e) "Brain state" picks out brain states by essential property of brain states, and "Pain" pain by an essential property of pains, and both terms are rigid designators, so (by [d]) the two things cannot be identical.

The argument here hinges on the claim that words for such "natural kinds" as "gold," "pain," "man," "brain state," etc. are rigid designators[2] – that they would pick out the same set of objects in any possible world in

---

[1] I am drawing primarily here on Kripke's discussion in "Naming and Necessity," in *Semantics of Natural Language*, ed. Donald Davidson and Gilbert Harman (Boston: D. Reidel, 1972), 253–355.

[2] Ibid., 331.

which they referred to anything at all.[3] Kripke's paradigm of a rigid designator – the case with the help of which he introduces the notion – is a proper name. His paradigm examples of designators which are not rigid are terms which signify accidental properties of individuals – thus, "the inventor of bifocals" picks out (in this world) Franklin by virtue of one of Franklin's accidental properties. When it comes to kinds rather than individuals, the distinction between rigid and nonrigid designators is not so clear. We are told that "pain" is a rigid designator and that it designates by means of an essential property of its referent and that "heat" is so also but that it designates by means of an accidental property of its referent – namely, the property of causing in us the sensation S. We are told that "C-fiber" may or may not be a rigid designator (or may or may not be used as one).[4]

The criterion for being a rigid designator is that the term would refer to the same object or kind of object in every possible world. This criterion, however, leaves one uncertain about the difference between "pain" or "heat" and "C-fiber," or about how to tell whether the phrase "whatever phenomenon causes sensation S" is itself rigid whether or not "heat" is. Kripke seems to want at least a fivefold classification: (1) proper names rigidly designating individuals; (2) terms designating individuals by means of accidental properties thereof (e.g., "the inventor of bifocals"); (3) terms designating kinds of things rigidly by means of necessary properties ("pain"); (4) terms designating kinds of things rigidly by means of contingent properties ("heat"); and (5) terms designating kinds of things nonrigidly ("C-fiber," perhaps).

Very roughly, we may say that the tradition Kripke opposes thinks of (2)-(5) as being more like each other than any of them is like (1), whereas Kripke thinks of (1) and (3) as being more like each other than either is like (2), (5), and perhaps (4). (The difficulty of the distinction between (4) and (5) will be discussed in more detail below.) Kripke resembles Aristotle in thinking that, for example, "Socrates" and "man" (as terms in what Aristotle called "the category of substance") have important features in common which neither shares with "philosopher" or "teacher of Plato" (terms in the "accidental" categories). To put it another way, Kripke would presumably think that there was something odd (or impossible?) about using "this very inventor of bifocals" as a rigid designator, picking out the same thing in all possible worlds in which bifocals had been invented (a thing which in one world had the property of being a black man; in

---

[3] Ibid., 269.   [4] Ibid., 337.

another, a white man named Franklin; in another, an ape; in another, an automaton; etc.). Similarly, Aristotle thought (at least in the *Metaphysics*, if not in the *Categories*) that such a phrase as "this white thing" (*hod' ho leukos*, with "*hod' ho*" translating "this very") was pretty fishy – for only a substance was a "this" (a *tode ti*).

To bring the issue between this neo-Aristotelian view and the mind-body identity theory into focus, consider the following line which the identity theorist might take. He might begin by granting that Kripke is right to distinguish the metaphysically necessary sort of identity which everything has with itself from modalities defined in terms of epistemological status. Consider the sort of identity which unites Hesperus and Phosphorus. These two, surprisingly enough, turn out to be the same object. So, to be sure, Hesperus cannot be other than Phosphorus. The temptation to say that the identity is contingent arises, just as Kripke says, from the situation in which we imagine something with some of the accidental properties of the one lacking some of the accidental properties of the other. But the fact that the weirdest things may turn out to be identical with each other, and, when they do so, will be seen to be metaphysically necessarily identical, just shows the triviality of the notion of metaphysically necessary identity. Once an identity is established, it will, to be sure, be seen to be a necessary identity. But when I call the identity between pains and stimulations of C-fibers contingent, the materialist continues, I am not denying that this very pain is necessarily identical with this very stimulation. Certainly it is, in the trivial sense in which Hesperus is necessarily identical with Phosphorus. Kripke's argument that they cannot be identical turns not on the claim that all identity-statements linking rigid designators attribute metaphysical necessity but on the claim that inquiry cannot rationally change our views about which terms signify essential properties. This claim, if true, would mean that there could never be a philosophically surprising reduction. Such reductions include the cases in which we want to say that the purported natural kind A is the same as natural kind B simply on the basis of Occam's razor. If A's and B's are constantly correlated, and if reference to B's can conveniently take the place of reference to A's in the overall pattern of explanation and prediction, then we have thereby discovered that any given A is probably necessarily metaphysically identical with some given B. Kripke sees a bar to this identity in the fact that we are able to imagine A's existing without B's – but this merely shows that what we can imagine is relative to our state of knowledge. These epistemic matters have nothing to do with metaphysical necessity. What Kripke should say is that we can imagine a world in which some of the properties of the thing which is both an A and a B – for example, the property of A-ness or that of B-ness – were had by other things than A's or B's. Instead his position suggests that in cases of purported identities of natural kinds, the only sort of identification which could work is what has sometimes been called the "disappearance form" of the identity theory – according to which there never were any A's at all, but only, so to speak "fool's A's," that is, B's.[5] Because Kripke thinks that in some cases he can pick out by thought experiments which properties of A's are necessary, without waiting for science – which terms are, so to speak, "in the category of substance" and thus essential to their bearers – he thinks that there is no such thing as imagining that the things picked out by these properties might turn out not to bear them after all. Yet if these things are in fact B's, it makes perfectly good sense for us to say that we once thought their essence was to be A's, but science (and Occam's razor) has shown that we were wrong – their essence is to be B, at most, and being A is, at most, just one more contingent property they happen to have. Essential properties, and discrete natural kinds, are discovered by scientific inquiry; they are not constraints upon it. Even in Aristotle's day, essentialism was a reactionary movement against the enlightened and progressive reductionist efforts of the Platonists and the atomists. The intuitions on which Aristotle drew – that some terms designate the same thing in any possible world in which it exists, that identity-statements linking such designators are, if true, necessarily so, and that some properties are essential to things and others accidental – can be preserved, but they must not be permitted to block the road of inquiry. They will not do so if we allow that terms which were once thought to pick out referents by way of their essential properties can be revealed not to have done so by further scientific developments and thus cease to be used as rigid designators. (Although, as was shown by the gradual abandonment of Aristotelian jargon in the seventeenth century, the Aristotelian intuitions do not look so important once this epistemological point is accepted.)

So much for the materialist's first line of defense against Kripke's argument. In rejoinder, it would be natural for Kripke to point out that he does in fact countenance plenty of "philosophically interesting"

---

[5] See "Naming and Necessity," p. 321, on cats and demons. I am not suggesting that Kripke would have any sympathy with the "disappearance" form of the identity theory. It is less easy to say that the things we thought were sensations turned out to be "fool's sensations" than to say that all the things we thought to be cats (and were actually demons) turned out to be "fool's cats." If one believes, as Kripke does, that an immediate phenomenological quality is an essential property of a sensation, it is not clear that there *could* be such things as "fool's sensations" – for nobody could be fooled.

reductions – for example, that of heat to molecular motion – but that there is a special feature in the case of sensations which makes the analogy inappropriate. The reductions which identity theorists like to cite are ones in which some term in what Aristotle would call "the category of relation" (e.g., "whatever phenomenon is the typical cause of sensation S") is used to pick out a referent which inquiry eventually discovers to have such and such an essence.[6] Heat thus has a nature (namely, molecular motion) which can be discovered but pain does not, for we already know the essence of pain. Thus, Kripke tells us:

> In the case of identity of heat with molecular motion the important consideration was that although "heat" is a rigid designator, the reference of that designator is fixed by an accidental property of the referent, namely the property of producing in us the sensation S. It is thus possible that a phenomenon should have been rigidly designated in the same way as a phenomenon of heat, with its reference also picked out by means of the sensation S without that phenomenon being heat and therefore without its being molecular motion. Pain, on the other hand, is picked out by the property of being pain itself, by its immediate phenomenological quality. Thus pain, unlike heat, is not only rigidly designated by "pain" but the reference of the designator is determined by an essential property of the referent.[7]

Putting the matter another way, Kripke explains that "the illusion of contingency" in the identity of heat and molecular motion is produced by the "epistemic situation" created by the way in which the "references of the designators are determined"; thus:

> In the case of molecular motion and heat there is something, namely the sensation of heat, which is an intermediary between the external phenomenon and the observer. In the mental-physical case no such intermediary is possible, since here the physical phenomenon is supposed to be identical with the internal phenomenon itself. Someone can be in the same epistemic situation as he would be if there were heat, even in the absence of heat, simply by feeling the sensation of heat; and even in the presence of heat, he can have the same evidence as he would have in the absence of heat simply by lacking the sensation S. No such possibility exists in the case of pain or in other mental phenomena. To be in the same epistemic situation that would obtain if one had a pain *is* to have a pain; to be in the same epistemic situation that would obtain in the absence of a pain is not to have a pain.[8]

---

[6] Kripke, "Naming and Necessity," 326.   [7] Ibid., 340.   [8] Ibid., 339.

Kripke sees three putative entities in the case of heat – the sensation of heat ("S"), heat, and molecular motion. Science can discover that these three are but two, since "heat-molecular motion" is true by virtue of the fact that "heat," though not synonymous with "phenomenon typically producing S"[9] nevertheless uses this latter "accidental" property of heat to pick out heat as its referent. In the case of pain, he sees only two entities – pain and constantly correlated brain states (C-fiber stimulations) – both of which are signified by terms which designate rigidly and presumably do so by means of essential properties of their referents. Pain is picked out by "an immediate phenomenological quality," but we pick out heat not by how it feels but, so to speak, at arm's length – as what is making us feel like that. The rationale for this distinction is presumably that there can be heat even if there are no sentient organisms, but there cannot be pain[10] – that is what makes pain "internal" and heat "external" and gives us an "appearance" of heat (the sensation S) but no "appearance" of pain.

This last point is brought out also in Kripke's appeal to our intuition of the "essentiality" of *being a pain* to pains:

> The difficulty [for the identity theorist] can hardly be evaded by arguing that although B could not exist without A, *being a pain* is merely a contingent property of A, and that therefore the presence of B without pain does not imply the presence of B without A. Can any case of essence be more obvious than the fact that *being a pain* is a necessary property of each pain? The identity theorist who wishes to adopt the strategy in question must even argue that *being a sensation* is a contingent property of A, for *prima facie* it would seem logically possible that B could exist without any sensation with which it might plausibly be identified. Consider a particular pain, or other sensation, that you once had. Do you find it at all plausible that *that very sensation* could have existed without being a sensation, the way a certain inventor (Franklin) could have existed without being an inventor?[11]

It will be convenient to take this last formulation first, and then work back to the notion of pain as picked out by "an immediate phenomenological quality." The comparison with Franklin highlights the way in which Kripke is insisting that only substance-terms get to designate rigidly and that only substances have essential properties. For consider the following reply. Granted that we cannot imagine that very sensation existing without being a sensation, we cannot imagine the inventor of bifocals existing without being the inventor of bifocals either. I can imagine Franklin existing without being the Inventor of Bifocals, but not the

---

[9] Ibid., 324.   [10] Cf. ibid., 340.   [11] Ibid., 335.

Inventor of Bifocals so existing (the capitalization indicating the trans-world identity of this figure, now incarnated as Franklin, now as Jefferson, now as a robot). It is of the essence of Franklin to be a man, but not of the essence of the Inventor of Bifocals. Similarly, it is of the essence of Pain (a natural kind which turns up in any world in which there are stimulated C-fibers) to be a stimulation of C-fibers, but it is contingent that in this world, in our sort of organism (or perhaps, as the solipsist suggests, just in me?) it comes on with a certain phenomenological quality. It all depends on what you think of as substrate and what you think of as property. We usually think of men as substratal and their achievements as properties, but we could do it the other way around. Since Descartes, the "immediate phenomenological qualities" have been prime candidates for "essential properties" of that great substrate, the "Mind" (the term that took the place of "man" as a paradigm of substance as a result of the scientific revolution of the seventeenth century). But in a materialist culture, where "the mind" was thought of as summarizing the way our ancestors talked about their brain states, the only substrate in the area would be the brain; by then, galactic ethnology will have doubtless found lots of different phenomenological qualities which turn up in conjunction with the stimulation of C-fibers. So Kripke's attempt to make our flesh creep by saying "Consider a particular pain, or other sensation, which you once had" begs the question: he wants us to consider the immediate phenomenological awfulness as of the essence, but what gets to be of the essence is determined not by a return *zu den Sachen* but by looking at the context of discourse about the thing in question. The identity theorist is suggesting a new context, which, he thinks, puts the whole matter in a new light and which has various philosophical advantages. The new light is shed, as usual, by changing old substrata into properties and old properties into substrata.

The strategy which I have been suggesting as available to the identity theorist is vulnerable to several objections – the most obvious being that the subject has been changed from pain to Pain and from Franklin to the Inventor of Bifocals. But (as the ambiguity of *hypokeimenon* between "subject of discourse" and "substrate of properties" reminds us) one man's changed subject is another's metaphysical discovery. Before taking up such objections, let me make a few historical remarks which I think help bring out the issue at hand. Kripke's essentialism is, of course, a scandal to Quineans, "cluster concept" philosophers of language, and Whiteheadian or Bradleyan metaphysicians. But moreover, his talk of picking out pains by their immediate phenomenological qualities is a folly to the Wittgensteinians. Kripke is going dead against practically all current fashions, as must any revival of Aristotelianism. For a great deal of twentieth-century philosophy is a reaction against Aristotelian notions of logic and language,[12] and against the lingering Aristotelian elements in Cartesian philosophies of mind.[13] On all fronts, the slogan common to this anti-Aristotelian reaction is that what counts as an individual, or a substrate, or an essence, is always relative to a description. The choice among alternative descriptions, it is tacitly assumed, is – when not simply a matter of taste or interest or rhetoric – a matter of suiting oneself to the needs of the onward march of empirical science. Thus, materialists feel themselves free, and indeed obligated, to construct philosophies of language which will make the philosophical world safe for materialism – confident that in doing so they are purifying us and themselves of the last vestiges of Aristotelian superstition. The counterintuitive consequences of such philosophies of language form the point of departure for Kripke's attempt to systematize the Aristotelian intuitions which twentieth-century philosophy has tried to repress or sublimate.

Before we reflect on the large question "Is all this just relative to a choice of description?" (and the larger one: "How would one tell whether it was?"), let us consider the various expedients open to the Wittgensteinian who feels suspicious as soon as immediate phenomenological qualities are mentioned. He can say, for example, that since there is no clear way to assure that I have the same immediate phenomenological quality as you do when we both use "pain" (or as I myself did yesterday), the term "pain" should not be thought of as having a referent, and the whole notion of "phenomenological quality" should be dropped. This "sensation-as-beetle-in-the-box" view, with the sensations "dropping out" when the epistemological difficulties are recognized, permits the Wittgensteinian to link arms with the Quinean, both using the slogan "No entity without identity." As a second possible move, he

---

[12] Consider, for example, Wolfe Mays's and David Harrah's accounts of the influence of *Principia Mathematica* on *Process and Reality*, as well as the obvious influence of the former on the *Tractatus*. Also consider Bradley's and Peirce's campaigns against the standard Aristotelian treatment of subject-predicate judgments, Dewey's and Quine's polemics against the notion of "essence," etc., etc. For a modern treatment of the Aristotelian doctrine that only substances have essences (*Metaphysics* VII, 4) see Manley Thompson, "The Distinction between Thing and Property," in *The Return to Reason: Essays in Realistic Philosophy*, ed. John Wild (Chicago: Henry Regnery, 1953). For a discussion of the view suggested in *Metaphysics* IV, 4 (1007a 20ff.) that rationality and necessity stand or fall with the notions of "substance and essence," see Anscombe's treatment of this passage in *Three Philosophers* (Ithaca, NY: Cornell University Press, 1961).

[13] I have in mind here Wittgenstein's attack, in the *Investigations*, on both the Cartesian notion of "immediate phenomenological quality" and the Aristotelian notions of "genus and species definition" and "essence," and his suggestion that both are examples of the same false picture of the relation between language and the world.

can say that the term "pain" does indeed refer, but we pick out its referents not by an immediately given phenomenological quality but by a pattern of causal relations (typical effects of hot stoves, dispositions to flinch and scream, etc., etc.). This will fit in with a "causal role" account of mental states generally and open wide the path for theoretical identifications of the heat–molecular motion sort. For now "pain" will just pick out C-fiber stimulations by the accidental property of being a node in certain causal patterns – in the manner suggested by Armstrong and David Lewis. As a third possible move, he can say that "pain" really does refer to an individual picked out by an immediate phenomenological quality but insist that the "identification" of such a quality is just a matter of having a certain linguistic practice, and that there is no sense in the question "Do the Martians, who have not heard of immediately given phenomenological qualities and who use the term 'stimulated C-fibers' where we use 'pain' (to explain writhing, screaming, etc.) have the same phenomenological quality immediately given to them?" On this third view, the fact that we use this quality to pick out pains is obviously no indication that that quality is of the essence of pain, since there is obviously no issue about whether we or the Martians use the "right" quality to pick it out, and so the skeptic about other minds has no foothold. All three of these strategies presuppose the notion that it is the way we talk that determines essence: the first will not let us refer to pains at all, whereas the second and third will let us refer by way of "accidental" properties. Only the latter two are congenial to materialism (the "translation" and "disappearance" forms of the identity theory, respectively), but both assume that we can tag anything we want to as an "essential" or an "accidental" property, depending on how it suits our ulterior scientific and philosophical purposes. All three ways pride themselves on getting rid of that Mind-Body Problem and the Other Minds Problem, and all three develop views on reference, meaning, etc., to suit this therapeutic end.[14]

---

[14] These various Wittgensteinian or quasi-Wittgensteinian tactics are to be found in various forms in various writers. The first is suggested as Wittgenstein's intention by George Pitcher in *The Philosophy of Wittgenstein* (Englewood Cliffs, NJ: Prentice-Hall, 1964) and by John W. Cook, "Wittgenstein on Privacy," *Philosophical Review* 74, no. 3 (1965), 281–314. The second is the so-called "behavioristic" treatment of Wittgenstein, refined and modified for materialistic purposes, by David M. Armstrong in *A Materialist Theory of the Mind* (London: Routledge, 1965) and by David Lewis in "An Argument for the Identity Theory," *The Journal of Philosophy* 63, no. 1 (1966), 17–25. I have argued for the third tactic in "In Defense of Eliminative Materialism," *Review of Metaphysics* 24, no. 1 (1970), 112–121, against the first tactic in "Wittgenstein, Privileged Access, and Incommunicability," *American Philosophical Quarterly* 7, no. 3 (1970), 192–205, and against the second tactic in "Incorrigibility as the Mark of the Mental," *Journal of Philosophy* 67, no. 12 (1970), 399–424. I do not think, however, that one's choice among these tactics is important in the present context.

Kripke, presumably, would resist all of these tactics and insist that "pain" is the name of a natural kind of particular which wears its essence on its sleeve. Wittgensteinians think of this insistence as a confusion between "the logic of our talk about physical objects" and "the logic of our talk about sensations."[15] How one is to know who is confused here is difficult, but one point seems clear. This is that everything turns on the notion of "identify by means of an essential (necessary) property" and nothing on "the principle of the necessity of identities using rigid designators."[16] This latter principle can be accepted with insouciance by any of the three suggested Wittgenstein tactics. They can cheerfully agree that the necessary identity of this very pain with some stimulated C-fibers is just as tight as the necessary identity of Hesperus and Phosphorus. When Kripke says that "the identity theorist cannot admit the possibility [that Jones' brain could have been in exactly that state at the time in question without Jones feeling any pain] and proceed from there,"[17] they can reply that they have no need to admit the possibility, any more than Kripke has to admit that Hesperus could exist without Phosphorus. They were talking about epistemological modalities; once Kripke switches to metaphysical modalities, he is of course quite right. What Kripke is imagining, they say, is perhaps a situation in which Jones's brain is in exactly that state, but Jones carries on with insouciance, denies that he feels pain, and so on. There will be dozens of reasons, they might say, why Jones does this. One is that he does not know about feeling pain – he has been brought up by Martians, and all he knows is that his C-fibers are being stimulated. (Notice that Kripke tends to identify feeling pain with being in a certain epistemic situation with regard to the pain – a suggestion which dubiously conflates feeling and knowing.) His insouciance is due to his masochism, his Spartan training, his mind being elsewhere, or what have you. Or perhaps Kripke is imagining a man so constructed that when his brain is in exactly that state he claims to feel enormous pleasure, capers about, demands to be kept in that state, etc. That is still all right – he is still feeling pain, but that is just the way pain feels to him: it gives him a different immediate phenomenological quality. But then it is not pain! Certainly it is, just as Hesperus would still be Hesperus if it had never appeared in the evening but had only been thought to do so as a result of mass-hypnosis-cum-mirrors. If this very pain is going to be treated on the lines of this very

---

[15] See, e.g., David Pears, *Ludwig Wittgenstein* (New York: Viking, 1970), 100ff., 159ff.; and also Cook, "Wittgenstein on Privacy," 313–314.

[16] Kripke, "Naming and Necessity," 335.   [17] Ibid.

star Hesperus, then it is no good saying that it cannot be pain if it does not come accompanied by certain behavior, immediate phenomenological qualities, etc. (any more than saying that it cannot be Hesperus if it does not appear in the evening sky). But pain *is* an immediate phenomenological quality! Well, in that case it certainly is not identical with the stimulation of C-fibers, but then it certainly is not a natural kind of particular picked out by means of one of its essential properties. Qualities do not have immediate phenomenological properties, nor essential properties. But that awful phenomenological quality is essential to pain! Well, that is just what we are arguing about – whether it is or not. There has to be some independent reason why it is essential, other than the claim that we can imagine Jones's brain state being exactly the same and Jones feeling no pain. For that claim is false if that phenomenological quality is accidental to pain, just as it is false that we can imagine Hesperus without Phosphorus if it is accidental to Hesperus that it appears in the evening.

The general dilemma which Kripke confronts when faced with these strategies is this: if names for natural kinds are like proper names in that they pick out an object perfectly well even though we do not know the object's nature and even though practically all our beliefs about the object are false, then there is never going to be any a priori argument for saying that two natural kinds may not turn out to be the same natural kind. If they are not like proper names, in that some criteria are available which would permit us to say "Well, we can no longer say that the term 'that very K' picks out that thing, now that we know we were wrong in thinking that it fulfilled the criteria for K-hood," then all the old epistemological considerations about cluster-concepts, and the relativity of essence to the current stage of scientific inquiry, recur. The only way to go between these horns is to use the notion of "pick out by means of an essential property" and to have a priori means of knowing which properties are essential. But any such a priori claim is going to be a disguised form of the notion of "criteria for being a K." Switching from saying "pain" means "the thing that has that immediate phenomenological quality" to saying that we pick out pain by means of that immediate phenomenological quality which is essential to it does not change anything. What we have, in either formulation, is just resistance (unimaginability? unwillingness? does it matter?) to using a certain word if the intended object does not have a certain feature. If there is such resistance in the case of pain, then that is why "that very pain" is unlike "Hesperus." For "Hesperus" could have picked out anything – a star, a flying saucer, a god in a chariot of fire – and it would not have been unimaginable to call it "Hesperus" once we had found out what we had picked out. On the contrary, it would have been as reasonable to call it Hesperus as it ever was. Once we found out that it was a star rather than a god, we could begin to say something about its essential properties – but that would be because we know something about the essential properties of stars, not because we know something about what has a right to be called "Hesperus."[18]

I conclude that the amalgamation of, so to speak, terms for primary substances and terms for secondary substances which Kripke proposes leaves the issue about mind-body identity where it stood. The old issues will go over into the new vocabulary – with less talk about meaning and more about reference, but without dialectical loss to either side. The identity theorist will, as always, have to say a number of paradoxical things to maintain his position, and a lot of the objections to his view can now be summed up in the form "You are confusing an accident of mental states with their essence" (the same thing that was said about Watson's behaviorism fifty years ago). But whether this confusion has been made will not be determined by reference to the necessity of identities using rigid designators. That principle is loose enough to be turned to the purposes of either side.

***

I have now argued my main thesis as well as I can, and I want to end with some general remarks about various topics I have touched on, in the hope that these will fill in the picture I want to draw. They concern: (1) the

---

[18] It may be thought that the dilemma I have offered hinges on a misunderstanding of Kripke's view about proper names. For the view may appear to be that we always associate a natural kind with a proper name from the first occasion of its use on. That is, Kripke's view might be that "Hesperus" does not refer unless Hesperus is a star; "Nixon," unless Nixon is a man; etc. But in fact this is not the view he wants:

> Some properties of an object may be essential to it, in that it could not have failed to have them; but these properties are not used to identify the object in another possible world, for such an identification is not needed; nor need the essential properties of an object be the properties used to identify it in this world, if indeed it is identified in the actual world by means of properties (273).

If Kripke would apply this last passage to kinds as well as to individuals – to terms like "pain" and "cat" as well as those like "Nixon" and "Hesperus" – then he would have to say either (a) that pain does not have to be picked out by a necessary (immediate phenomenological) property, but it just happens that we have lit on one to pick it out; or (b) that there is something special about pains (and presumably mental states generally – perhaps it is "direct acquaintance") which fixes it so that we always catch on to their essence – what they *are* – right off the bat. But then, once again, what we are arguing about is just whether we have caught on to the essence of pain. The materialist thinks not, and whether he is right or wrong has nothing to do with his views on the issues between Kripke and Mill, Kripke and Russell, etc.

notion of "rigid designator"; (2) the notion of "essence"; (3) what I have been calling "Aristotelianism"; and (4) materialism.

Rigid Designators. Kripke has defined "rigid designator" as "a term that designates the same object in all possible worlds." This is a fairly clear notion for terms applying to individuals or to their properties. I think intuition is more shaky when we come to natural kinds. Kripke does not argue, as far as I can see, that terms for these are rigid designators,[19] and it is hard to be clear about just what the claim comes to. To clarify it, we would need examples of terms which are neither rigid designators nor properties of individuals. At one point Kripke suggests that the only general terms which are not rigid designators are those which express properties – for example, "foolish," "fat," and "yellow."[20] Elsewhere, however, he suggests that "hot," "loud," and "red" are rigid designators too.[21] The notion of picking out the same thing in any possible world (any counterfactual situation) does not seem to give us anything to go on in the case of "red" or "cat" or "pain" – apart from a knowledge of the necessary properties of any of these kinds of things. In the case of proper names, one can say "I am talking about, no matter what the counterfactual situation, a reactionary thirty-seventh US president generally called 'Nixon' and looking like this photograph," or one can say "I am talking about, no matter what the counterfactual situation, this very man here." Doubtless Kripke is right in saying that most of us usually use proper names so that the latter remark would be appropriate. But is a parallel choice of intentions possible for words like "cat," "pain," and "yellow"? We can grant that, as Kripke says, the reference of these terms usually gets fixed in terms of the property of "being the kind instantiated by this sample,"[22] rather than by a Mill-like dictionary specification of necessary and sufficient conditions.[23] But, once reference is so fixed, what would we do to distinguish between picking out cats by means of the notion "whatever, in any counterfactual situation, has the following list of qualities among those instantiated by this sample" and by means of . . . ? What? Just by whether they are cats, whether or not the list applies? But what is it to use the notion of "cats, whether or not . . . " unless we have some other list made up?

Kripke explicates the notion of "rigid designator" further by saying:

[19] Cf. Kripke, "Naming and Necessity," 329f, where the thesis is put forward.
[20] Cf. Ibid., 322 – but I may misinterpret him here.   [21] Ibid., 327.   [22] Ibid., 328.
[23] Ibid., 322.

What I mean by saying that a description might have referred to something different, I mean that in *our* language as *we* use it in describing a counterfactual situation, there might have been a different object satisfying the descriptive conditions *we* give for reference. So, for example, we use the phrase "the inventor of bifocals," when we are talking about another possible world or a counterfactual situation, to refer to whoever in that counterfactual situation would have invented bifocals.[24]

But this does not help with our problem. The single-minded historian of optometry designates the same thing (now Franklin, now Jefferson, now an ape) by "the Inventor of Bifocals" as he surveys various counterfactual situations. (If one prefers a more realistic example, consider "The Dalai Lama"; for Tibetan Buddhists, there has been and could be only one of them, no matter what the counterfactual contingency.) We, finding it counterintuitive to think of Franklin and Jefferson as the same thing, find his usage odd. We mark this, in Kripke's vocabulary, by saying that we use "inventor of bifocals" nonrigidly – which is a way of expressing our intention to let Franklin and the counterfactual Jefferson who invented bifocals count as different things, rather than as the same thing wearing different sets of properties.

But what corresponds to this sort of intention in the case of cats or pains or yellowness? The substrate-property distinction is prima facie up for grabs in the case of individuals (and so also, then, is the rigidity of one's designator). But in the case of the kind cat there does not seem anything to be up for grabs until one has made up one's list of salient properties (and thus no way to test rigidity). What is then up for grabs is the essence-accident distinction. One can differ about what to call the original sample if all or most of its members turn out to lack what one has now intuited or discovered to be the essence of cat. One can, with Kripke, call them "fool's cats"[25] and conclude, given some other conditions, that there never were any cats. Or one can keep right on calling them "cats" and say that the so-called intuition or discovery about the essence of being a cat was all wrong. But before somebody has broached a view about essence, while we are just confronted with the original sample and have not even gotten around to listing qualities yet, what does it mean to say that we are then using "cat" "so as to refer to whatever (not necessarily including this sample) in any counterfactual situation, would be a cat" (nonrigid) or perhaps "so as to refer in any

---

[24] Saul Kripke, "Identity and Necessity," in *Identity and Individuation*, ed. Milton Karl Munitz (New York: New York University Press, 1971), 145.

[25] Kripke, "Naming and Necessity," 321.

counterfactual situation to, at a minimum, those things before us" (rigid). Kripke's use of the notion of "rigid designators" for natural kinds seems to want to abstract altogether from the epistemological question of whether we have as yet grasped, or thought ourselves to have grasped, the essence of the kind. But I do not see how it can be so abstracted.

Knowledge of Essential Properties. The notion of a property which a thing could not lack and still be the same thing seems an innocuous one, once separated from epistemological problems. But it rarely has been so separated, and its unpopularity in recent philosophy is due to the fact that nobody has ever figured out how to tell whether we were right in our hunches, or intuitions, or theories, about what was essential to what. Thus, the notion of internal properties and relations has succumbed to verificationism and suffered the ultimate indignity of being relativized to "a choice of descriptions" or "a motive for inquiry." Kripke wants to restore its metaphysical purity and thus its respectability. This would be harmless enough, except that he calls upon the notion to decide particular metaphysical disputes. In the mind-body case, Kripke wants to use the epistemological notion of "imaginability." But he thereby deprives himself of the advantages of having made essence a metaphysical notion, since he is now drawn into quarrels about competing intuitions, intuition vs. the needs of unified science, and the rest. In particular, he has to have a view about when, if ever, inquiry can enlarge the scope of imagination, when inquiry can go wrong about essence, and how one knows that it has. Could heat turn out not to be molecular motion? Could it stay molecular motion and yet turn out to be the cause of sensation S? All these tricky Putnamesque questions – the ones which, when formulated in terms of meaning, give rise to the "cluster concept" theory which is anathema to Kripke – also arise when formulated in terms of "properties by which we pick out referents." The Quinean view that when things get fuzzy it does not much matter whether we say that we are talking about the same thing but saying mostly new things about it, or instead say that we are now talking about a different thing, retains all its force even when the "principle of the necessity of identities using rigid designators" is adopted. For, as I have been arguing above, in the case of kind-words the rigid-vs.-nonrigid distinction cannot be given a clear sense except by reference to the essence-accident distinction, and neither distinction can be applied to the mind-body problem without getting involved in precisely the epistemological questions Kripke wants to avoid.

Aristotelianism. Are, then, essence, what counts as substance rather than quality, and necessity all "relative to a description"? Was Aristotle just wrong, and is Quine right in his "only shades of grey" view of necessity and his dismissive attitude toward essence? Kripke is certainly right that the notion of necessary property is much more than "a philosopher's notion with no intuitive content"[26] – it is pretty basic to the way we speak. But, like many another such notion (e.g., "just plain wrong, intrinsically wrong" as in "Premarital sex is just wrong") it becomes philosophically controversial when somebody asks "How do you know?" The spirit of philosophy since Kant has been verificationist – saying that if this latter question could not be answered, then the notion in question might as well be dropped. To put it another way, the whole spirit of philosophy since Kant (and, indeed, since Descartes) has been not to recognize the sort of distinction between "epistemological" and "metaphysical" concepts which Kripke wants to draw.[27] So the natural thing to do with the intuitive content of the notion of "necessity" has seemed to be to relativize it: to say that at any given state of inquiry (or, if you like, of the history of language, or the history of the imagination), you can block things out into essences and accidents in the good old Aristotelian way – by, for example, taking advantage of the latest scientific notion of what things are made of. Common sense, on this view, will always be Aristotelian – it will just be Aristotelian in a different way in every generation. It will not be a background for scientific inquiry; it will just be inquiry frozen at some selected point. We can be Aristotelian when coping with the needs of the moment but Deweyan when contemplating time and eternity.

I confess I have no idea how to argue the question of whether this verificationist spirit (of which the latest flowering is Searle's and Putnam's approach to names and concepts) is a mistake on a world-historical scale or whether it is genuine progress. I am inclined to say that no real issue has been drawn. Thus, for example, Kripke quotes Searle as saying that "It is a necessary fact that Aristotle has the logical sum, inclusive disjunction, of properties commonly attributed to him" and comments that "Such a suggestion, if 'necessary' is used in the way I have been using it in this lecture, must clearly be false."[28] Indeed it must be, but why not just have two senses of "necessary," one to suit the man who wants his reference to be determined by, for example, the causal roots of the use of the vocable (as on Donnellan's view), and another for the man who cares nothing for the roots and wants to talk about whatever man it was who . . . ? Must one of

---

[26] Ibid., 265.   [27] Ibid., 260–261.   [28] Ibid., 279.

these be the right sense? To put it another way, must there be a notion of "reference" which is such that the latter man is referring to the end of that causal chain whether he wants to or not? Well, this just shoves things one step back. Is there a relation called "reference" which is something beyond – more metaphysical than – finding out what people are talking about by asking them (or what you are talking about by asking yourself)? If there is such a relation, does its existence make any difference to other philosophical topics?

I have been arguing that the refurbished Aristotelian notions Kripke wields do not affect the issue about mind-body identity, but I have no confidence that they do not affect some other interesting philosophical issues. Further, I think that Kripke is right in trying to systematize some of the commonsense intuitions which have gotten lost in the recent movement to relativize everything in sight. There ought to be some way in which we can adopt the lofty world-historical perspective common to Hegel, Dewey, and Quine while still speaking with Aristotle and the vulgar, and thus avoid flashy relativistic paradoxes. Nobody has managed this much tact so far, and maybe some of the old Aristotelian distinctions will help. (Although if they do, their use will have to be disassociated from such brand-new paradoxes as that "no counterfactual situation is properly describable as one in which there would have been unicorns."[29]) But first we will have to get a clearer idea about the method of metaphysics-as-abstracted-from-epistemology, and about how to adjudicate disagreements within this field.

Materialism. I shall end with a few words about Pain and painfulness. By the former I shall refer to a natural kind of particular (a nonextended substance) which turns up here and there in sentient organisms and which some have suggested is actually *not* nonextended, but has, as its intrinsic metaphysical nature, the stimulation of C-fibers. The latter is an immediate phenomenological quality, which pains usually have in humans. Some philosophers think it is a contradiction to think of nonpainful pains. They say that painfulness is of the essence of pains. They claim to know this a priori – and to have a belief to which empirical inquiry is irrelevant – by virtue of an analysis of meanings, or phenomenological bracketing, or just plain *nous*. They would not usually claim to know a priori about the essence of any sort of particular other than mental states, but these, they

---

[29] Saul Kripke, "Addenda to Saul A. Kripke's 'Naming and Necessity,'" in *Semantics of Natural Language*, ed. Donald Davidson and Gilbert Harman (Boston: D. Reidel, 1972), 763.

think, have especially easily knowable essences. A philosopher who takes this position is on solid ground in resisting mind-body identity. All that remains is for him to develop an epistemology and a methodology which accounts for our a priori access to the mental. This is not easy.

Philosophers who resist mind-body identity but who (frightened, perhaps, by Wittgenstein) are not sure they want to resurrect the Cartesian view that "nothing is easier for the mind to know than itself" try to sidestep the epistemological issue. They say that the immediate phenomenological quality itself is what is in question and that this is "irreducible" – not to be identified with C-fiber stimulations, nor the quality of having one's C-fibers stimulated, or anything else. So we can forget about Pain and just contemplate this irreducible quality. What is it a quality of? Not pains, they are gone. Experience? Certainly, but this is no great help, since every "immediate (i.e., noninferentially reportable) quality" is a quality of experience. What about experience? Is it a name for a bunch of qualities, or is it a nonextended substance? If the former, what are these bunch of qualities attached to? Maybe brains; nobody seems to have any better idea. If the latter, how do we know the essence of this nonextended substance? Are we really sure that it is nonextended? What a priori method do we bring to bear to confirm our intuition here? Back to epistemology again!

I have constructed these dilemmas to suggest that questions like "substance or quality?" "essence or accident?" are not in place. I agree with the Wittgensteinian view (cited above) that philosophers have unfortunately insisted on taking sensations as if they were pretty much like physical objects and applying the same vocabulary to them as to cats and demons and mountains. The reason why we should not do this, I think, is not that their "logics" are different, or anything of that sort, but just that in-principle-unanswerable questions arise if you think of them this way. Such questions used to be called pseudoproblems, and it was said that their irreality was exposed once we realized that all sides in the controversy agreed on "the facts" and that all that was left over was the "verbal" question of how to express these facts. Nowadays we are not so sure about this factual-vs.-verbal distinction, but I think the force of it is just that certain disagreements are sterile, in that they do not hook up in any interesting way with disagreements about anything else. ("Differences which do not make a difference," in James's phrase.) Materialists disagree among themselves and with their opponents about (a) whether there are particulars called pains constantly correlated with stimulated C-fibers; or whether instead (b) these fibers have, when stimulated, certain awful phenomenological qualities; or whether instead (c) these fibers do not have these qualities but instead produce them somewhere else (in our minds, say); or whether perhaps (d) "stimulation of C-fibers" and "that awful phenomenological quality" are not just two names for the same property; or whether . . . .[30] But most people agree that, if physiology lives up to our expectations, a brain-state language would do just as well as a sensation-language for coping with the hazards of life. The latter admission takes most of the interest away from dualism, and a whole-hearted Austinian refusal to use the "essence-accident, substance-quality" vocabulary on sensations would take most of the punch out of materialism. Once we got rid of the specter of ghost-substances or ghost-properties, even if physiology did not come out right (i.e., no decent psychophysical correlations appeared), nobody would think that there was a mind-body problem anyway.

I have argued elsewhere that once we can get straight about the *epistemological* issues concerning our knowledge of the mental, there are not going to be any metaphysical problems left over in this area (just as there were none for Aristotle).[31] One reason why I think it important to *not* bring back Aristotelian metaphysical notions (via the philosophy of language) with reference to the mind-body problem is that I think that the problem was created by a bad picture of human knowledge and is dissolved by a better one. To put it crudely, epistemology can cure the ills which epistemology caused. But this is a view which I cannot defend here. I hope, however, that this discussion of Kripke's view on mind-body identity shows that the intuitive objections which arise to the assertion of such an identity neither gain nor lose force if one adopts the views about reference, naming, and necessity which Kripke advances.

---

[30] This sentence ends with the ellipses in the original. – *Eds.*

[31] "Incorrigibility as a Mark of the Mental," cited in fn. 5 above and "Cartesian Epistemology and Changes in Ontology," in *Contemporary American Philosophy*, ed. John B. Smith (New York: Humanities Press, 1970), 273–292.

II

Later Papers

9

Philosophy as Epistemology: Reply to Hacking and Kim

Both Ian Hacking and Jaegwon Kim speak as if "knowledge" and "philosophy" named natural kinds – as if both were the sorts of thing which had essences, natures, which we might get right or get wrong. Although both are prepared to dispense with foundationalism, and with "eternal problems," they think that there is a distinctive philosophical interest and that it has something to do with knowledge. Hacking says, for example, that "thinking about knowledge has been integral to philosophy."[1] Kim would like philosophy to be, at least, "*intra*paradigmatic inquiry concerning the conceptual, foundational, and regulative aspects of a given paradigm."[2] To get my disagreement with these claims into focus, I want to distinguish two relevant senses of both "philosophy" and "knowledge." The first sense of each is too broad to be interesting or to suggest the possibility of inquiry into essence. The second sense is so narrow that it names only an outworn artifact. Hacking and Kim are working with what is either a third sense (invisible to me) or an oscillation between the narrow and broad sense.

In its broad sense, "philosophy" means, as Wilfrid Sellars, has put it, "seeing how things, in the largest sense of the term, hang together, in the largest sense of the term."[3] In its narrow sense, it may be defined as an effort to improve the amount or quality of our knowledge by picking out a privileged group of assertions, claiming that they are in some special way in correspondence with some extralinguistic entities, and then imparting this special relation to as many more assertions as we can. In the broad sense, "philosophy" is roughly synonymous with "high culture." In the narrow sense, the term is used to divide thinkers like Plato and Locke and Dewey from thinkers like the pseudo-Dionysius, Goethe, Kierkegaard, and Matthew Arnold.

---

[1] Ian Hacking, "Is the End in Sight for Epistemology?," *The Journal of Philosophy* 77, no. 10 (1980): 586.
[2] Jaegwon Kim, "Rorty on the Possibility of Philosophy," *The Journal of Philosophy* 77, no. 10 (1980): 595.
[3] Wilfrid Sellars, *Science, Perception, and Reality* (New York: Humanities Press, 1963), 1. – Eds.

In the wide sense of "knowledge," the term applies to all warranted assertions – or, rather, all those which will still look warranted at the Peircean end of an indefinitely continued Habermasian undistorted conversation. Candidates for this latter class include, for example, "If you paint her that way, she will look lopsided," "If you build it that way, it will look ugly," "Equals added to equals give equals," "We must love one another," "God is Three Persons in One Substance," "Wintergreen is the best candidate," "F equals MA," and "The cat is on the mat." In the narrow sense of "knowledge," the term applies to a much more restricted class, whose exact limits are decided by philosophical reflection on how to shortcut the conversation by "methodological" means. Popular candidates for inclusion in this latter class used to include "God is Three Persons in One Substance" and "We must love one another." At the moment, the most favored candidates are "Equals added to equals give equals," "F equals MA," and "The cat is on the mat." Roughly speaking, an assertion is a candidate for the narrow, privileged, class if it seems likely that nobody will turn up anything new which will make it seem unjustified, or suggest a new vocabulary which will make the terms in which it was cast seem obsolete.

If both "philosophy" and "knowledge" are taken in the narrow sense, then it is analytic that, as Hacking says, "most of those whom we include in our canon (of great philosophers) have been fascinated by the best knowledge of their time."[4] The reason why we shelve Plato and Locke and Dewey in the philosophy section of the library is because they hoped to find out the secret of some disciplines which were doing nicely in their time and to apply this secret of success to new areas. We shelve the pseudo-Dionysus and Goethe and Arnold elsewhere because their attempts to make things hang together, to see life steadily and see it whole, did not have much to do with isolating privileged assertions and trying to specify just why they were privileged. But I think it worth noting that when Hacking says that the reason why the metaphor of a Mental Eye is so popular is that the ancients' "most permanent contribution to knowledge is geometry,"[5] he is begging a lot of questions. Certainly the ancients whom we call "philosophers" thought a lot of geometry. But is Euclid's work really more permanent than, say, the knowledge of how to govern cities through democratic assemblies? Of how to represent the moving human body in stone? Of how to secularize, intellectualize, and sublimate our religious instincts? Hacking's unhesitating choice of geometry seems to me to illustrate the philosophers' habit of using the narrow sense of "knowledge" in order to

---

[4] Hacking, "Is the End in Sight for Epistemology?," 585.   [5] Ibid., 584.

demarcate something which they can then proceed to make look like a natural kind. The "what if?" questions which Nietzsche asks in *The Birth of Tragedy* and Heidegger in *Introduction to Metaphysics* seem to me useful ways of reminding ourselves that there are a lot of ways the West could have gone in the fourth century BC, and that it is only certain handpicked ancients who "well knew" that "their most permanent contribution to knowledge" was geometry.

Coming back now to my distinction between broad and narrow senses of "philosophy," my objection to philosophy in the narrow sense – philosophy as centering around something like epistemology – is historical and empirical rather than principled. It looks to me like an enterprise which simply never panned out. Efforts to figure out which of our warranted assertions will still be being made at the end of inquiry are probably not worth making. Even if we guess right about which of our contributions are going to be permanent, it seems unlikely that we are going to find some special ingredient in those contributions which we can isolate and use to make more contributions. However, I do not think there is any neat a priori way to show that this is *impossible*. My point is rather that the history of attempts to do this is sufficiently long and sufficiently discouraging to suggest that it was not a very good project in the first place. But if we do not have such a project in mind, then I do not think we shall be able to make sense of what Hacking calls "an attempt to understand the possibility and nature of the various kinds of knowledge and styles of reasoning."[6]

On one interpretation, Hacking's phrase can be taken simply as a reference to philosophy in the large sense – something done by Goethe as much as by Dewey. Such an attempt might just be seeing how the various human activities that culminate in warranted assertions resemble and differ. This is what philosophers would do if they adopted what I am calling a hermeneutic rather than an epistemological attitude toward culture – an attitude which would lead, I suspect, to the gradual loss of a professional sense of autonomy and a gradual coalescence of philosophy with history and literature. But Hacking would, I take it, resist such blurring of the genres. Hacking finds unattractive the role of "informed dilettante, compromising or transcending disciplines and discourses" which I recommend for philosophy. In particular, he thinks that "history and sociology are not successor subjects to epistemology, but only among

---

[6] Ibid., 586.

the tools by which the epistemologist will pursue his questions."[7] My trouble is that I do not see what these questions might be.

I find Hacking's phrase the more puzzling because Hacking and I are both admirers of Foucault. I would take Foucault's *The Order of Things* (or *Discipline and Punish*, or *Madness and Civilization*) as a good illustration of how the history and sociology of various disciplines can do more for us than epistemology can. I know that Hacking takes Foucault to be doing something distinctively epistemological, but I have trouble seeing what it is. Nor am I helped by Hacking's references to Chomsky and Kuhn. I do not see Chomsky as telling us something constructive about the nature and possibility of human knowledge, but as making a negative point about Skinner-type research programs. Similarly, I do not see Kuhn as telling us something of that sort, but as making a negative point about the so-called "received view" in philosophy of science. Both negative points have been enormously helpful, but I cannot see how they can be viewed as answering epistemological questions. On my view, Chomsky's own self-descriptions of his work in terms of rationalism and innatism, and Wolfgang Stegmüller's attempt to use Kuhn to recreate old-style criteria of theory-choice,[8] are exactly the wrong ways to go. They are attempts to pour new wine into old bottles, thus killing the taste. I suspect that Hacking's treatment of Foucault is something of the same sort, but I may simply not understand his view of Foucault properly.

To bring my reply to Hacking to a close, I can sum up what I have been saying as: it only makes sense to ask about the nature of something if you have some particular puzzle which you want to solve. In the case of "knowledge" in the *broad* sense, I do not think we have any clear idea of what we mean by "the nature of knowledge," because we cannot put our finger on any particular difficulty which "knowledge of the nature of knowledge" would resolve. In the abstract, there seems no better chance of coming up with something which makes all warranted assertions warranted than of coming up with something which makes all good manners good. If it is knowledge in the *narrow* sense that is in question – if we are asking what Euclid's axioms, laws of mechanics, and reports of the positions of cats have in common – then I take it that Hacking and Kim and I agree that this is just the discredited search for foundations. So I am inclined to suspect that "the nature of knowledge" is an empty phrase.

---

[7] Ibid., 587.
[8] Wolfgang Stegmüller, *The Structure and Dynamics of Theories* (New York: Springer-Verlag, 1976). – Eds.

"The nature of science" might seem a bit more promising, but I doubt that it is. I do not think that we are going to find a common strategy which was used to put, successively, mathematics, physics, chemistry, biology, economics and philosophy on a "scientific basis." In all the attempts to make this and that scientific which we have witnessed, methodological kibitzing has never done much good. What did the trick was somebody coming up with a new substantive vocabulary which worked. I think it is the beginning of wisdom in this area to see Galileo and Dalton and Darwin as scientific because they were successful, not successful because they were scientific. "The secure path of a science" seems to me just the honorific which gets applied to any discipline which seems to have done something pretty impressive and is now the scene of a reasonable amount of consensus and teamwork. "Science," on my view, is a sociological rather than an epistemological notion.

As for the possibility of knowledge, this only seems to me an interesting question if somebody can suggest why it should not be possible. Since Kant, philosophers have developed a bad habit of explaining what they do by saying that they are investigating the "conditions of possibility" of this and that, in some sense of "condition" which is as vague as Kant's sense of *Grund.* Perhaps, however, Hacking has in mind straightforward causal conditions of the sort Foucault describes – changes in jargon and in institutions which leave an open space for some genius to make his name. But I do not see how to get from the old Kantian sense of "possibility" to this sociological sense. Hacking does not like the constant reference to "practices" in my *Philosophy and the Mirror of Nature.* He says, "But to talk about practices is not even to begin to ask a question."[9] This remark seems to me to beg the question about what questions to ask. The reason I talk so much about practices is the same as Wittgenstein's – it makes it that much more difficult to ask the bad old questions.

Hacking says that I am wrong in saying that "when a practice has continued long enough the conventions that make it possible are relatively easy to isolate." "For," he says, "we can isolate no pertinent conventions" which "made possible the practice of chemistry from the time of Lavoisier."[10] What I meant by conventions, however, was just what people learn in learning how to be, for example, chemists. We do not, to be sure, give them a list of conventions to memorize, as we give soldiers the list of General Orders. But it goes with being on the secure path of a science that there is an initiation procedure – for example, graduate education – which makes a scientist out of

---

[9] Hacking, "Is the End in Sight for Epistemology?," 587.   [10] Ibid.

you. What you learn is how to carry on a practice, and "familiarity with the relevant conventions" seems a reasonable, if not particularly informative, term for part of what it takes to do that. Hacking thinks it too uninformative. So my basic difference with him is about whether we can hope for more information. I do not think we can, but, once again, I have nothing but the record of past failures to justify my pessimism. At a certain point, it is reasonable to take past disappointments as a reason for abandoning a project which may still look good on paper. The history of answers to questions about the nature and possibility of knowledge seems to me to show that there was something wrong with the epistemological project.

***

I turn now to Kim's remark that Platonism cannot be blamed for begetting epistemology. Kim regards notions of "correspondence with nature" and "accurate representation" as used by Plato as harmless and commonsensical, while joining me in being dubious about Cartesian mentalism and Kantian universalism.[11] I have to reject the proffered compromise, because it is precisely such Platonic notions which enable Kim to use the "cognitive vs. noncognitive" distinction to criticize my conception of philosophy. That latter distinction seems to me unintelligible without the Platonic assumption that some of our warranted assertions correspond to reality and some do not. Without that notion, we would never have developed philosophy in the narrow sense, nor given the term "knowledge" its distinctively philosophical sense. We would not have thought that "2 + 2 is 4" or "The cat is on the mat" has some clearer and more basic sort of truth than is possessed by "There ought to be more love in the world." Without the notion of "correspondence" and "accurate representation," we should not have had the project of looking for ties between thoughts (or sentences) and the world around which philosophy in the narrow sense has entered.

We can drop Plato's notions of correspondence and representation, however, while still having what Kim calls "the assertorial function of language." It seems to me precisely the glory of Dewey, Wittgenstein, and Sellars to have shown how, on a "language-game" analysis, we can distinguish assertions from other noises (e.g., coughs and commands) without using Platonic, neo-Sellarsian notions.[12] The virtue of such an analysis – and more generally, of such an approach to thought and

---

[11] Kim, "Rorty on the Possibility of Philosophy," 589–590.
[12] Brandom's "Asserting" is a particularly elegant example of what can be done along these lines. See Robert Brandom, "Asserting," *Noûs* 17, no. 4 (1983): 637–650.

language – seems to me precisely that it removes part of the temptation to think that "There ought to be more love in the world" has some sort of unperspicuous, dubious, second-rate sort of truth as compared to the intelligible and clear-truth of "The cat is on the mat." Language-game analyses permit us to say that both sentences are true without having to worry about what "makes" them true.

I suspect that Kim thinks this is a worry we ought to have, and, as a good Platonist, thinks that truth without truth-makers is not good enough. I do not know how to debate this point, except to say that here again I think we have to rely primarily on how the Platonic research program, so to speak, has worked out in practice. I do not think that analyzing what we mean by "true" is going to be of much help, because the Platonist and the Wittgensteinian have such different notions of what it is to "give an analysis." I suspect that one's view on this matter is ultimately going to be determined by looking over the contemporary philosophical scene and deciding which way to go – where the more promising work is being done. The question of whether to stick with Platonism – with what Heidegger called "the metaphysics of presence" – is the question which currently divides "analytic" from "Continental" philosophers. People like Derrida and Foucault take the anti-Platonist view for granted, have gotten accustomed to truth without truth-makers, and have tried to envisage a form of intellectual life which does not revolve around the cognitive vs. noncognitive distinction. It seems to me that this form of life has more promise than the form which is defended and explicated in Russell and Reichenbach. But, once again, I have no knock-down arguments to offer – only the suggestion that we see the choice as a practical rather than a theoretical one, more like a choice about what discipline to pursue than like a choice between two competing theories within a single discipline.

Wherever one stands on truth-making and the metaphysics of presence, however, one should be clear about the difference between saying

(a) there are no such things as truth-makers and
(b) social approval is the only truth-maker.

I am saying the former rather than the latter. Kim speaks of me as "socializing" truth, but it would be more accurate to say that, like James and Dewey, I am trying to moralize it. Current social approval – current warrantedness – does not, of course, guarantee that an assertion will still be warranted at the end of inquiry, that it will survive the conversational twists and turns of the future. Nor is any society ever going to be in a position to claim that the conversation is finished. It is true that any society can – and most societies have – tried to put forward such a claim in respect to certain conversational topics. They have thus, in Habermas's phrase, "distorted communication," constrained conversation. But they should not have done this. The reason they should not have is not that undistorted communication is the best way to get accurate representations of reality but because undistorted communication is a morally good thing. Whereas Hacking thinks that what makes the West Western is its attachment to "knowledge of truth as a value for its own sake,"[13] I think that what makes us Western is our willingness to keep talking, to try out new vocabularies, to break through convention in the hope of still more interesting conversation. Hacking and Kim tend to identify the special virtue of the West with an interest in getting things right. I identify it with keeping people free to talk in ways they never talked before – with Pericles rather than with Euclid. As long as we think of truth as made by powers not ourselves, we shall be looking for constraint and security – the secure path of a science – rather than testing our freedom. The alternative is not to think of truth as made by us but to think of truth as not made at all. If, with James, we see the true as what is good in the way of belief, then we shall reject the question "What makes truths true?" for the same good reasons as we reject the Platonic question "What makes goods good?" Both are questions which look worse and worse the more one tries to answer them.

Turning now from what Kim says about knowledge and truth to what he says about philosophy, I should like to offer some criticisms of his view of philosophy as Handmaiden of Science. Roughly, my view is that science does not need what Kim calls "intraparadigmatic inquiry concerning the conceptual, foundational, and regulative aspects of a given paradigm."[14] I may just be speaking out of ignorance of the history of science, but I cannot think of a good example of a discipline doing itself much good by meditating on its foundational, conceptual, and regulative aspects – by turning philosophical. It seems to me that such meditation is an Owl of Minerva phenomenon – caused either by what Kuhn calls the piling up of anomalies which precedes a revolution, or by sheer boredom. Recurring to a point I was making earlier, what keeps the conversation going is somebody having a bright idea about a new way to talk. Self-reflection seems to me useful only when an old, mature, self-satisfied paradigm has been impudently challenged by such a new idea. It is a defensive maneuver, useful only when there is in fact an enemy to be defended against.

---

[13] Hacking, "Is the End in Sight for Epistemology?," 585.
[14] Kim, "Rorty on the Possibility of Philosophy," 595.

A practice only needs to bother to make itself "internally coherent and consistent,"[15] it seems to me, if there is some concrete doubt about whether it is a good practice. When there are no such doubts, then we get the sterility typical of books on "Conceptual Foundations of . . . " The philosophical, Socratic, imperative to be critical and reflective seems to me better interpreted as the imperative to try to have some new ideas, rather than the imperative to examine "conceptual, foundational, and regulative questions" in abstracto. I take the central Western value as keeping conversation moving and open, rather than ensuring that inquiry is solidly based or in touch with the real. So I do not think that systematicity is an intrinsic virtue. It is simply the normal style of intraparadigmatic reasoning.

Mention of systematic philosophy brings me to the last point I want to make about Kim's paper. He says that on my conception philosophy does not aim "at the attainment of intellectual truth"[16] – it becomes noncognitive, a sort of art form. Here again I want to insist that it aims at just the sort of truth which physics and politics aim at. Insofar as a human activity produces assertions, it aims at "intellectual truth" – the only sort of truth there is. I may have seemed to be invoking a form of cognitive vs. noncognitive distinction by distinguishing between "systematic" and "edifying" philosophy, but this is a misleading appearance. Rather, I want to blur the distinction between art and science by saying that the interesting distinction is between normal forms of both and abnormal forms of both.

I think that I caused needless confusion by using the word "edifying," since Hacking finds it a demeaning term to apply to, for example, Wittgenstein. Further, several reviewers of *Philosophy and the Mirror of Nature* have assumed that "edifying philosophy" and "hermeneutics" are roughly synonymous. I meant to keep them far apart. Hermeneutic philosophy is just what Hacking calls "a concern for styles of reasoning" when this concern is freed from worry about "the nature and possibility of knowledge" and from the cognitive vs. noncognitive distinction. Anybody can do this sort of philosophy, simply by commenting on the state of the culture, the passing scene, from a certain pragmatical stance. My book is hermeneutic philosophy in this sense, a sense in which philosophy blends into history and sociology. By contrast, "edifying philosophy" is something which only the occasional genius can give us. Only a few times in a century do we get a philosopher who breaks through into a whole new way of talking about things in general. Wittgenstein, Heidegger, and Dewey seem

---

[15] Ibid., 593.   [16] Ibid., 594.

to me our century's candidates. They did not try to be critical and reflective from within a mature and comprehensive paradigm, but rather challenged the reigning vocabulary of high culture with better ideas.

I do not know how to imitate these edifying philosophers, and I am certainly not suggesting that philosophy as an academic discipline should cease to be systematic and become edifying. As long as it remains a discipline, it will of course be systematic. There is no way to train students to be edifying, any more than there is a way to train them to be original. We can train them to be hermeneutic by assigning Nietzsche rather than Russell, Derrida rather than Trilling, Foucault rather than Parsons. But that will not necessarily have edifying results. Indeed, it opens the terrifying possibility of doctoral dissertations on "the conceptual, foundational, and regulative aspects" of hermeneutics.

***

I should like to conclude with a few words about two of Hacking's claims that I do not get the history right. He says that Kant was not the first to use the distinction between sense and intellect, particular and universal, as a clue to writing the history of philosophy. He is right about this. I overstated my case when I said that Kant gave us a "history of our subject." My point was that up until Kant's time, there were lots of distinctions (e.g., between faith and reason, nature and spirit) which could have been used to pick a canon, to divide philosophy in the broad sense into philosophy in the narrow sense plus a lot of nonphilosophical thinkers. Kant provided the paradigm which made his distinctions the ones to look for. The new kind of "histories of philosophy" which get written in the 1780s and 1790s seems to me good evidence for this claim. Hacking is doubtless right that Kant took his cue from Leibniz, who in turn took it from the quarrel between Augustinian and Aristotelian schoolmen, about whether there was something in the intellect not previously in the senses. Highlighting this distinction perhaps goes back to Plato's "quarrel between the gods and the giants."

On the other hand, it is not clear that the bits of Plato and Aristotle which Leibniz and Kant thought central were central to Plato and Aristotle themselves. There is very little evidence that they were. Once we have the canon which Kantian historiography gives us, we should not be surprised to see Kantian distinctions turning up everywhere, and texts which mention those distinctions highlighted. But I do not think that we have a good answer to the question "Is that canon the 'right' canon, as Hacking suggests, or is it just the 'neo-Kantian' one, as I am suggesting?" I am not even sure what sort of question this is. It is a bit like the question "Are the poets whom Hume lists in 'The Standard of Taste' the touchstones of the right canon or just a typical eighteenth-century canon?" I am not sure what would count as "getting history right" in the case of such questions. I do think that there is evidence that Kant was the figure who made it possible for holders of the ancient professorial chairs Hacking mentions to develop the self-image which we have today – as practicing a "formal" discipline which is autonomous and critical, neither dependent upon the current state of science nor responsible to the religious sentiments of the community. This was not the image had by pre-Kantian holders of those same chairs, and I think we need an explanation of how we got it, of the Foucauldian "rupture" involved. What Hacking calls "the standard reading" does not help here (though Foucault's *The Order of Things* does).

Another point which Hacking makes in the first section of his paper, commenting on p. 149 in *Philosophy and the Mirror of Nature*, is headed: "The validity of the interest in universal and particular."[17] Here he says that my project is such that I do not wish to argue, with Russell, that the particular-universal distinction is an accident of language, nor with Ramsey that it is a mistake. Indeed I do not, and I do not see why Hacking thinks I should. In the sense in which this distinction is an "accident of language," so is every other distinction. I do not see what a distinction which was *essential* to language," as opposed to a distinction which any language could be used to paraphrasistically translate, would be like. Nor do I see any sense in which it could be called "a mistake." At most, Ramsey showed that you could get along without it for various purposes. The quarrel between Strawson and Quine about the irreducibility of singular terms is not without interest, but the topic shares the vagueness of all quarrels about "reducibility" – reducibility for what purposes? Hacking seems to think that I should argue about whether or not the particular-universal distinction corresponds to reality – whether it is "really there." The last thing I want to do is to say that it does or does not so correspond. I just want to say that, like the distinction between faith and reason and between nature and spirit, it has been hashed over too long with too little profit. There is nothing "invalid" about an interest in such distinctions. It is just that – like the distinctions between Aryan and Orthodox, Catholic and Protestant, Marxist and non-Marxist – they no longer seem to have much point. Perhaps this is only semblance. As Kim says, we might have lucked into "the right philosophical questions."[18] But I would take this to be a prediction

[17] Hacking, "Is the End in Sight for Epistemology?," 582.
[18] Kim, "Rorty on the Possibility of Philosophy," 595.

that some genius will come along and revitalize empiricism or rationalism, nominalism or antinominalism, idealism or realism, so that such issues will not look as merely scholastic as they do now. Maybe this will happen. So maybe systematic, epistemologically centered, philosophy will get a new lease on life. At the moment, however, systematic philosophy seems to be in pretty poor shape. I cannot prove that it will not recover, but I do not think we should strain to keep it alive simply because we have no better idea of what to do.

10

Naturalized Epistemology and Norms: Replies to Goldman and Fodor

Everybody is in favor of knowing as much truth as possible, just as everybody is in favor of doing as much good as possible. But opinions diverge on whether there is anything general and useful to be said about how to go about doing either – and on whether there can be an interesting general theory about knowledge or truth or goodness. Just as Aristotle was dubious about Plato's attempts to define terms like "virtuous" and "pious" and "good" in ways which might help those who were unsure about the right thing to do, or the nature of a good life, so philosophers like Reid and Dewey had been dubious about the efforts of post-Cartesian philosophers to get theories of knowledge and truth which would be helpful to truth seekers. Contemporary Aristotelian ethical theorists like Iris Murdoch are suspicious of general moral principles. They suggest that in the clinches, the principles always let you down and leave you to muddle through on your own. Contemporary writers on science like Paul Feyerabend and Marshall Swain are suspicious of the sort of general precepts which Descartes advanced in the *Discourse on Method* and the *Rules for the Direction of the Mind.* When Descartes says, for example, that we should "carry on our reflections in due order, commencing with objects that are the most simple and easy to understand, in order to rise little by little, to knowledge of what is most complex,"[1] this seems about as helpful as being told to inquire whether you can will the maxim of your action as a universal law for all rational agents. There are too many criteria of simplicity – too many vocabularies in which different terms are taken as undefined and primitive – to make Descartes's rule of much use, just as there are too many vocabularies in which a given action can be described to make Kant's of much use.

---

[1] René Descartes, *Discourse on Method; and Meditations on First Philosophy*, 4th ed., trans. Donald A. Cress. (Indianapolis, IN: Hackett, 1998), 11 – Eds.

I am sympathetic to the view that the search for rules of knowledge seeking has never gotten us anywhere and thus that the idea of "epistemology" may have been a bad one – just as I am sympathetic to the idea that general moral principles have not done much to guide action and that the idea of "ethical theory" may have been a bad one. I agree with Marshall Swain's comment on a previous paper of Alvin Goldman's[2]: Swain says he is as "skeptical about the likelihood of philosophical progress [in normative epistemology] . . . as [he is] about systems that would purport to tell us how to lead the good life."[3] I do not think there are, or could be, any general knock-down arguments against the very possibility of useful epistemic rules or moral principles, but I think that the search for them has now gone on long enough for us to consider whether further effort has any chance of paying off. If one follows Murdoch and Sartre in being skeptical about ethical theory, and Feyerabend in being skeptical about the idea of "scientific method," one will suggest that what we really need are examples rather than rules or principles. To learn how to act rightly and live well, on this view, one will read Plutarch or Balzac rather than Kant or Mill. But the best means will be association with the right sort of people. Similarly, the best means of directing one's mind and making progress in the scientific, or other intellectual, discipline of one's choice, will be the study of recent paradigmatic achievements in that discipline. But even better will be initiation into what Kuhn calls a "disciplinary matrix"– the acquisition of the know-how possessed by those who are in fact making some progress in the area in question. None of these means are infallible – since one may get involved with a morally bad lot or initiated into the arcana of a scientific-research program which is just about to be supplanted by the work of some ingenious revolutionary. But no principle will help one avoid such pitfalls.

On this view of epistemology, the importance of Descartes's *Discourse on Method* was to direct people's attention toward Galileo's achievements and away from the Aristotelian tradition. This was a good thing to do, but unfortunately Descartes suggested that Galileo had discovered "how to be scientific" rather than simply a better vocabulary for describing motion than Aristotle's. Descartes thus popularized the unfortunate notion that Galileo had been "rational" in a way that Aristotle had not, and the notion that there are such things as "canons of scientific procedure," obedience to

[2] See Alvin I. Goldman, "Epistemics: The Regulative Theory of Cognition," *The Journal of Philosophy* 75, no. 10: 509–523. – *Eds.*
[3] Marshall Swain, "Epistemics and Epistemology," *The Journal of Philosophy* 75, no. 10 (1978): 524.

which could lead to discoveries in other fields comparable to Galileo's in mechanics and Descartes's own in geometry. It is, I have argued elsewhere,[4] doubtful that these notions could have survived had not Locke taken up the challenge and developed the idea that rationality could be studied by studying the mind as if it were a machine for the production of truth – a machine which took "simple ideas" as input and produced things like Newton's laws as outputs. This suggestion chimed with Ramist and Leibnizian notions of grinding out "analyses" by quasi-mechanical procedures. The combination led, in the fullness of time, to Goldman's Principle I:

> *A person's doxastic state D (at time t) is justified if and only if D results from a history of cognitive-state transitions that conform with (are permitted by) the correct epistemic rules.*[5]

From the skeptical point of view I have suggested, the question which this principle raises is "Are there any such rules which are more enlightening than such platitudes as 'Try to avoid inconsistency' and 'Keep your eyes open for new evidence'?" The suspicion that there are not is what leads people like Gilbert Harman to pooh-pooh the idea that the rules of deductive logic can take one from "basic statements" to interesting new discoveries.[6] The old idea, common to Aristotle and Locke, that to be rational is to start from the right sort of premises and then "think logically" is viewed, by people like Harman, Keith Lehrer, and antifoundationalist writers generally, as outmoded. On their view, the only sort of general epistemological principle we can hope for is something like the following:

> S is completely justified in believing that *p* if and only if, within the corrected doxastic system of *S*, *p* is believed to have a better chance of being true than the denial of *p* or any other statement that competes with *p*.[7]

In such a principle, everything turns on what a "corrected doxastic system" is. Lehrer defines this notion as follows:

> The *doxastic* system of a person *S*, is a set of statements of the form, *S* believes that *p*, *S* believes that *q*, and so forth, which describes what *S* believes. The *corrected* doxastic system of *S* is that subset of the doxastic

[4] See Richard Rorty, *Philosophy and the Mirror of Nature* (Princeton, NJ: Princeton University Press, 1979), chap. 3. – *Eds.*
[5] Alvin I. Goldman, "The Relation between Epistemology and Psychology," *Synthese* 64, no. 1 (1985): 36.
[6] Gilbert Harman, *Thought* (Princeton, NJ: Princeton University Press, 1973), 157.
[7] Keith Lehrer, *Knowledge* (Oxford: Clarendon, 1974), 198.

system resulting when every statement is deleted which describes *S* as believing something he would cease to believe as an impartial and disinterested truth-seeker . . . a *veracious* inquirer.[8]

Lehrer goes on to explain that "the way for a man to find out what he would believe as a veracious inquirer is for him to strive for that ideal and see what he believes."[9] He admits that "it remains a logical possibility that the beliefs of a man about the world within his corrected doxastic system could be entirely erroneous"[10] – the traditional objection to coherentist epistemologies. But he is content to leave this objection unanswered, as Descartes was not.

In commenting on my own view of the role of epistemology in modern philosophy, Goldman has suggested that I have confused epistemology with a specifically Cartesian variety of epistemology, and have taken justified criticisms of the species as criticisms of the entire genus. He writes:

> One needn't espouse Cartesian foundationalism to be a foundationalist. Even if there is no "immediate givenness" of the mind, knowledge or justification may have a vertical structure. Finally, foundationalism is not the only going theory of epistemic justification, coherentism is a viable option. Why can't one espouse coherentism and still be doing "epistemology"?[11]

Harman's point, cited by Goldman in "The Relation between Epistemology and Psychology," that deductive logic may always lead one to question premises rather than adopt conclusions seems to me enough to show that the cases in which "justification has a vertical structure" are just the cases in which nobody needs any epistemological advice. Those are the cases in which everybody has already agreed to play by some rules – namely, rules which forbid fighting the data or forbid throwing over the traditional vocabulary or the traditional principles. As to coherentism as a variety of epistemology, there is clearly a difference between the sort of thing searchers for "correct epistemic rules" are hoping for and the sort of moral uplift which is all coherentists like Lehrer and Habermas can offer. If you wanted rules for directing your mind and are told that you should be an impartial and disinterested truth seeker trying to keep the speech-situation undistorted, you will probably feel cheated. So I would suggest that once one espouses coherentism, one will be just as dubious about epistemic rules as one who espouses Sartre will be about the notion of moral principle.

---

[8] Ibid., 189–90.   [9] Ibid., 190.   [10] Ibid., 213.
[11] Alvin I. Goldman, "Review of *Philosophy and the Mirror of Nature*, by Richard Rorty," *The Philosophical Review* 90, no. 3 (1981): 425.

To make this issue more precise, let me turn now to Goldman's distinction between descriptive, analytic, and normative epistemology. I agree with him that many textbook accounts of epistemology are disingenuous. One cannot disjoin epistemology from psychological description in the usual priggish Frege-Husserl manner, while continuing to cite Locke and Hume as distinguished practitioners of epistemology. I applaud his bringing in "the sociology of science and knowledge, the history of science, and cultural anthropology" as branches of "social descriptive epistemology."[12] I would, however, want to add to these intellectual history generally – including the work of such writers as Comte, Hegel, Marx, Nietzsche, and Dewey. These writers describe the defective conceptual instruments used by our ancestors. They also go on to draw normative morals by warning us of the lingering traces of those concepts found in our contemporary vocabularies and presupposed by our cultural institutions.

I would suggest, however, that within the field of descriptive epistemology thus widely defined, the place of psychology – as, in Goldman's words, "*individual*" descriptive epistemology – may be rather slight.[13] If one wants to be more of a disinterested truth seeker than one is, if one worries about being caught in the prejudices and illusions of one's time as the Aristotelian astronomers at Padua were caught in theirs at the time of Galileo, then it will be the descriptive *social* epistemologists one will want to read. Individual psychology does not seem likely to do much. To offer an analogy which I shall return to later, intellectual history – my favorite sort of descriptive social epistemology – can be viewed as giving hints about how to reprogram human organisms in order to make them serve the ends of the race better. Psychology can then be viewed as the study of the – unfortunately unchangeable – wetware of those organisms insofar as it makes difficulties for such reprogramming. This analogy seems to me to help explain why the hopes which the seventeenth century thought might be fulfilled by the Lockean discipline we now call "psychology" in fact got fulfilled by disciplines which only emerged in the eighteenth and nineteenth centuries. It was in those centuries that the historical consciousness became the powerful engine for intellectual progress which we now recognize it to be.

Returning from this prolepsis to Goldman's threefold division, let me now leave descriptive epistemology behind and consider "analytic epistemology." Goldman describes this field as "only interested in the *ordinary* person's *concept* of knowledge and *concept* of justified belief."[14] I take it that

---

[12] Goldman, "The Relation between Epistemology and Psychology," 31.   [13] Ibid.   [14] Ibid., 33.

he has in mind, for example, attempts to provide a fourth criterion for knowledge in order to solve the Gettier problem.

I sympathize with William W. Rozeboom's claim that there is no reason to think that the ordinary person's use of "know" gives us resources for deciding whether to call various complicated Gettierological puzzle cases "knowledge" – just as the ordinary person's concept of "moral" lacks resources for resolving complex moral dilemmas. So I doubt that there is any future in analytic epistemology, in the sense defined by Goldman. The current vogue for giving necessary and sufficient conditions for truth of "S knows that p" seems to me analogous to the recurrent vogue for giving necessary and sufficient conditions for the truth of "A was the right thing for S to have done." A lot of interesting issues can be mooted within the stylistic confines of such analyses, but the idea of an analysis which is both informative and proof against counterexamples is a will-of-the-wisp. As Fodor has said, "surely it is the lesson of modern philosophy that interesting ideas don't get analyzed."[15]

Turning now to Goldman's third division – normative epistemology – I agree with him that this is where the action is. I would argue that the hope that we might find epistemic rules is the original source of the idea that there might be a discipline called "theory of knowledge." The hope for a normative epistemology was what called descriptive and analytic epistemology into existence. The hope was that we could make ourselves more efficient truth seekers by reprogramming ourselves, not just with new vocabularies for particular domains (as in the case of Galileo) but by isolating what Goldman calls "domain-independent rules."[16] The real question which divides him and me is whether there is any likelihood of getting domain-independent rules out of individual psychology.

My hunch that this is not likely results from the reflection that the hopes of epistemology would be gratified only if we got rules which were not only *domain*-independent but *task*-independent. What I mean by a task-dependent rule is exemplified by the one implicit in the example Goldman cites from Lawrence Powers: when asked to find a word whose first letter is missing, use visual rather than auditory imagery. Another example would be: when

---

[15] Jerry A. Fodor, "Psychosemantics; or, Where Do Truth Conditions Come From?," in *Mind and Cognition*, ed. William Lycan (Oxford: Basil Blackwell, 1990), 333. – Eds.

[16] Goldman believes, despite Kuhn, that the various disciplines *do* supply themselves with methodological canons, domain-independent rules. He thinks that epistemology should supply still more general canons. I side with Kuhn in thinking that the various disciplines merely supply know-how rather than domain-dependent methodologies. But this is a side issue which can be neglected for present purposes.

composing new knock-knock jokes to amuse the children, try out various auditory images rather than relying on visual ones. This is, I take it Goldman would grant, not the sort of rule normative epistemology wants. But it seems the only sort psychology is likely to give us. My reason for thinking this can perhaps best be put by recalling an analogy I mentioned earlier: the analogy between psychology and hardware considerations, on the one hand, and between intellectual history and programming considerations, on the other. Consider a systems analyst in charge of a room full of computers (all of the same model). He is trying to get them to serve the company's interests better. He will spend most of his time thinking up new ways in which to present them with data, new problems for them to solve, new languages in which to program them, and the like. He will need to know very little about their hardware, except for quite specific little tasks which arise in the course of programming. He may be able to take advantage of some engineering detail to save a bit of running time, or he may have to complicate a program in order to get around some other engineering detail which he heartily wishes had never been built into his machines. But when he asks himself large questions about what operations will be most likely to lead to the sorts of answers he wants to get, he will draw on his experience with all the discarded programs and formats of the past – the stories told of their success and failures by his fellow systems analysts. This lore will be his equivalent of intellectual history. He will be unlikely to think that further details about the way the model he is stuck with works – his equivalent of individual psychology – will help.

However, it could be suggested that the analogy might be turned around so as to work in favor of Goldman. For whereas the systems analyst presumably has the engineering details of his machines ready to hand in a manual, we are still trying to find out the details about the machine which is our body. Cognitive psychology may be viewed as discovering the program of the human organism – or, rather, the programs of the various relatively independent mechanisms which compose it. So there is no a priori reason to think that once the manuals for our organism are written, we shall not get domain- and task-independent epistemic rules – directions for reprogramming ourselves – out of it. Still, there is an a posteriori reason for doubt. This is that most of the interesting results of psychological experiments which epistemologists and philosophers of mind cite are just too far down from the level of abstraction at which epistemologists work, the level at which domain- and task-independent rules could be formulated. This is a point made by Daniel Dennett in his review of Fodor's *Language of Thought*. Dennett notes that although one may usefully and correctly remark of a chess-playing program that "It thinks it should get its queen out early,"

> for all the many levels of explicit representation to be found in the programme, nowhere is anything roughly synonymous with 'I should get my queen out early' explicitly tokened. The level of the analysis to which the . . . remark belongs describes features of the programme that are, in an entirely innocent way, *emergent* properties of the computational processes that have 'engineering reality'.[17]

Dennett sums up by saying "I see no reason to believe that the relation between belief-talk and psychological-process talk will be any more direct."[18] Goldman, it seems to me, would need to satisfy Dennett's doubts by giving us an example of some bit of psychological research which gives promise of telling us something about general intellectual strategies.

A historical comparison is, I think, instructive at this point. It was Hume's exhibition of the gap which yawned between Lockean talk of the association of ideas and scientific talk of substances and causal laws which led Kant to conclude that psychology – what he called "Locke's physiology of the human understanding" – was not going to be of much use to normative epistemology. Kant – the normative epistemologist *par excellence* – wanted to sort out the promising from the unpromising research programs in the culture of his day. He suspected that Newtonian physics was all right, vitalistic biology dubious, and Leibnizian metaphysics hopeless. In order to argue for these suspicions, he found it necessary to transform epistemology from Lockean attempt to describe transitions from mental state to mental state into something quite different. For him, it became a series of thought experiments designed to show what would happen if one tried to overstep what he thought of as the bounds of human knowledge. Such thought experiments gave him reasons for saying, for example, that Leibnizian metaphysics was never going to get on the secure path of a science.

Kant's transformation of epistemology quickly engendered, in Herder and Hegel, the beginnings of what Goldman calls "social descriptive epistemology" – the attempts to envisage new forms of intellectual life which might perhaps extend these bounds. The kinds of intellectual history and cultural anthropology which these successors of Kant founded here, as I said earlier, largely displaced psychology (not to mention epistemology) as sources of advice for intellectuals who want to know how to

---

[17] D. C. Dennett, "Critical Notice," *Mind* 86, no. 342 (1977): 279.   [18] Ibid.

direct their minds. In order to get Lockean *individual* descriptive psychology – the study of transitions between mental states – back to the position it had before Kant, and thus to give Goldman what he needs, the psychologists will have to come up with something which looks like a real advance on Locke. About the only candidates for such an advance which come to mind are Freudian theories of unconscious motivation. But such theories seem, if anything, grist for the mill of intellectual historians like Foucault, rather than a source of examples for Goldman. It is true that there are a bag of tricks peddled by PhDs in psychology which purport to bring Freudian discoveries to bear on personnel management, marital counseling, and the like. But, once again, these tricks seem too task-dependent to fill the role of Goldman's "epistemic rules."

I can sum up my reaction to Goldman's paper as follows. I agree with him that, given the meta-epistemological principles which he puts forward, psychology is relevant to epistemology. Further, I think he does a very nice job of showing the failure of various attempts to marry logic to epistemology, while freezing out psychology. A great many of the particular things he says about what it would be nice to have in the way of epistemology seem to me right and very clearly argued. But I still cannot get myself to believe that there will be any epistemic rules of the sort his meta-epistemological principles require. So I view his demonstration of the relevance of psychology to epistemology as resembling a demonstration of the relevance of particle physics to alchemy. I see no reason to think that we need to revise the decision which the intellectuals made early in the last century – to get their hints about how to think from history rather than psychology, from social rather than individual descriptive epistemology.

***

Turning now from Goldman to Fodor, my doubts about his paper[19] are of the same level of generality as my doubts about Goldman's. They concern the project as a whole rather than the details of its accomplishment. I am dubious about the notion that we might explain "the intentional properties of mental states as inherited from the semantic properties of the mental representations which . . . are involved in their tokening."[20] More specifically, I am not clear what "inherited from" means here. The intentional properties of mental states, Fodor says, include their aboutness and their possession of a truth-value. What one would need to feel that Fodor had

---

[19] Fodor, "Psychosemantics; or, Where Do Truth Conditions Come From?" – *Eds.*
[20] Ibid., p. 313.

solved a real problem would be to imagine somebody who felt that it was puzzling how mental states could have such properties. These people would also have to be people who would feel their puzzlement vanish when they were told that we can follow the procedure Fodor sketches toward the end of his paper[21] – finding entry conditions for a mental representation which are both the content of the subject's belief and the truth-condition of the representation – and thus give semanticity to mental representations. That is, one has to imagine Fodor's intended audience as philosophers who believe the following things:

(a) It is not enough to understand the intentionality of mental states to understand, in the manner of Ryle, how we verify ascriptions of such states.
(b) It is enough to understand the semanticity of mental representations to understand, in the manner of Fodor, how we verify ascriptions of truth conditions to such representations.
(c) Understanding the latter verification process somehow legitimizes the former verification process because we can now see the intentionality of the states as inherited from the intensionality of the representations.

I do not know any philosophers of this sort. It seems to me that nobody nowadays gets shook up by the Brentano thesis – the thesis that there are no necessary and sufficient behavioral conditions for the truth of ascriptions of intentional states. This is because we have all absorbed what Fodor calls "the lesson of modern philosophy," that there are no interesting necessary and sufficient conditions for anything. There are, I admit, philosophers who, even though they no longer hanker after biconditionals, still feel that intentionality is deep and mysterious. But I think that these philosophers will not feel that Fodor has resolved the mystery. Searle and Dreyfus, for example, are philosophers who think that there is something called "intrinsic intentionality," which we shall only understand if we understand much more about the brain than we do now. Dreyfus sees the quest for intrinsic intentionality as the continuation of the phenomenologist's insistence on the importance and "irreducibility" of intentionality. But neither Dreyfus nor Searle would feel that the secret of intrinsic intentionality had been discovered by the realization that we can ascribe truth conditions to neural events in the manner Fodor suggests. They would reply that we can ascribe such truth conditions to inner states of computers – or, for that matter, of thermostats – just as readily, and that

---

[21] Cf. ibid., p. 332.

this ability does not illuminate "the nature of intentionality." For, on their view, it is an unquestioned standing point of cognitive science that computers and thermostats do not have intentional states. An explanation of how one can treat such gadgets as containing inner representations of the environment by assigning truth conditions to inner events would leave Dreyfus and Searle cold.

If they are told that the thermostat can "inherit" intentionality from the semanticity of some of its inner states, they will have just as strong prejudices against allowing that those inner states really are semantical as they do against allowing that the thermostat as a whole really has beliefs.

Let me sketch the picture of the current scene in philosophy of mind which I see as the dialectical background to Fodor's efforts. On the left wing, there are people like Dennett and me who blithely ascribe aboutness, and possession of truth-value, to anything which it seems handy to describe in intentional terms. It is certainly handy so to describe for people and computers, handy but optional for thermostats and record changers, and quite probably useful for states of brains. As Fodor says, a theory of inner representations is the only idea anybody has had about how to do non-behaviorist psychology, and since behaviorist psychology never did much, there seems no harm in giving cognitive psychology a whirl. So, Dennett would say, let us go ahead and ascribe "content" to states at the "sub-personal" level. But let us not worry about whether we have any philosophical justification for doing so. Newton postulated action at a distance despite screams that he was resurrecting the occult qualities of the scholastics. It paid off. Maybe it will pay off to ascribe truth conditions to brain events or maybe not – but at any rate, we can safely neglect the screams of the philosophers.

On the right wing, there are the people given to this sort of screaming – Dreyfus and Searle. They see people like me and Dennett as verificationists who confuse the shadow of intentionality – the behavior which Dennett would adduce as evidence for the thermostat's intentionality – with the substance. They see a real difference between the "intrinsic intentionality" possessed by people and dogs and the "pseudointentionality " possessed by machines. Presumably they would see a parallel difference between the intrinsic semanticity possibly possessed by brain events and the pseudosemanticity possessed by transistor events. So they would say that Fodor has sold the path to verificationism by demystifying the semanticality of brain states. The question which needs answering, on this right-wing view, is not "How do we go about ascribing truth conditions to brain states" but rather "What is that brains have got that transistors do not which makes it the case that we should not ascribe truth conditions to machine states?" Fodor dodges this question, they would say, by giving us procedures for ascribing semanticity which would work for anything of a reasonable degree of complexity.

Fodor stands in the middle, having sympathies with both the right and the left wing. Fodor thinks that Dennett is too casual and insufficiently "realistic" about assigning intentionality. He agrees with Searle and Dreyfus that

> instantiating the same program that the brain is not, in and of itself, a sufficient condition for having those propositional attitudes characteristic of the organism that has the brain.[22]

Fodor thinks that a further condition which must be satisfied is that there be "the right kind of causal linkages" – the same kind "that holds between our brains and our transducer mechanisms on the one hand and between our brains and distal objects on the other."[23] Presumably he also thinks that the right kind of causal linkage is one which would provide for the "inheritance" of intensionality from symbolic events in the brain to state of the organism. So perhaps Fodor would reply to Searle and Dreyfus that they should not complain about his analysis of what it takes for an inner event to have a truth-condition, but rather about his failure to specify what causal linkages brains have got that computers lack. Fodor suggests that we simply do not know whether anything except brains bears the right sort of causal relation. So he might say that there were two steps necessary in demystifying what Searle and Dreyfus call "intrinsic intentionality," of which he has only taken one. The first step is to show how inner events can have truth conditions; the second is to show what causal relations constitute the "inheritance" relation which links the semanticity of the representations to the intentionality of the states. He could then cheerfully admit that the second step remains untaken.

I am not, however, sure how the debate between Fodor's centrist position and Searle's right-wing position should proceed, since I feel as vague about Fodor's use of "inheritance" as I do about Searle's use of "intrinsic." Fodor says that the strategy "of reducing the problem 'what makes mental states intentional' to the problem 'what bestows semantic properties on (fixes the interpretation of) a symbol'"[24] goes back to Locke. He says that Locke, too, held that "the intentional properties of mental states are inherited from the semantic (referential) properties of mental representations."[25] Maybe Locke did, though I am not sure how to

---

[22] J. A. Fodor, "Searle on What Only Brains Can Do," *Behavioral and Brain Sciences* 3, no. 3 (1980): 431.
[23] Ibid.   [24] Ibid.   [25] Ibid.

rephrase the point in Locke's jargon. For Locke, after all, the defining feature of an "idea" was that it be "before the mind," not that it have semanticity. Possibly Locke believed that ideas had other features which somehow communicated themselves to the minds which had them – but I do not recall anything in Locke which explains what this communication amounts to. So I suspect that if Locke did hold this view, his form of it needs as much explaining as Fodor's does.

Perhaps I am pressing Fodor's use of "inherit" too hard, but I would want to insist that he owes us a fuller account of the nature of the problem "what makes mental states intentional" before we can evaluate his proposal to reduce this problem to the problem of the semanticity of inner representations. For left-wingers like Dennett and me, there is not any problem of this form. We already know all about what makes mental states intentional – they are said to be about things and to have truth-values. In our light-minded and pragmatic way, we are not troubled by the question "How could anything have such weird properties?" since having a truth-value seems no weirder than being red or being good, or having an atomic weight. The question "Do thermostats really have beliefs and brain-states truth conditions, or is it just convenient to say that they do?" strikes us left-wingers as silly as the question "Are things really red or is it just convenient to use the predicate 'red' in describing and explaining them?"

I suspect that the underlying issue between Dennett and me, on the one hand, and Fodor, on the other, is just the question of whether there is an interesting difference between truth and convenience. In a criticism of Dennett's "Intentional Systems,"[26] Fodor quotes Dennett as saying, "The decision to adopt the strategy (of taking the intentional stance) is pragmatic and is not intrinsically right or wrong," and glosses this as follows: "Dennett's analysis ... explains the utility ... of the intentional idiom without assuming that there are facts that intentional ascriptions correspond to."[27]

My problem here is that I do not see what more one could do by way of "assuming that there are facts to which such ascriptions correspond" than expatiating on the utility of the ascriptions. Again, Fodor says that

> if we start out by thinking of our intentional stance theories (for example, our logic) as simply computational devices from which predictions about mental phenomena are somehow to be elicited, then the question "What

[26] Daniel C. Dennett, "Intentional Systems," *Journal of Philosophy* 68, no. 4 (1971): 87–106. – *Eds.*

[27] Jerry A. Fodor, *Representations: Philosophical Essays on the Foundations of Cognitive Science* (Cambridge, MA: MIT Press, 1981), 105.

licenses the transition from interformulaic relations in the theory to causal relations in the mind?" surely does arise.[28]

I do not see that it does arise. But even if it does, I cannot see that the answer to such a question could be the one Fodor recommends – namely, that "it's the assumption that the [intentional stance] theory is *true*."[29] That does not license a transition – it simply asserts an intention to make the transition.

Fodor would presumably rejoin that I have the wrong view of truth. When he says "the theory is true," he goes on to explain, he means that "in something spiritually similar to the technical sense, the mental processes of the agent constitute a model of the theory."[30] Fodor thinks that when you say something like that you have given a reason for using a theory which adds something to your hope or belief that the theory works – that it actually enables you to predict and control. I do not. Further, Fodor thinks that the burden of proof is on people like Dennett and me to give "an argument that the Realist construal cannot be sustained."[31] Here we have a dialectical impasse. For me, if not for Dennett (who sometimes, alas, displays Realistic yearnings which betray his notably pragmatical approach) the burden is on Fodor and other Realists to explain what kind of additional reason you have given for using theory when you say "and furthermore I assume that it corresponds to reality." This seems to me like bolstering one's belief that opium will put you to sleep by reminding yourself that it has dormitive powers.

Let me now try to connect this impasse with the question of whether there is a problem about "what makes mental states intentional." I do not see a problem here because I translate this question into the Rylean question "What verification procedures do we have for ascribing beliefs and desires to organisms?" Fodor will not make such a translation because he thinks that questions about the nature of something – for example, of intentionality – are questions which remain after we have said everything we have to say about verification procedures. Such a view is what one would expect of a Realist, and my view is what one would expect of a Pragmatist. Since this latter, wider, issue, is too wide to discuss here, I now drop it.

Let me conclude, however, by pointing out a more general way in which the realism-vs.-pragmatism issue is relevant to our discussions. Consider the question: What does Fodor's attempt to answer the question "What

---

[28] Ibid., 113.   [29] Ibid., 114.   [30] Ibid.   [31] Ibid.

makes mental states intentional?" have to do with epistemology? Or, more broadly, what does the question "What is the nature of the mind?" have to do with the question "What is the nature knowledge?" The Pragmatist answer to this latter question is: probably not much. That is, the Pragmatist suspects that all there is to say about knowledge gets said when we study verification procedures, the language-games inquirers play. This is the task, as I said before, of what Goldman calls "social descriptive epistemology" – intellectual history and the like. So the Pragmatist does not care – as far as epistemology goes – whether the mind is a Cartesian spiritual substance or a bunch of brain states with semantical properties or just a bunch of pulleys and levers without semantical properties. I suspect that for a Realist like Fodor, on the other hand, to say "Knowledge is possible only because we have internal representations of reality" is epistemologically enlightening. For the Pragmatist, however, it is no more enlightening than saying "Knowledge is possible only because we have a nervous system." The Pragmatist views knowledge as something which you study at the rather lofty level of programming, not at the level of wetware – not even of the wetware considered as computational device. For the reasons I suggested earlier, the wetware details seem ones by which he can probably just divide through. So the Pragmatist wishes the cognitive psychologist well with Representational Theory of Mind, as he wishes Newton well with action at a distance. But he does not expect epistemological enlightenment from the one, any more than he expects metaphysical enlightenment from the other.

The Objectivity of Values

1. Introductory

Many people think that philosophers should be able to tell you what is real and what is not – as if there were some special philosophical way to second-guess science and common sense and get at the real nature of things. Many people also think that it is part of a philosopher's job to tell us whether values are real – whether words like "right" and "good" refer to "objective" properties which situations or actions have, or instead refer to something which is merely "subjective" or merely "relative" – something like emotional reactions or social customs. These notions of what philosophers ought to do seem to me quite wrong. I do not think that philosophers have any special methods for deciding that science is right and religion wrong, or vice versa, nor for adjudicating conflicts between science and common sense. Rather, all philosophers can do is try to find a vocabulary in which one can see how everything – science, religion, common sense, morality – hangs together. To put it another way, all philosophers can do is to try to iron out conflicts between these areas of culture, so as to permit us to keep as much of religion as possible in the face of science, as much of science as possible in the face of common sense, and so on. To put it still another way, philosophers cannot come up with surprising new discoveries that God does not exist, or that morality is an illusion, or that modern science is just a "conceptual" distortion of reality. Philosophers say this sort of thing, to be sure, but their doing so should be seen as mere sloganeering, as dramatizations of their new way of looking at things. They have not made a discovery in the sense in which an astronomer might discover a new planet or a chemist might synthesize a new compound. Nor have they proved anything in the sense in which a mathematician might prove a theorem or a lawyer might prove the validity of a contract. The announcements they make are really just announcements of a new vocabulary, a new perspective, a suggestion about how to restate what we have been saying in terms which will give us a more coherent view, one less open to objections, one that makes more sense of the various things we talk about.

If this view of philosophy is right, then the notion that philosophers ought to tell us whether values are real or not is misguided. The question "Are values objective or subjective?" is a bad question. There are lots of things to be said about the relations between moral values and emotions, moral values and God, moral values and social customs, and so on – but it is silly to think that philosophers could discover that moral values are emotional reactions. Nor would it make sense to imagine reading in the newspaper that philosophers had discovered that moral values were, surprisingly enough, just as real and objective as planets or chemical compounds. Nor are philosophers going to discover that there are new, previously unexpected, moral values which nobody has noticed until now but which make all the difference to how one should live one's life or to social policy.

To put my point another way: talk about moral values is just misleading jargon for talk about what people ought to do – how they ought to live, how they ought to treat other people, how they might balance conflicting obligations, how they can organize themselves into societies. It is an unfortunate metaphor to describe decisions on such matters as made by looking at something called "the realm of values" or by studying something called "value theory" or by deciding on the relative rankings of various different values. This makes it sound as if lives or actions or situations came with little tags attached which told you how much of which values each exemplified (in the way in which other tags list fiber content or nutritional content). It makes it sound as if the only problem were to rank those values in order. But if I conclude that Goethe was high in self-fulfillment and low on altruism, or that Lenin was high in boldness, altruism, and cruelty and low in charity and piety, I am not making it any easier to decide whether to take these men as models. If I say that killing a terminally ill patient who is in agony would be high in eliminating suffering but low on respect for human life, I am not making progress toward a decision on whether to kill or not. If I say that Chinese society is high in discipline and social concern and that American society is high in freedom and leisure, I am not making any headway toward deciding how society should be organized. To deliberate on moral questions is not, or at least should not be, a matter of isolating special moral properties and then ranking them. The philosopher's jargon of "values" makes it harder for us to remember what real-life moral and political deliberation are like.

It is only if we have this misleading picture of values as little tags attached to things that it occurs to us to raise questions about whether the tags are really there or whether they are just in our minds, or whether the tags really and truly belong to the things or are simply attached by the culture or society to which the things belong. If, instead, we think of the problems of how to achieve a decent society or how to live so that one can respect oneself or how to help someone caught in a moral dilemma, the whole question of "objectivity" seems beside the point. Whatever philosophers say about the metaphysical status of values or about the meaning of sentences used to make moral judgments, the moral problems remain as real and as pressing as ever.

The reason the bad question about the objectivity of values is raised is, I think, twofold. First, we have inherited from the seventeenth and eighteenth centuries the notion of an opposition between clear-headed, tough-minded "science" and tender-minded, muddle-headed "prejudice" or "superstition." We think, therefore, that it is necessary to be "scientific" about morals and that this means getting straight about whether moral values are "out there" or are just "in us."

Second, ever since Thrasymachus challenged Socrates to explain why justice pays – why it profits one to care what happens to other people – it has seemed that we could answer Thrasymachus only if something like Plato's Form of the Good was real. Philosophers sometimes suggest that unless the nature of the world is at least as different from common sense as Plato said it was, then there is no answer to Thrasymachus or to Hitler – no answer to the person who simply does not care what happens to others.

It seems to me that the seventeenth century notion that what science does not know about is not real is a mistake. It also seems to me that Plato's notion that unless philosophers can discover a new and special kind of object – for example, a realm of Forms, a realm of values – we cannot answer Thrasymachus is also a mistake. In the rest of this paper, I shall try to explain why I think these are mistakes and thus explain why I think that the question about "the objectivity of values" is a bad question. In the next section, I shall argue that it is pointless to make a distinction between qualities of objects which are "in them" as opposed to those which are "in us." In section 3, I shall criticize some arguments offered by a recent defender of the view that there are no objective values – the late J. L. Mackie of Oxford. In section 4, I shall take up a variation on the notion of "objective moral value" – that of "moral principle." I shall argue there that although there is no way to "answer" Thrasymachus or Hitler by deduction from principle, this fact does nothing to show that morality is "subjective" or "personal" or "relative." Finally, in section 5, I shall argue that the idea of "moral philosophy" is obsolete – that, as a secular alternative to religion, moral philosophy has been replaced, in our century, by the novel, on the one hand, and by the social sciences, on the other.

2.   The Subjective-Objective Distinction

The idea that although tables are really sharp and hard, they do not really have colors, much less beauty or ugliness, goes back at least to Galileo. But if we ask what it means to say that a table is objectively hard but only subjectively brown or ugly, it is not easy to say. One way to explain the distinction is to say that it remains hard under all conditions, but is brown only in certain lights and for certain people (e.g., those who do not have jaundice). But this will not work. What does it mean to say that it remains hard under all conditions? Suppose one pours some glop on it which softens it up? Why does this not count as changing the conditions? Alternatively, suppose somebody comes along demanding something hard, and one suggests that he try the table. Suppose that he explains that since what he wants to do is cut glass, he needs something really hard, like carbon steel or a diamond. Well, it might be said, at least the table has a certain hardness at a certain time – yet much resistance to pressure at this particular moment (before one pours softener on it). Maybe that shows that its hardness is a real, intrinsic, objective property of the table? Well, suppose one narrowed things down in the case of color and said that at this particular moment, in this particular light, the table was objectively, intrinsically brown. One might reply that it still would not look brown to people whose eyes were in a certain state. But that seems like saying that the table would not be hard if measured by a pressure meter which was on the blink. Under abnormal conditions, of course, things will not seem to have their normal properties. But what basis do we have for dividing up the normal properties into two classes – one intrinsic and the other extrinsic, the one "primary" and the other "secondary"?

I suggest that the reason we are inclined to do this is that we confuse two questions: (i) how debatable is the attribution of the quality to the table? and (ii) is the quality in the table or in our minds? The first question is reasonable enough, and we might say that the table's hardness, brownness, and ugliness, can be arranged in that order on a scale of debatability. It is very hard to get up an argument about how hard something is, slightly less hard to get up an argument about what color it is, and considerably easier to get one up about how ugly it is. But when we identify increased debatability with increased likelihood of being "merely subjective," what are we adding? The notion of being "in the mind" is obviously metaphorical – nobody thinks that we have a little immaterial box inside our skull filled with objects like brownness or ugliness. But if we try to cash the metaphor, we do not seem to come up with anything. To say that opinions on what is beautiful or right or good vary with people's upbringing – that these are particularly debatable matters – is uncontroversial. To explain this fact by saying that these are intrinsically subjective matters seems hopeless. Consider the different views cultures have about what the universe is like – on whether it is filled with demons, on whether it is subject to mechanical laws, on whether its nature is essentially linked with human destiny, on whether it is finite or infinite, on whether it is under the control of a benevolent creator, and so on. One's opinion on these matters will obviously vary with one's culture, upbringing, and so on. Should we explain this variation by saying that there is no objective truth about the structure of the universe? If so, maybe it would be better just to abandon the notion of objective-vs.-subjective, because one half of the distinction is never going to apply to anything. If not, what criteria do we have for saying that scientific theories are about objective matters of fact whereas moral theories are not?

I think that there is no good answer to this latter question and therefore no good use for the subjective-objective distinction. We would do better to replace that distinction by the more straightforward distinction between what modern physical science talks about and what it does not talk about. If one carefully delimits "physical science" so as to include optics but to stop short of psychophysiology, then one can say that science talks about hardness and the length of light waves, but does not talk about either brownness or ugliness. So far so good. But we should not go on to say that what physical science does not talk about is automatically "subjective." If we do, we seem to be saying that there is not really any rational way to settle debates about whatever science does not deal with. But this seems obviously false.

I think that our use of fuzzy notions like "subjective" and "objective" is just a case of cultural lag. We are still suffering from the effects of the scientific revolution of the seventeenth century – the period in which the humanly scaled cosmology of Dante's *Divine Comedy* was replaced by the terrifying cosmology of Galileo and Laplace – the universe in which everything that happens can be predicted by knowing some simple laws and the positions of the elementary particles. Locke was so impressed by this new science that he built the primary-secondary–quality distinction into modern philosophy, formulated as the distinction between being really there and just one of our "ideas." But we should no longer be impressed. We have lived with modern physical science long enough to see it as not a revelation about the human condition but simply a new and better way of figuring out how things work and predicting what will happen next.

This point can be put in another way by considering the relation between science and religion. The god whom Christians worshipped before Galileo presided over a finite, picturable, homey, universe. Despite professional theological talk about his "existing everywhere and nowhere," the ordinary Christian-in-the-street knew that God occupied a certain position within that universe – up at the top, so to speak. Once the universe was pictured as infinite and mechanical, however, this picture was shattered. So it became the mark of the intellectual to abandon hope, the comfort of religious belief. Intellectuals prided themselves on coming to terms with a universe of atoms blindly charging about. But in their anxiety to show themselves liberated from superstition, they overshot the mark. They created a bad philosophical distinction between what science talks about and everything else by saying that everything that science does not talk about counted as "subjective" or "relative" or "cultural" or "in the eye of the beholder."

This simple-minded distinction should just be dropped. We should replace it with a sliding scale of controversiality. At one end of the scale are logic and mathematics, where a statement is either provable or not. Slightly further along are uncontroversial empirical matters – like whether a given tree is an elm or a beech, whether a given compound contains carbon, whether a given table is brown, whether a given disease is measles. Still further along are such more controversial matters as whether a given table is ugly, whether a given marriage can be saved, whether a given politician should be elected. At the far end of the scale are such issues as that between Marxist and liberal ways of writing history, between Christian and Buddhist conceptions of the divine, between Aristotelian and Galilean conceptions of the universe, between Kantian and Nietzschean conceptions of how to live one's life, between the kind of painting which takes David as a paradigm and the kind which takes Cezanne.

This scale that runs from algebra at one end to art at the other seems to be preferable to the objective-subjective distinction because it does not depend upon the quaint notion of "being in the mind" as opposed to "being out there," nor on a misguided overestimation of the significance of physical science. On the conception I want to recommend, the degree of controversiality of a question is not a function of the metaphysical character of its subject matter. Nor is it a function of a distinction between human faculties – for example, "reason" as opposed to "taste" – nor between methods of inquiry – for example, "logic" as opposed to "observation." All such distinctions strike me as too simple to really illuminate anything. If we want to understand why physicists often agree and theologians often do not, or why mathematicians often agree and literary critics often do not, we shall not be helped by traditional philosophical distinctions like "objective-subjective" or "rational vs. irrational" or "conceptual vs. empirical." We will only be helped by looking at how people actually go about resolving disputes in these various areas.

3.　Mackie's Arguments for the "Subjectivity" of Values

In order to spell out more clearly why I think "subjective" and "objective" are unhelpful terms, I want to criticize some arguments which purport to show that they are subjective. In the first chapter of J. L. Mackie's recent book *Ethics: Inventing Right and Wrong*, Mackie quotes another Oxford philosopher – Richard Hare – as saying that he "does not understand what is meant by 'the objectivity of values'" and that he "has not met anyone who does." Hare had argued as follows:

> Think of one world into whose fabric values are objectively built; and think of another in which those values have been annihilated. And remember that in both worlds the people in them go on being concerned about the same things – there is no difference in the "subjective" concern which people have for things, only in their "objective" value. Now I ask "What is the difference between the states of affairs in these two worlds?" Can any answer be given except "None whatsoever"?[1]

I think that Hare is absolutely right about this. The same argument, it seems to me, would work to show the silliness of the claim that "colors are not objective properties of material objects"; suppose there were one world in which they were and another in which it just looked to people, always and everywhere, as if they were. How on earth are we supposed to worry which world we are living in? As William James said, every difference must

---

[1]　J. L. Mackie, *Ethics: Inventing Right and Wrong* (New York: Pelican Books, 1977), 21.

make a difference. The real problem with the subjective-objective distinction, whether applied to colors or to beauty or to goodness, is just that it makes no difference to our lives whether something is subjective or objective. To dispute that question is, as James said, like disputing whether it is elves or brownies who are at work behind the scenes. What does make a difference is whether we have usable procedures for resolving disputes about colors or about values. But this is a question about our practices, not about "what is out there in the world."

Mackie replies to Hare's argument as follows:

> Hare's argument is similar to the positivist claim that there is no difference between a phenomenalist or Berkeleian world in which there are only minds and their ideas and the commonsense realist world in which there are also material things, because it is logically possible that people should have the same experiences in both. If we reject the positivism that would make the dispute between realists and phenomenalists a pseudo-question, we can reject Hare's similarly supported dismissal of the issue of the objectivity of values.[2]

Mackie means by "positivism" the claim that questions which we do not know how to decide are not real questions, that they are "meaningless." The logical positivists said that the issue between phenomenalists and realists about whether there really are material objects was "verbal" because no sensory evidence could ever help decide it – since both sides agreed that our sense would give exactly the same reports no matter who was right. I think, unlike Mackie, that the positivists were on the right track here. Maybe we should not say that the issue is "verbal" or "meaningless," but we can reasonably say that unless somebody thinks of a way of arguing it, we might well forget it. So it seems fair to ask Mackie how he thinks the objectivity of values could be argued about. He produces three arguments for the claim that they are not objective, and I shall briefly take up each of them.

His first argument is that "from relativity" and says that

> the actual variations in moral codes are more readily explained by the hypothesis that they reflect ways of life than by the hypothesis that they express perceptions, most of them seriously inadequate or distorted, of objective values.[3]

What is it to explain a difference of moral code as a reflection of a way of life? Presumably what Mackie has in mind are such examples as the claim

[2] Ibid., 22. [3] Ibid., 37.

that certain tribes have certain taboos, because of their socioeconomic needs. But this sort of explanation also works pretty well for science – pre-Galileans accepted an Aristotelian cosmology in part because they had no technology which allowed them to construct telescopic lenses. Galilean science might not have become widely known and accepted had it not been for the Reformation. And so on. To make his point, Mackie would have to show that explanations by "extrinsic" factors are more appropriate for differing moral codes than for different scientific beliefs. His argument from relativity hinges on the notion that we explain choice among scientific theories in terms of better or worse perception of external objects, but do not do the same in choosing moral views. But this is a simple-minded empiricist notion of how science works. It is the account of science which Kuhn's *Structure of Scientific Revolutions* has helped us set aside. Mackie is picturing the physicist as being constrained to get the structure of matter right by encounters with that structure, but refusing to see the moralist as getting moral obligation right by encounters with the moral law. One can make such a distinction, but only if one is antecedently persuaded that atomic structures are out there to constrain our beliefs and that the moral law is not.

In the absence of any such presupposition, one would not be able to employ an "argument from relativity." But such a presupposition can only be established by something like what Mackie calls an "argument from queerness." This is, in fact, his second argument against the objectivity of values. Mackie says that this argument has two parts: one metaphysical and the other epistemological. The metaphysical part says that "if there were objective values, then they would be entities or qualities or relations of a very strange sort, utterly different from anything else in the universe."[4] The epistemological part says that "if we were aware of them, it would have to be by some special faculty of moral perception or intuition, utterly different from our ordinary ways of knowing everything else."[5] The reason values would have to be utterly different, Mackie says, is that they are "intrinsically action-guiding or motivating," but we know of no other sort of object which is. Furthermore, he says, there is a problem about "how such values could be consequential or supervenient upon natural features" – by which he means that we would need to explain how these values fit into the scientific account of the world, what place physics can allow for them.[6]

I think that if, like Locke and Mackie, one accepts the principle that anything which does not occur in a scientific account of the world cannot

---

[4] Ibid., 38.   [5] Ibid.   [6] Ibid., 49.

be real, then one will indeed find values queer. But otherwise it will not seem odd that there should be entities in the world which are intrinsically motivating or action-guiding. If we think of a prospective sexual partner or a piece of food as common sense thinks of it, then it will seem natural to say that it is intrinsically motivating or action-guiding. If we think of either as "really" just an assemblage of atoms, then we will not. Similarly, we think that the spectacle of heroic human life – that of Socrates or St. Francis or Sakharov – is intrinsically action-guiding, that one could only fail to be moved by such a life if one's faculties were somehow impoverished. But, of course, there are lots of vocabularies in which one could tell the story of such lives – for example, a physicalistic vocabulary in terms of their component particles, a behavioristic vocabulary, a psycho-analytical vocabulary – which would not suggest that these lives ought to be imitated. Mackie thinks it queer that something should be "intrinsically" action-guided because he thinks that any description of that object which is action-guiding smuggles in some extrinsic, merely relational, property. But he would only think this if, like Locke, he assumed that any vocabulary other than those of the physical sciences introduced such properties. Once again, it seems to me, his argument reduces to the claim that the vocabulary of physical science is not the vocabulary of moral choice. One will only feel that there is a problem about the relation between values and "natural" qualities if one has previously defined "natural" qualities in such a way that only those named in the vocabulary of physical science count.

Turning now to the epistemological side of Mackie's argument from queerness, he says that it seems ad hoc to postulate a special faculty of moral intuition which recognizes the values of objects or events. So it does, but it does not seem ad hoc to say that our ability to reach rational agreement on moral issues is much like our ability to reach rational agreement on scientific theories. Again we come back to Mackie's rather simplistic empiricism. He thinks that all knowledge either must come through the five senses or be clearly based on knowledge which does come that way. He thinks there is no argument from "is" to "ought," because he thinks that all "is"-premises must ultimately boil down to premises about what somebody would see or hear or feel. But this sort of empiricism can make no more sense of theory-choice in science than it can of theory-choice in morals. If we really thought that we have "objective knowledge" only where we can tie theory-choice down to sense perception, we should have to conclude that we have practically no objective knowledge. Mackie is not prepared to accept any account of our knowledge of objective values except some sort of sixth sense – some faculty modeled on sight. But this limitation on an epistemological account presupposes that knowing about values is much like knowing about shapes or sizes. But why should it be? Why should getting an understanding of the best sort of life for a human being to lead be anything like seeing how big something is?

Mackie's third and final argument against the objectivity of values is that it is easier to explain people's moral beliefs by appealing to their desires, their power relations within their society, their fears and hopes, and the like, than by appealing to moral facts with which they become acquainted. This argument is repeated in a succinct form by my colleague Gilbert Harman in his book *The Nature of Morality*, when he says that the great difference between science and ethics is that

> you need to make assumptions about certain physical facts to explain the occurrence of the observations that support a scientific theory, but you do not seem to make assumptions about any moral facts to explain the occurrence of the so-called moral observations.[7]

As an example of "so-called moral observation," Harman offers "rounding a corner and seeing a group of young hoodlums put gasoline on a cat and ignite it." Here we are tempted to say that we just see that an action is wrong. But, Harman asks, "is our reaction due to the actual wrongness of what you see or is it simply a reflection of your moral 'sense', a 'sense' that you have acquired perhaps as a result of your moral upbringing?"[8] He is inclined to think that the best explanation for our reaction is always the latter, and Mackie agrees. Mackie points to the same considerations which he used to back up his argument from relativity – the ability of psychologists and anthropologists and historians to explain why people claim to see that this and that is right or wrong, good or bad, without ever mentioning objective moral facts.

In order to evaluate this point, we need to consider whether the best explanation of somebody's making an observation in nonmoral cases is the presence of what he claims to observe. Harman says that in the case of a scientist watching a cloud chamber, seeing a vapor trail, and saying "There goes a proton," the best explanation of his observation includes the fact that there was indeed a proton going through the chamber. In the case of the person who says "That's wrong" to the hoodlums torturing the cat, however, Harman says that "it would seem that all we need assume is that he has certain more or less well articulated moral principles ... It

---

[7] Gilbert Harman, *The Nature of Morality: An Introduction to Ethics* (New York: Oxford University Press, 1977), 6.
[8] Ibid., 4.

seems completely irrelevant to our explanation whether his intuitive immediate judgment is true or false."[9] I think that Harman is right about this but wrong about the proton example. There, too, it seems to me, it is completely irrelevant to an explanation of the scientists' observation whether or not there are protons. Suppose nuclear physicists begin to tell us that there never were any protons, that the very concept of a "proton" was a confused way of describing the structure of matter, and that there is no neat way of matching types of vapor trails in cloud chambers with types of elementary particles. Indeed, suppose that the very notion of "elementary particle" comes to seem a misleading and primitive way of talking about discontinuities in space-time, or some other far-out, new-fangled kind of entity. All these changes seem to leave our explanation of the observation of a proton untouched. We know how the observer was trained to make reports of protons, and we know that he did what he was told; so we know why he reported what he did. The question of whether he was trained to use the terms of a false physical theory simply does not arise. Similarly, we can explain why we have a negative reaction to torturing cats by our having been raised in a Christian, sentimentalist, bourgeois atmosphere. That explanation is quite sufficient, and it would be irrelevant to raise the further question of whether sentimental views about kindness to animals get the moral facts right or not. But that does not mean that it is not as objectively right or wrong to torture cats as it is objectively right or wrong to say that there are protons.

The point I want to make here against Harman and Mackie is, once again, that their attempt to distinguish between science and ethics is built around a simple-minded empiricist approach to scientific truth. Mackie thinks that scientific theories can somehow be boiled down to reports of sensory observations. Harman thinks that "you need to make assumptions about certain physical facts to explain the occurrence of the observations that support a scientific theory." Neither view seems to me plausible. Scientific theories, as Quine and Kuhn have said, touch our experience only intermittently and incidentally. They have this in common with moral outlooks. We no more develop scientific theories by trying to account for the sensory appearances of things than we develop moral theories by trying to account for our offhand moral reactions, although we may occasionally do both.

---

[9] Ibid., 7.

I can make this criticism more specific by citing one last passage from Mackie. Mackie sums up his view about the good for man, or the goal of human life, by saying,

> Moral reasoning consists partly in achieving a more adequate understanding of this basic goal (or set of goals), partly in working out the best way of pursuing and realizing it. But this approach is open to two radically different interpretations. According to one, to say that something is the good for man or the general goal of human life is just to say that this is what men in fact pursue or will find ultimately satisfying, or perhaps that it is something which, if postulated as an implicit goal, enables us to make sense of actual human strivings and to detect a coherent pattern in what would otherwise seem to be a chaotic jumble of conflicting purposes. According to the other interpretation, to say that something is the good for man, or the general goal of human life, is to say that this is man's proper end, that this is what in fact he *ought* to be striving after, whether he in fact is or not.[10]

My view is that there is only a stylistic difference between these two interpretations. If we find a way of detecting a coherent pattern in what would otherwise seem a chaotic jumble of conflicting purposes, and if acting according to this pattern is ultimately satisfying, what is added by saying that this is in fact "man's proper end"? Mackie thinks that the difference between the two interpretations is the difference between making a descriptive and making a prescriptive statement, between saying something about psychology and making a claim about objective values. I think that the difference is like the difference between saying "This theory of the physical universe appears to account for all the phenomena better than any of the competitors, and we have used it to gain an extraordinary mastery of nature" and saying "This theory tells us how the physical world actually works." There is no way to drive a wedge between the one statement and the other, as far as I can see. We cannot have good reasons for saying that a theory will work beautifully forever, in every area, yet does not actually tell us anything about the world. Similarly, I do not see any way to drive a wedge between Mackie's two interpretations so that it would make sense to say that a moral theory fulfilled all the aims which systems of ethics had ever hoped to fulfill but unfortunately was merely "subjective." I can see a difference between saying, as a matter of psychological fact, that most people enjoy torturing cats and saying, prescriptively, that they should enjoy this. But when it is a matter of a global theory about right

---

[10] Mackie, *Ethics,* 46–47; italics added.

and wrong – one which is ultimately satisfying – I do not see how or why one would make such a distinction.

4.   Moral Principles

This is all that I shall say about Mackie's attempt to give sense to the notion that values are merely subjective. But I want to press my point about the analogies between science and ethics a bit further by taking up the topic of moral principles. Philosophers of Mackie's persuasion often say that a statement like, "One ought to repress one's impulses to be cruel to cats" cannot possibly be true in the way in which "Bodies attract one another with a force proportional to the square of their distances" is true. The idea is that "ought"-statements are not intended to tell us how objects are, whereas statements about, for example, gravity, are. On this view, it is just a mistake to look for objective values – objects for "ought"-statements to be true of – because "ought"-statements are incapable of being either true or false. On my view, "ought"-statements about cruelty are true in exactly the same way as "is"-statements about gravity. Neither is true of objects. In neither case is there any point in thinking of truth as "correspondence to reality." There is no object called "gravity" to correspond to, any more than there is an object called "oughtness" to be respected. Both statements have their sense and importance as excerpts from large-scale views about how we ought to live or how we ought to understand what is going on. They cannot be matched against reality point by point, nor can they profitably be thought of as "reporting what is really out there." They both resemble statements like "There are numbers such that the square of the number is equal to the number itself." This is part of a theory and is accepted as true because the theory as a whole meets the needs for which theories about numbers are constructed – but there is no way to confront it with objects. Yet it would be silly to say that it was "merely subjective" or "merely relative" or "merely conventional."

The main reason people say that "ought"-statements cannot be true in the same sense in which scientific theories are true is that it seems relatively easy to imagine competing theories of morality based on opposing first principles. Suppose one theory starts from the premise that one should express one's sadistic impulses and the other from the premise that one should repress them. Given such an opposition, we are told, there will be no way to resolve the issue between the two theories, which are equally consistent and defensible. But this claim seems to me blatantly false. The whole idea of a moral theory which starts by encouraging cruelty is just a philosopher's fiction – there are no such theories, any more than there are mathematical theories which set off from the proposition that there are no infinite numbers or that long division does not work. You cannot show the relativity or the subjectivity of morals by saying that somebody might stubbornly and consistently hold a silly view any more than you can show the relativity or subjectivity of physical science by saying that somebody could consistently claim that the earth was flat or that what Newton called "gravity" was really the work of invisible gremlins. To be taken seriously, a scientific theory must not just deny the first principles of another theory – it must go on to give its own account of how something works and display the advantages of this account. Similarly, for a view about morality to be taken seriously, it cannot just proclaim that cruelty and selfishness are good; it has to go on to develop a view of human life and society which incorporates these claims, makes sense of them, and displays their advantages. This is not easy to do – no easier than explaining that the earth only seems to be round but is really flat.

This point can also be put in terms of the claim that there is no way to refute a man who says that his moral position is that everybody should sacrifice themselves to him, because he is more important than anybody else – or, like Hitler, that nobody except right-thinking Germans have any rights that need to be respected. It is true that there is no way to refute people like that, but there is no way to refute somebody who says that there are no numbers larger than a million or that the world is run by a committee of elves and brownies or that everybody but himself is a robot. There are lots of silly or pointless or crazy things one can say and not be refuted. This is because the notions of argument, disagreement, refutation, controversy, and the like only make sense in situations where both sides share a certain minimal agreement. One can only refute somebody who shares some of one's premises. People who share too few premises are not treated as unrefutable opponents, but as too childish or nutty or uneducated or whatever to get into the conversation. Every sphere of discourse – moral, scientific, mathematical, literary – has, so to speak, certain admission requirements, certain credentials which have to be presented before one is taken seriously. The difference between Hitler and, say, Nietzsche, is that Hitler lacks the credentials and Nietzsche has them. Nietzsche shares the concerns, the interests, the vocabulary of Aristotle and Mill and Kant. Hitler does not. Nietzsche can be argued with, though perhaps not "refuted" in the sense in which one mathematician or lawyer can refute another. Hitler certainly cannot be refuted. But that is not because he has an irrefutable position but simply because he cannot be argued with at all.

The difference between Nietzsche and Hitler is parallel to that between Einstein and the Flat Earth Society. Einstein said some weird, paradoxical, almost nonsensical things, but he said them in the context of the physical theory of his time, in response to problems within that theory. He managed to transform physical theory by showing that you could get better explanations by accepting the paradoxes. The people in the Flat Earth Society, on the contrary, neither know nor care what is being said within scientific theory; all they want to do is show that nobody can prove the earth is round. They are quite right about this, just as a Society for Cruelty to Cats would be right in saying that nobody can prove that you should not torture cats. But that is not to say that either has much to contribute to rational discussion of their respective subjects.

5. Philosophy, Literature, and Social Science

I think that one reason that the issue about the objectivity of values seems more interesting and serious than it is is that people think that moral knowledge is the province of a group of specialists – the moral philosophers. Some philosophers like to give the impression that if you really want the true word about how to live your life or how to organize your society, you naturally turn to people like Plato, Kant, Nietzsche, Rawls, and the like. This impression seems to me terribly misleading. During the eighteenth and nineteenth centuries, when religion was losing its prestige as a source of counsel and illumination, philosophy put itself forward as a replacement. That was the great age of moral philosophy. In that period, Kant and Bentham put forward nice, simple, abstract formulae which were supposed to sum up and clarify all our moral intuitions. They were even supposed to enable us to resolve agonizing moral dilemmas by a nice straightforward application of deductive or inductive reasoning. But almost as soon as the categorical imperative and the utilitarian principle had been put forward, people came to realize that these were as hopeless as the Ten Commandments or the Golden Rule. Whatever moral knowledge is, it is not achieved by memorizing rules or formulating principles. General principles are the last things one wants when confronted by a genuine ethical or political dilemma.

This remark may sound shocking. We often describe a morally bad person as "unprincipled," and we often praise good people for having "firm" or "high" principles. So it may seem terribly important to formulate principles. But what we really mean by these phrases is simply that there are some things a good person simply will not do under any circumstances – he will not betray his friends, he will not cheat his clients, he will not violate trust. A person of high principles is not necessarily one who can formulate a general principle and deduce particular actions from that principle. Rather, to describe him as having firm or high principles is much like describing him as having an upright character, or great moral dignity. It is a remark not about what he knows but about the kind of thing he can be expected to do in the clinches. If we actually met someone who attempted to deduce what he should do from general principles, we would, I think, be somewhat wary of him. For there is something odd about the notion that moral dilemmas can be solved in this way – as odd as the notion that one can pick a friend or a lover by drawing up a list of values which he or she should exemplify and then finding somebody who maximizes those values.

We in the twentieth century think of ourselves as more advanced morally, as making more sophisticated and clearer-headed and wiser ethical choices than previous generations. But this is not because we think we know more general moral truths than they did. Rather, it is because we are more experienced, in the sense that we have a livelier sense of the alternatives, of the consequences that may follow various choices. In particular, we do not have this livelier imagination and broader culture because we have more sophisticated systems of moral philosophy – more convincing general principles or more clearly defined scales of value. Rather, it is because we are the beneficiaries of two cultural developments which were only getting underway in the times of Kant and Bentham. These are, roughly, modern literature and the social sciences. In Kant's time, novels like those of Dostoevsky and Dickens, Balzac and James, Kafka and Proust, Nabokov and Lessing were as yet undreamt of. Reflection on the course of human life and on the possible ways in which it could be lived still had to be fitted within notions left over from Stoicism and from Christianity; the incredibly various ways of describing oneself which we owe to these novelists were simply not available. Even Goethe, whose imagination was so vast as to leave his contemporaries awestruck, could not have envisaged a fraction of the kinds of human life which were to be put forward as alternatives within a hundred years of his death. In our century, it is in novels rather than in sermons or in works of moral philosophy that we find the vocabularies we use in formulating moral choices. We ask ourselves whether, if we adopt this and that sort of plan for our lives, we shall not run the danger of being like some particular figure – sometimes a historical figure, but more often a figure in a novel. When we try to find ways of formulating why we abhor certain people and admire others, it is comparisons between these people and people in literature which supplies the easiest way of making our criteria clear to ourselves. In everything that concerns private rather than public ethics, to be morally sophisticated is not to have advanced philosophical views but to have an imagination schooled by literary works.

In what concerns public rather than private decisions – social ethics as opposed to personal ethics – we get our sophistication not from philosophical reflection on the nature of social justice but from anthropology, psychiatry, political and cultural history, comparative politics, and sociology. Our century has profited from an extraordinary proliferation of attempts to understand strange cultures, strange sorts of personality, strange ways of arranging political life. Thanks to geniuses like Marx and Freud, but thanks also to the sheer accumulation of anthropological and historical data, we have acquired a much more tolerant and broader-based view of the possibilities open to human beings and societies. This increased tolerance, the increased ability to see other social classes or groups or cultures or political systems as strange but not necessarily immoral, is a large part of what we mean by saying that we are morally more sophisticated than our ancestors in the last century.

Let me illustrate my point about the role of literature and the social sciences by discussing the following question: given that the enormous change in the treatment of blacks by whites in the United States during the last thirty years is a moral advance, on the basis of what knowledge was that advance made? The civil rights movement was primarily a matter of moral pressure rather than of force. The whites, after all, controlled the police and the military and could have savagely suppressed the movement by throwing its leaders into concentration camps and increasing the rigor of discriminatory legislation. But they did not. Was this because philosophers had found new arguments in favor of a moral principle – namely, that skin color does not count – a principle which had previously been doubtful? Or because they had learned something about the ranking of various objective values which they had previously been ignorant of? I doubt that any such explanation would work. We shall understand the phenomenon better if we remember that the generation of the white middle class which was running America in the 1950s and 1960s had been brought up reading novels like Richard Wright's *Black Boy* and sociological treatises like Gunnar Myrdal's *An American Dilemma*. They had had their noses rubbed in what it was like to be black in America and had been made to feel guilty. When the civil rights movement came along, they responded accordingly. This is an example of what I mean when I say that it is literature and the social sciences which are our moral educators rather than philosophy.

Philosophers' attempts to formulate principles and to rank values are not useless, but they are useful only if other areas of culture have made us morally sensitive.

My conclusion from all this is that it would help if we did away not only with the distinction between subjective and objective but with that between facts and values, empirical description and evaluation of the state of affairs described. These distinctions have made moral reflection more difficult rather than easier. Since I have been rather hard on philosophy as a discipline in this paper, let me conclude by trying to rectify the balance. Most of what I have been saying in this paper has been lifted from Wittgenstein, Dewey, and Heidegger – who seem to me the great philosophers of our century. Their attempt to break down traditional philosophical dualisms of the sort I have been criticizing, and to get us back in touch with actual moral deliberation, seems to me to show that the only cure for bad philosophy is more philosophy. So, despite all the nasty things I have been saying about traditional philosophical distinctions, I think that the philosophers still have a social function. This is not to discover unexpected facts, nor to prove anything. Rather it is to suggest a vocabulary, a way of stating our concerns, which will help us make sense of what we do, will make us more aware that we might be wrong, and will increase our sensitivity to new possibilities.

What Is Dead in Plato

It is quite true that the history of Western philosophy is a series of footnotes to Plato, but in the last few centuries, many of these footnotes have been saying, "Notice how much harm this particular bad Platonic idea has done." Dante Germino is quite right that Plato has frequently been oversimplified and caricatured. But he has also been disagreed with, on fundamental points, by people who can claim a good understanding of his work. I agree that Karl Popper's Plato is a caricature. But I think that philosophers like Nietzsche, Dewey, Wittgenstein, and Heidegger have not caricatured Plato and that they have given us good reasons to discard most of Plato's central doctrines.

These philosophers have believed, as I gather Germino does not, that Plato put forward an "intellectual system." It may be, as Germino suggests, that the system which commentators have found in the central books of *The Republic* and in such dialogues as the *Phaedo* and the *Theaetetus* does not represent Plato's actual view – that this system is a sort of elaborate joke, or a pedagogic device designed to lead beyond itself. Plato does indeed say, in one of his letters, that his true doctrine cannot be written down. Commentators have been baffled to know what to make of that letter, and so am I. So the "Plato" whom I shall discuss is the author of the intellectual system known as Platonism – the system which contains such doctrines as that of the Forms, and which integrates this doctrine with the distinctions between knowledge and opinion and between the soul and the body. My excuse for discussing this system, despite the "Seventh Letter," is that it is this system to which Western philosophy is a footnote. It is these doctrines which, from Aristotle and Cicero down to Allan Bloom, people have been discussing. These are the doctrines which have sprung to their minds when the name "Plato" was mentioned. So I, too, shall discuss them.

Most criticism of Plato in recent times does not concern his politics but rather his conception of human beings and particularly his conception of truth as correspondence with a transcendent reality. Germino agrees with

Plato that some of our experiences are of a transcendent being. He agrees with him also that "knowledge is ultimately not induction but recollection" and that "the true philosopher is ... a teller of a story of a reality moving through him and through all of us as we grapple with the meaning of life, suffering, death and immortality." I disagree with him on all these points.

Philosophers who think that Plato started off on the wrong foot believe that there is no such thing as a reality moving through all of us. There is nothing like a "transcendence" to be experienced or attained. Nor is there anything "good and true deep within us." From our point of view, Platonism is a secular version of religion. It shares both the advantages and disadvantages of religious faith. The principal advantage of both is that they make life easier to bear. The principal disadvantage of both is that they make a distinction between the world of appearance – the world associated with time, the body, and the senses – and a True World, the world of eternal truth, the immaterial world of the spirit. Many recent philosophers think the advantage is outweighed by the disadvantage, and I agree.

Plato's principal legacy to our civilization has been otherworldliness, the idea that there is something beyond the world of time and space, that we human beings somehow have a foot in this other world, and that true knowledge consists of recollection of this nonspatiotemporal reality. Plato's principal critics have been those who say that both the idea of God and the idea of a true world have done more harm than good. These critics think, and I agree, that it would be better to think of human beings as merely temporal, merely mortal creatures. It would be better to give up the idea that human beings have a nature and a duty to achieve that nature. It would be better to think of ourselves as creating ourselves as we go along. It would be better to drop the idea that there is something called the truth, knowledge of which will make us free.

There is no quick, knock-down argument to show that it would be better to give up these religious and Platonic ideas, anymore than there is a quick, knock-down argument for or against God's existence. All that anyone can do in this area is develop alternative visions, alternative ways of looking at the situation which human beings find themselves in at the present time. I shall try to develop the anti-Platonic picture by expanding on the idea that human beings are makers rather than, as Plato thought, knowers.

Plato's philosophy centers on an attempt to take the mathematician, rather than the poet, as a model. The mathematician can give conclusive arguments for his beliefs. The poet cannot, nor can the literary critic – the person who wants to insist that one work of art is better than another. Plato thought that the kind of certainty which the mathematician had was preferable to the sort of uncertainty under which the poet or the critic or the politician must labor. He set himself the task of asking, What would human beings have to be like, if they were in principle capable of attaining such certainty? What would they have to be like, if there were right answers to the questions which Socrates went around asking – questions about the nature of justice, of virtue, and of knowledge?

His answer was that time and space must be, in the end, an illusion – a veil behind which stands something to which the human soul is akin. Just as the Christian believes that there is a world beyond the grave, where we shall see as we are seen, so Plato believed that the world around was not the True World, not the world which could answer the questions we find ourselves driven to ask. Unless there were some transcendent reality with which we could get in touch, Plato thought, Socrates would have lived in vain. Unless there were a truth out there waiting to be discovered – an absolute truth, not relative to changing human circumstances – there would be no way for human beings to become free.

The contrasting view, best exemplified by Dewey, is that the point of Socrates's life was not to discover a permanent and absolute truth but rather to keep people thinking, to keep them inventing, to open up their imaginations to alternatives. The point of Socratic questioning is not to home in on a transcendent reality but simply to make people ask the question: Are our customs and institutions the best we can imagine, or can we do better than this? On Dewey's view, there is no built-in criterion for being better. We do not have any recollection of the nature of goodness which will serve to judge between proposed alternatives. All we can compare new customs and institutions with is old customs and institutions, in the experimental and tentative way in which we compare new friends, jobs, or environments with old ones. If experience leads us to prefer democratic to monarchical or oligarchic or totalitarian institutions, we shall have no justification of democracy save Winston Churchill's. Churchill said, supposedly, "Democracy is the worst form of government imaginable, except for all the others which have been tried so far."

If a Deweyan is asked what his criterion for truth is, all he can do is say "Free discussion – discussion between people who do their best to think of all possible alternatives, and then go over the advantages and disadvantages of each." The only test of truth is that it is the view which wins in a free and open encounter. But that test only works until somebody comes up with a new proposal – a new scientific theory, a new artistic style, a new political institution. Then the discussion will have to be undertaken again. We are never going to arrive at something which we can be sure is the last word, the final, absolute truth. For we can never be sure that all the possible alternatives have been canvassed. There will never be a time when Socratic questioning has become unnecessary.

I can put this Deweyan view another way by raising the question: Why are we so sure that truth cannot be defeated in a free and open encounter? The Platonic answer to this question is that knowledge is recollection, that we shall recognize the truth when we see it. The Deweyan answer is that, in our liberal democratic society, free discussion has become the criterion, the only criterion, of truth. For Dewey, there is nothing more to be said about the nature of truth or knowledge except that it is what such discussion produces. For Plato, there is a lot more to be said: there are a whole range of metaphysical questions about the nature of human beings and epistemological questions about the nature of human knowledge to answer. For Dewey, metaphysics and epistemology are parts of Plato's legacy to the West, a legacy we should be better off without.

How do we decide between Plato and Dewey? As I said earlier, I do not think there is any knock-down argument. It is a matter of whether one wants to see humanity as contained within something larger than itself to which it must be faithful or whether one wants to see humanity continually creating itself by creating new forms of science, art, and community. The Platonic view is comforting, and the Deweyan view is liberating. The Platonic view runs the danger of encouraging dogmatism; the Deweyan view runs the danger of encouraging anarchism. In deciding which philosopher to follow, we are weighing these various advantages and disadvantages against each other.

The reason that there is so much Plato bashing these days is not, I think, ignorance or prejudice but rather the conviction that the shift to a secular culture should now be followed by a repudiation of secular versions of religious comfort. Many people think, as I do, that we are, on balance, better off now that theological issues have been separated from political issues. They see the Enlightenment as having freed questions about how to deal with injustice and suffering from questions about the will of God. They would now like to free these questions from questions about the nature of man or the nature of truth. They would like to de-philosophize politics, just as Mr. Jefferson and the other Founding Fathers de-theologized it.

Just because Western philosophy is a series of footnotes to Plato, to free politics from philosophy is to free it from the need to pay further attention to Platonism.

13

The Current State of Philosophy
in the United States

We are constantly told that there has, of late, been rapid change in the academic disciplines lumped under the term "the humanities." Sometimes we were also told that there is now a "crisis" in the humanities. This is not true of philosophy in the United States or Britain. Philosophy in those countries revolutionized itself by becoming "analytic" during the 1950s. It has remained self-confidently and proudly analytic ever since. There has been nothing remotely like generational warfare, or even like a crisis, in the discipline since the 1950s. No structural changes have taken place in that period, and there seems little prospect of large-scale change in the foreseeable future.

The first version of analytic philosophy – the logical empiricism of the 1930s – declared its independence from the philosophical tradition and from the humanities. It insisted that philosophy should cease to think of itself as a neighbor of history and literature and should do its best to become a science. Carnap and Reichenbach were quite sure that studying geology would be a better preparation for philosophical work than reading George.[1] They suspect that Gadamer's immersion in Plato and the poets unsuited him for serious philosophical work. Their declaration of independence held it to be self-evident that there is a nice, sharp distinction between questions of language – questions of how words are or should be used – and factual, empirical, questions. It went on to argue that Plato – and most other writers in the Western philosophical canon – had created innumerable pseudoproblems, in part because they had ignored this self-evident truth.

This neat linguistic-empirical distinction, along with the idea that concepts could be "analyzed" and "clarified" by discovering necessary

---

[1] We have been unable to establish with certainty to whom Rorty is referring here. One possibility is the American economist and journalist Henry George. – *Eds.*

and sufficient conditions for the applications of the words which signified those concepts, lasted about twenty-five years. It did not survive the criticisms offered by Quine and by the later Wittgenstein, circa 1950. But the pre-Quinean rhetoric of "powerful analytic methods" was not supplanted by a new metaphilosophy. Rather, the second generation of analytic philosophers tacitly abandoned their old charter without attempting to draw up a new one. The philosophers who were writing their first books or articles in the 1960s were united by a sense of shared know-how, rather than by an explicit commitment to a method or a program. The same holds true of the generation presently emerging from graduate school. It is substantially the same know-how in both cases.

This sense of shared know-how, combined with a sense of moral and intellectual superiority to philosophers of other ages and lands (not to speak of professors of literature[2]), has sufficed to keep analytic philosophy intact and self-assured for half a century. Analytic philosophers are not much good at explaining to outsiders what they do and why they do it, but they usually feel that this is no more harmful or embarrassing than similar disabilities on the part of topologists, statisticians, or Sanskritists. They know that they are good at what they do, and they are not much concerned to explain why it needs to be done. They typically regard criticism by outsiders as a symptom of vicious anti-intellectualism. When the criticism comes from self-described humanists – people who would like philosophy to be more like it was in the good old days – they assume that their critics are animated by the suspicion and fear typically felt by the flabby minded whenever they encounter rigorous argumentation.

Despite the lack of an explicit metaphilosophical or methodological program, however, most analytic philosophers would probably feel fairly comfortable with David Lewis's account of philosophy as a matter of reconciling conflicting intuitions. Lewis says:

> One comes to philosophy already endowed with a stock of existing opinions. It is not the business of philosophy either to undermine or to justify these preexisting opinions, to any great extent, but only to try to discover ways of expanding them into an orderly system. A metaphysician's analysis of mind is an attempt at systematizing our opinions about it. It succeeds to the extent that (1) it is systematic, and (2) it respects those of our prephilosophic opinions to which we are firmly attached.[3]

---

[2] One of my old colleagues at Princeton began a book with the remark: "If, as is often said, there are basically only two kinds of people – the logical positivists and the goddamned English professors – then I am a logical positivist."

[3] David Lewis, *Counterfactuals* (Oxford: Blackwell, 1973), 88.

As specialists in making things hang together systematically, all the members of a philosophy department will dutifully troop in to hear visiting philosophers speak on topics as diverse as the reducibility of consciousness to brain processes, the existence of God, the nature of linguistic reference, human rights, and the implications of quantum indeterminacy for moral responsibility. They may all take a vigorous part in the subsequent discussion. For they view themselves as people who can, as long as technical vocabularies are avoided, tell a good from a bad argument and an intuitive plausible claim from a counterintuitive one. Analytic philosophers share the skills of judges, who also must consider a bewildering variety of issues. Given a confusing tangle of conflicting considerations, both sets of specialists are good at separating the skein into separate threads and seeing how these threads can be woven together into a coherent pattern.

What makes analytic philosophers analytic is their assumption that exercising this skill in some particular sub-area of the discipline is *all* that a philosophy professor can be expected to do. People who want more from philosophy than that – especially people who, despite Lewis, *do* want philosophy to undermine or to justify preexisting intuitions, tend to be dubious about analytic philosophy. Typically, such people think that philosophers should suggest large changes in the way we think about the world and ourselves, rather than simply inventing small distinctions in order to resolve clashes between small intuitions. What seems to the philosophy professors like desirable professionalism seems to such people like being stuck in a rut.

In order to discuss such doubts, I need to discuss the relations between analytic philosophy and other sorts of philosophy, and between it and other areas of contemporary American culture. I shall do so under four headings: the history of philosophy; philosophy in non-Anglophone countries; other disciplines in the university; and contemporary political issues.

I.   The History of Philosophy

The most conspicuous difference between philosophy in America before World War II and at present is the role, in graduate training, of the history of philosophy. In the old days, a graduate student was expected to acquire some familiarity with Plato, Aristotle, Augustine, Aquinas, Descartes, Spinoza, Leibniz, Locke, Berkeley, Hume, Kant, and Hegel. Nowadays one can get along with a nodding acquaintance with three or four of these figures. Quine's contempt for the history of philosophy is notorious, and his remark that two sorts of people go into philosophy – those interested in the history of philosophy and those who are interested in *philosophy* – reflects the attitude of many analytic philosophers.

Although many contemporary graduate students write their dissertations on historical subjects – more now than a decade ago – these students usually do not have a big sweeping story to tell about the course of philosophy from the Greeks to the present. They tend to specialize in a period or a school, just as teachers of literature specialize in a century. If you know a lot about Berkeley or Kant, you will not therefore be expected to have interesting things to say about Plato or Hegel.

More generally, it is much more important for philosophy graduate students to know what is happening right now than to be familiar with the canon. So the change which is said to be happening in literature departments these days happened quite a while ago in philosophy departments. The "star" PhDs in analytic philosophy are the people working on currently hot topics – the topics which are being discussed most intensively in the most prestigious graduate departments. These can usually be discussed without much knowledge of the past.

This decline in the prestige of the history of philosophy has been accompanied by a consensus that knowledge of foreign languages is not particularly important for a philosopher. There is a general feeling that an overwhelming percentage of good philosophy is written in English, and a general expectation that, in the fullness of time, philosophy in all countries will become analytic. Although American philosophers in the first half of the century were not particularly cosmopolitan, they are certainly less cosmopolitan now.

II. Philosophy outside the Anglophone World

In France, Germany, Italy, and Spain, the history of philosophy still occupies the place in the philosophy curriculum which it occupied in America before World War II. Debate about the significance of canonical figures is still an indispensable form of communication between philosophers in those countries. Habermas and Derrida, the two leading figures in so-called Continental philosophy, both have big, sweeping stories to tell about the career of philosophy since the Greeks. The direction of their work was largely determined by their reactions to the stories told about this career by Hegel, Marx, Nietzsche, and Heidegger.

You cannot be a very good reader of Derrida or Habermas if you are not familiar with the latter authors. Analytic philosophers typically are not. The result is that in the United States, Habermas is taught more in political science departments, and Derrida more in literature departments, than in philosophy departments. A whole tradition of European philosophical thought, stretching over the last two centuries, is rarely mentioned in American philosophy departments.

Although nonanalytic philosophers are not treated with quite as much contempt by the analytic establishment as they were fifteen years ago, eyebrows are still raised if a graduate student in one of the major American philosophy departments takes an interest in Heidegger or Derrida. If such a student goes on to write his or her dissertation on either author, his or her chances of a good teaching job are diminished. Philosophy departments typically employ (because of undergraduate demand) one person who teaches Continental philosophy, but rarely more than one. By contrast, they are likely to have three or four people working in analytic philosophy of language and mind.

The neglect of the past and of foreigners is by now so deeply entrenched in American and British philosophy departments that it seems likely that the analytic-Continental divide will persist indefinitely. By changing people's ideas of what counts as respectable philosophical work, and of what one needs to know to be a philosopher, analytic philosophy may have rendered itself immortal. I think it likely that "philosophy" will continue to denote two quite distinct, geographically separated pursuits for the next few centuries.

III.   The Relation of Analytic Philosophy to Other Disciplines

Analytic philosophy started out as an attempt to get philosophy out of "the humanities" and to put it on the secure path of a science. This attempt was accompanied by an attempt to explain and exalt the distinctive nature and methods of the natural sciences. In the 1950s, philosophy of science was at the heart of analytic philosophy, and the contrast between Carnap and Heidegger was seen as the contrast between a scientific approach to philosophy and an unscientific, and therefore irrationalist, one, an approach biased against democracy and toward fascism.

The scientists themselves, however, were not particularly interested in philosophy of science. Attempts to link up philosophy with particular natural or social sciences have not been very fruitful, except perhaps for cooperation between philosophers and cognitive psychologists in investigations of artificial intelligence. Since the philosophers had already cut themselves off from the humanities, and in particular from history and literature, the result has been that philosophy has become a pretty isolated discipline. Most faculty members in the university have little sense of what their colleagues in philosophy do and little interest in finding out.

This isolation has been only slightly mitigated by the rise, during the 1970s and 1980s, of programs in "applied philosophy" – particularly applied ethics. There are now well-established programs in medical ethics within medical schools, and in business ethics within business schools, staffed largely by people with PhDs in philosophy. But the philosophers who work in such programs quickly drift out of contact with their university's philosophy department. The literature in these areas of applied ethics is by now so vast that those working in them have little time to keep up with other areas of philosophical inquiry.

IV. Contemporary Political Issues

However things may be in other traditionally "humanistic" disciplines, there has been no politicization of philosophy. Philosophy professors were active in the 1960s in the movement against the Vietnam War, and the American Philosophical Association passed anti-war resolutions. But the idea of making philosophy more relevant to struggles for social justice has never really caught on among analytic philosophers. Their rhetoric remains one of pure, quasi-scientific, disinterested search for truth.

Political philosophy is a flourishing sub-area, but it is largely a matter of sorting out our intuitions about, for example, the respective weights to be given to liberty and to equality in constructing sociopolitical institutions. Almost nobody in a US philosophy department seriously questions the tradition of political liberalism. Most teachers of political philosophy in the United States would identify with the left wing of the Democratic Party.

The shift in style and problematic which characterized much of analytic philosophy did not, however, lead to any great change in English-language political philosophy; Rawls, for example, would have written much the same book if the linguistic turn in philosophy had never been taken. By now the only difference between a political theorist trained in a political science department and one trained in a philosophy department is that the political scientist will probably be a bit more familiar with the history of his subject.

Feminism is perhaps the only sociopolitical initiative which has been important to Anglophone philosophy in recent years. As in many other areas of scholarship, some of the most interesting books in philosophy these days have a feminist slant. But most of these books are written by women whose favorite philosophers are Continental rather than analytic. Writers like Derrida have suggested ways in which the Western philosophical tradition reflects specifically male assumptions and have attempted to change the intuitions to which this tradition has given rise. Analytic philosophy has not been particularly useful to feminists.

***

So much for description. I turn now to the question of whether, as is often suggested, the growing isolation of analytic philosophy departments is a symptom that analytic philosophy has become a sort of decadent scholasticism. Hilary Putnam, for example, quotes the passage from David Lewis which I cited above and reacts by saying that "the intuitions to which David Lewis himself gives weight – for example, the intuition that if properties are simples, then it is unintelligible how one property can 'entail' another property – seem to me very far from having either practical or spiritual significance."[4] Putnam remarks that "the method Lewis recommends was the method of philosophers in the Middle Ages."[5]

Putnam certainly has a point. Once philosophers decide that it is not their business either to undermine or to justify existing intuitions, one cannot expect the rest of the culture to take much notice of them. Putnam's impatience with the contemporary situation in analytic philosophy is shared by many philosophers in non-Anglophone countries. These foreigners typically admire the analytic philosophers' esprit de corps but are not sure whether they are writing anything which needs to be read.

On the other hand, it is always hard to tell the difference between undesirable scholasticism and desirable professionalism. Whatever analytic philosophers may not be, they are certainly skilled, hard-working, enthusiastic professionals. But, of course, so were the Ockhamists and Scotists of the fifteenth century. Considerations of academic freedom and autonomy suggest that when such a group of professionals comes into existence, the rest of the university and of the culture should assume that these people know what they are doing and should leave them alone to get on with it. Historical reflection, on the other hand, suggests that there have been long periods in which a humanistic discipline simply marched in place and achieved nothing of interest.

My own sense of the situation is that it was a mistake to try to put philosophy on the secure path of a science but that it is also a mistake to ask whether a given discipline is currently doing its assigned job. I am inclined

---

[4] Hilary Putnam, *Renewing Philosophy* (Cambridge, MA: Harvard University Press, 1992), 139.
[5] Ibid., 136.

to say that analytic philosophy as a movement has by now run out of steam (the sort of thing people started saying about the New Criticism along about 1960). But movements, and indeed disciplines, just do not matter all that much. New Criticism produced several-hundred-thousand trite and boring books and articles, but people will read Empson and Eliot, Brooks and Tate with interest and pleasure for quite a long time. Analytic philosophy has produced almost the same number of trite, formulaic, narrow, incestuous pieces of writing, but people may read Ryle, Sellars, Davidson, Dennett, and a few others with pleasure and interest for some time to come.

Good work in the humanities, as in the arts, is not produced by methods or movements or teams but by idiosyncratic imaginations. No matter what is fashionable in departments of English – whether it be the discovery of organic form or the discovery that all forms tear themselves apart – there will always be the occasional Harold Bloom or Kenneth Burke, an occasional original mind. Such minds are so wrapped up in the books they discuss, and the contribution of those books to their own sense of who they are, that it does not matter much to their work what fashions are current.

Even if 99 percent of the issues discussed by contemporary analytic philosophers of language will seem artificial and verbal fifty years from now, a few books which emerged from that discussion will still be worth reading. Russell and Moore are as boring and dated as philosophers get, but if he had not read their work, Wittgenstein would never have written *Philosophical Investigations*. Nobody now wants to read Christian Wolff, but without him we should not have had *The Critique of Pure Reason*. Nobody reads the Oxford philosophers of 1600, but if they had not been as decadent as they were, we might never have had the surly polemics of *Novum Organum* or of the section of Hobbes's *Leviathan* called "The Hot-Houses of Vain Philosophy." Perhaps a movement has served its turn well enough when it has produced three or four violent and interesting manifestoes and has provoked (a generation or two later) three or four violent and suggestive reactions.

14

Brandom's Conversationalism: Davidson and Making It Explicit

Robert Brandom's very ambitious, impressive, long, and complicated book offers what he calls a "unified vision of language and mind." To master the book, and the terminology it deploys, one will need to teach it a couple of times. Since I have read it only once, have not yet taught it, and am still digesting it, I am not in a position to give a balanced account of its achievement. So I shall try only to assign the conclusions of the book a tentative location in contemporary philosophical space. This will mean neglecting the extraordinary elegance, and the striking originality, of the inferential path by which Brandom reaches his conclusions.

More specifically, I shall say how *Making It Explicit* looks to somebody who shares Brandom's conviction that Wilfrid Sellars's work is central to the philosophical progress made in our century, but who has been as much influenced by Davidson as by Sellars. As a Sellarsian who has been trying to work through the implications of Davidson's work, I found myself continually comparing and contrasting what Brandom is doing with what Davidson is doing. I see the two men's work as complementary, and unlikely to conflict, although very different in emphasis and in terminology. Both Brandom and Davidson are concerned to complete the replacement of empiricism by naturalism, which was initiated by "Empiricism and the Philosophy of Mind," on the one hand, and by "Two Dogmas of Empiricism," on the other. In this effort, Brandom is to Sellars what Davidson is to Quine.

In particular, both Brandom and Davidson attempt what Brandom calls "an account of propositionally *explicit* saying, judging, or knowing-*that*, in terms of practically *implicit* capacities, abilities, or knowing-how."[1] Viewing rationality and cognition as a matter of terms of complex know-how chimes with Davidson's suggestion that we drop the idea of language

[1] Robert B. Brandom, *Making It Explicit: Reasoning, Representing, and Discursive Commitment* (Cambridge, MA: Harvard University Press, 1994), 135.

having a *structure* and that we erase "the boundary between knowing a language and knowing our way around in the world generally."[2] When this move is conjoined with an abjuration of residual atomistic doctrines (Quine's unfortunate Skinnerian attempt to interpose "stimulus meanings" between judgments and the world, on the one hand, and Sellars' unfortunate enthusiasm for Tractarian picturing, on the other), we get a nonempiricist, and thoroughly holist, view of mind and language. The principal virtue of such a view is that it eschews what Davidson calls "the third dogma of empiricism," the distinction between scheme and content. It does not start with a picture of a scheme-enforcing subject and a content-producing object which meet in the middle at a place called "experience," the place where the scheme put forward by spontaneity encounters the content provided by receptivity. Instead, it starts with people doing things and asks what particular things they have to do in order to be said to use languages and to have minds.

Brandom ends his book by saying that what he has just given us – "an expressive account of language, mind, and logic," which explains all three in terms of know-how – is an "account of who *we* are."[3] Slightly earlier he has said that "conversation is the great good for discursive creatures."[4] One handle by which one can pick up his massive book is by contrasting this conversationalism with the traditional idea that the great good for discursive creatures is getting the Way the World Is right. One can, in other words, contrast Brandom's account of human beings as conversationalists with the Platonic/Aristotelian account of human beings as distinguished from the brutes by their ability to penetrate through appearance to reality.

The latter account is the one which says that, though human beings start out with descriptions of reality which are dependent upon human needs and interests, they can eventually transcend these and move on toward something like Bernard Williams' "absolute conception of reality." We can call this latter view "realism" if, as I do, one agrees with Plato, Aristotle, and David Lewis that, in Lewis' words, "realism that recognises a nontrivial enterprise of discovering the truth about the world needs the traditional realism that recognizes objective sameness and difference, joints in the world, discriminatory classifications not of our own making."[5]

To be a realist in this sense is to urge that any philosophical account of language, mind, and logic must divide discourse up into the part in which

[2] Donald Davidson, "A Nice Derangement of Epitaphs," in *Truth and Interpretation: Perspectives on the Philosophy of Donald Davidson*, ed. Ernest LePore (Oxford: Blackwell, 1986), 445–446.
[3] Brandom, *Making It Explicit*, 650.   [4] Ibid., 644.
[5] David Lewis, "Putnam's Paradox," Australasian Journal of Philosophy 62, no. 3 (1984), 228.

we are trying to get something right, and so are under what Crispin Wright calls "Cognitive Command," and the areas in which we are *just* conversing. In the first part, the discriminatory classifications come from the world, and in the latter they come from us. This is the sort of division which Locke put forward and which the logical positivists revived. Contemporary philosophers like Wright and John McDowell, who value what they call "our realistic intuitions," are still tempted by such a division of discourse. But any such division requires an account of a special word-world relation, such as "accurate representation" or "correspondence," which will separate, for example, objective physics from subjective aesthetics.

Davidson, who treats physics and aesthetics as on a semantic par, has suggested that it would be well to get rid of the idea that language and mind represent anything, since *any* use of the concept of representation seems bound to plunge us first into skepticism and then into relativism.[6] Davidson would like to drop the whole topic of the purported independence of world from mind, and thus set aside the debates about realism and antirealism. His repudiation of the distinction between representational scheme and represented content amounts to the suggestion that we no longer inquire, as realists must, about which discriminatory classifications are the world's and which ours – which are part of the representing scheme and which of the represented content.

Brandom, too, wants to get rid of the traditional dualisms. He says that "discursive practices incorporate actual things" and "must not be thought of as hollow, waiting to be filled up by things; they are . . . as concrete as the practice of driving nails with a hammer."[7] He is insistent that his own distinction between norm and fact is not a dualism of subjective scheme and objective content but merely a way of emphasizing the need for two ways of describing a single set of interactions between human beings and the rest of the world.[8] "Facts," he says, "are just true claims," for "there is no strictly nonnormative realm – no realm where concepts do not apply."[9]

But Brandom is, to my regret, less dismissive than Davidson of the notion of representation. He recognizes that the "issue of objectivity is perhaps the most serious conceptual challenge facing the attempt to ground the proprieties governing concept use in social practice"[10] – an attempt which eschews such "representational primitives" as "perceptual experience." So he devotes his final chapter to arguing that his account can

---

[6] See Davidson, "The Myth of the Subjective," in *Relativism: Interpretation and Confrontation*, ed. Michael Krausz (South Bend, IN: Notre Dame University Press, 1989), 165–166.
[7] Brandom, *Making It Explicit*, 332.   [8] Ibid., 624.   [9] Ibid., 622, 624.   [10] Ibid., 137.

"explain the representational dimension of thought and talk."[11] This last chapter's thesis is that "the *representational* dimension of propositional content is conferred on thought and talk by the *social* dimension of the practice of giving and asking for reasons."[12]

For Brandom, however, the idea that propositional content has a representational dimension boils down to nothing more than the claim that our conversational practices institute "implicit norms according to which the truth of claims and the correct use of concepts answer to how things objectively – rather than how things subjectively, or even intersubjectively – are taken to be."[13] Brandom undertakes to show us how "the notion of propositional contents as truth conditions – as depending for their truth on the facts about the objects they represent – gets its grip."[14] It gets its grip from the fact that "commitments undertaken against one doxastic background of further commitments available for use as auxiliary hypotheses can be taken up and made available as premises against a different doxastic background."[15] Their use in this way results in *de re* ascriptions, and Brandom thinks the ability to make such ascriptions is all that is needed for objectivity to be distinguished from intersubjectivity. As he says, "Locutions such as 'of', 'about' and 'represents' play the expressive role of representational locutions in virtue of their use in *de re* specifications of the contents of ascriptions of propositional attitudes."[16]

Philosophers with strong realistic intuitions, however, are going to say that there is a lot more to the notion of representing X as it really is than the ability to say that we all were mistaken in thinking that X has the property P. They will be inclined to insist that Brandom's inferentialism can indeed explicate "about" and "of," but that there is more to representing reality than being about it. Brandom himself admits that "the notion of *de re* belief that has exercised philosophers since Quine has more epistemic oomph to it than the thin notion reconstructed here." This is because, as he goes on to say, the former notion "involves being en rapport with a particular object in a stronger sense than merely having some way or other of denoting it."[17]

Brandom will have no truck with the idea that "directly referential expressions, paradigmatically indexical ones, make possible a fundamental sort of cognitive contact with the objects of thought, a kind of relational belief that is not conceptually mediated – in which objects are directly present to the mind."[18] For Brandom is loyal to Sellars's

[11] Ibid., 495.   [12] Ibid., 496.   [13] Ibid., 498.   [14] Ibid., 517.   [15] Ibid.   [16] Ibid., 584.
[17] Ibid., 548.   [18] Ibid., 551.

psychological nominalism – the doctrine that all awareness of anything, even of particulars, is a linguistic (and thus a conceptually mediated) affair. He has no sympathy with Kripke's attempt to squeeze realism out of indexicality by construing *de re* ascriptions as latching on to objects by a reference relation which swings free of the inferences made to and from such ascriptions.

One might epitomize the difference between Brandom and Davidson, on the one hand, and the self-proclaimed defenders of our realistic intuitions, on the other, by saying that the former reduce all word-world relations *other than causality* to word-word, conversational, relations, whereas the latter insist that there is at least one such relation – representation, correspondence, or what Wright calls "being under cognitive command" – which is reducible neither to causal relations nor to conversational relations. Then one might say that the only interesting difference between Davidson and Brandom is that Brandom talks about norms and Davidson about behavioral regularities.

The latter difference, however, seems insignificant. Consider Davidson's claim that "the ultimate source of both objectivity and communication is the triangle that, by relating speaker, interpreter and world, determines the contents of thought and speech."[19] Compare it with Brandom's claim that the only difference between objectivity and intersubjectivity is that we have, in *de re* ascriptions, a way of saying that everybody has always been wrong in one or more of their beliefs about X. If Brandom would accept Davidson's point that everybody could hardly have been wrong in *most* of their beliefs about X, there seems little for them to disagree about.

I shall return to the question of whether Brandom would accept this point below. But first I want to remark on a few more parallels between Brandom and Davidson. Brandom quotes Davidson's claim that "one cannot be a thinker unless one is an interpreter of the speech of others" approvingly.[20] Davidson, I think, would approve of what Brandom calls "tactile Fregeanism" – the view that our practice puts us in touch with facts and the concepts that articulate them.[21] As far as I can see, he would have no reason to object to Brandom's claim that enough has been said about objectivity once we have explained our ability to understand the possibility of perpetual and unanimous false belief.

This agreement is possible because, if I read them aright, neither Brandom nor Davidson has any use for the notion of "how the object is in itself," nor that of "correspondence to the intrinsic nature of the object." Both explicate the idea of objectivity without reference to such ideas. So neither, as far as I can see, can or should grant the realist his claim that there was a Way the World Was prior to the emergence of mind and language. For both, the idea of distinguishing joints in the world which coincide with present linguistic discriminatory classifications and those which do not is, at most, a gesture toward a possible future, in which human beings may deploy more useful linguistic discriminatory classifications than those we are presently making. It is a contrast between poorer and richer discursive practices rather than David Lewis' distinction between the world's discriminatory classifications and ours. Both Brandom and Davidson would presumably say that there were as many Ways the World Was before language and mind as there are descriptive vocabularies which language-users will manage to formulate and that none of these vocabularies is more closely related to the world than any other. Lewis, Bernard Williams, and Crispin Wright, however, all seem committed to saying that the vocabulary of physics is more closely related to the world than that of aesthetics. They take the photons of the prehuman world to be part of the Way the World Was, but claim the beauty of the prehuman sunsets was not part of this Way.

Brandom should, it seems to me, endorse Davidson's doctrine that most of anybody's beliefs must be true. This claim seems implicit in Brandom's own doctrine that linguistic ability, rationality, and *cognitive* ability are three ways of describing a single skill.[22] That doctrine would seem to entail that the idea of pervasively false belief systems makes no sense and that, as Davidson puts it, "belief is in its nature veridical." For both men, saying something true should not be seen as the result of a desirable noncausal relation between a description and an undescribed world – a relation which holds only if these two relata divide up along the same lines – any more than winning a game should be seen as a relation between a social practice and something outside that practice. For both, I take it, the only relevant relations between the described and the description other than aboutness are causal ones. These causal relations are far too complex to be described in terms of matching, corresponding, or fitting. The holism involved in ascribing truth, like that involved in ascribing belief, defeats attempts to cut nonlanguage up into fact-sized chunks which stand in causal relations to sentences.

---

[22] Ibid., 203.

Nevertheless, it may seem that a great gulf divides Davidson's Tarskian approach to semantics from Brandom's insistence that "representational locutions [such as 'true' and 'refers'] are not suited to play the role of primitives in a semantic theory."[23] One can easily imagine Davidson balking at Brandom's claim that "truth and reference are philosophers' fictions, generated by grammatical misunderstandings."[24] Davidson explicitly says that Tarski's truth predicate is a "legitimate" predicate,[25] whereas Brandom explicitly says that one can avoid the paradoxes of deflationism only by denying that it is a predicate.[26]

However, I am not sure that these differences between Brandom and Davidson make any difference. For both agree on the indefinability of the word "true." Both would disagree with critics of Tarski, such as Hartry Field, and for the same reasons. Both think that we are never going to have more of an understanding of how words hook on to the world than we have now and that we do not need anything like a new, improved theory about how either truth or reference works. Both ridicule the idea of "truth-makers" – of chunks of the world which nestle up against sentences and thereby make them belief-worthy.[27] Davidson could, I think, cheerfully grant Brandom's point that there are no such things as semantic facts, since "mastering semantic vocabulary just gives us a new way ... of getting at a range of nonsemantic facts we already had access to."[28]

But surely, one might expostulate, Davidson could never agree with Brandom's claim that "one ought not to explain propositional contentfulness in terms of truth conditions."[29] Notice, however, that Brandom is not denying that anything that has a propositional content has truth conditions.[30] He is simply saying that what gives it both that content and those conditions is the same social practice. Philosophical perspicuity in this area consists in saying that both logic and semantics are just ways of calling attention to features of that practice. Notice also that Davidson is not about to answer the question "Why do you think that this noise has propositional content?" by saying "Because it has truth conditions." He would presumably agree with Brandom that this would be a "dormitive power" sort of explanation. He certainly would agree that "This sentence is true because it corresponds to reality" is that sort of explanation.[31]

Brandom endorses Davidson's view that "the *only* constraint on an assignment of denotations to subsentential expressions ... [is] that it makes the truth

---

[23] Ibid., 285.   [24] Ibid., 324.   [25] Davidson, "The Structure and Content of Truth," 285.
[26] See Brandom, *Making It Explicit*, 326–327.   [27] See ibid., 328.   [28] Ibid., 329.   [29] Ibid.
[30] Ibid., further down.
[31] See ibid., 330; compare with Davidson, "The Structure and Content of Truth," 305.

conditions come out right"[32] – truth conditions which have been determined by noting social proprieties. Consider a field linguist constructing a truth theory for a natural language, trying to attain the know-how necessary to bicker with the natives like a sister. She looks for evidence of social norms which regulate which marks and noises are acceptably made in which environments, and which actions, linguistic and other, typically ensue upon the production of these marks and noises. She may, as she builds up her interpretive know-how, convert it into knowing-that by writing down T-sentences. But if she has never read Tarski or Davidson, she may do the same job by composing an old-fashioned Berlitz-style translation manual. The difference is merely that between using "is true if and only if" as the term which connects native sentences with sentences of her mother tongue and using "means" as such a connective. She would do no better or worse if she waved both truth and meaning aside and confined herself to saying "They find it appropriate to say so-and-so only in the conditions under which we should find it appropriate to say such-and-such." The difference between converting knowing-how into knowing-that by using "true," by using "means," and by using "socially approved of" seems, once again, a difference that makes no difference.

   If Davidson were asked whether he, like Brandom, takes truth-locutions to be force-indicating rather than content-specifying,[33] I can imagine him demurring at having to choose. But I take his view that the word "true" is indefinable and unanalyzable to amount to agreement with Brandom. Davidson, I take it, shares Brandom's enthusiasm for Frege's insistence that "truth is indefinable, something the understanding of which is always already implicit in claiming."[34] And, as far as I can see, the line between indefinable words and definable ones is pretty much the line between words used to indicate force and words used to specify content – between words whose use you have to just pick up and words whose use can be explained by other words without obvious circularity. Brandom thinks that both logical terms like "and" and semantical terms like "true" indicate force. This is why he says that "the truth condition on knowledge" is best thought of not as the claim that what is known must have a property called "truth" but simply as the trivial point that an endorsement of someone's claim to know something is automatically an endorsement of what she says she knows.[35]

***

So much for my suggestion that Davidson and Brandom should be viewed as part of the attempt to naturalize semantics and philosophy of mind. This

---

[32] Brandom, *Making It Explicit*, 364.   [33] See ibid., 296.   [34] Ibid., 112.   [35] See ibid., 297.

project culminates, it seems to me, in Davidson's claim that once we admit that we are not going to be able to define truth, we do not need to be, and indeed cannot be, either realists or antirealists. Davidson puts the point by saying: "Realism, with its insistence on radically nonepistemic correspondence, asks more of truth than we can understand; antirealism, with its limitation of truth to what can be ascertained, deprives truth of its role as an intersubjective standard."[36]

Brandom agrees with Davidson that we should not try to reduce objectivity to intersubjectivity by defining the former, with Peirce and Putnam, as what we shall get at the end of inquiry. But I suspect that realists are going to insist that some such reduction is implicit in his view, as well as in Davidson's. I think that there is a sense in which they are right about this. More generally, I think that once you naturalize semantics and philosophy of mind, you can give a respectable sense to William James's notorious claim that truth is utility to human beings, and also to the claim that objective truth is a matter of what human beings can agree on. I think that Davidson and Brandom should both be more willing than they are to say that James had a good point.

The standard argument for assimilating truth to utility is that words and concepts are tools developed to serve human purposes. So, if Brandom is right in saying that there is "no realm where concepts do not apply," then James must be right in saying that "the trail of the human serpent is over all" and Williams and Lewis wrong in suggesting that we can find a realm free of the traces of this serpent. We must say that there is no Way the World Is except one of the various ways in which human beings have found it useful to describe the world and that all such ways are equally closely tied to human needs and interests.

It seems to me that Brandom ought just to grant this point. If he did, however, he would have to revise at least one passage in his book. This is the passage which says that "the nonlinguistic facts could be largely what they are, even if our discursive practices were quite different [or absent entirely,] for what claims are true does not depend on anyone's claiming of them. But our discursive practices could not be what they are if the nonlinguistic facts were different."[37]

In the passage I have just quoted, Brandom falls back into something much too much like the scheme-content distinction. What he should have

---

[36] Davidson, "The Structure and Content of Truth," 309.
[37] Brandom, *Making It Explicit,* 331 – a page that does not chime with p. 624, nor even with pp. 332–333.

said is that there are no nonlinguistic facts – which seems to me what his previous claim that "there is no realm in which concepts do not apply" amounts to. Then he could have said that there is no point in trying to distinguish what we contribute to facts and what the world contributes to facts – no way to separate off a scheme part from a content part of facts. He could do justice to James as well as to "our realistic intuitions" by agreeing with James that it is equally pointless to say that a belief is true because it useful or that it is useful because it is true.[38]

On the same page on which he puts forward the view I have just criticized, Brandom says that

> it is not up to us which claims are true (that is, what the facts are). It is in a sense up to us which noises and marks express which claims, and hence, in a more attenuated sense, which express true claims. But empirical and practical constraint on our arbitrary whim is a pervasive feature of our discursive practice.[39]

I should rejoin that the need for ever richer and more complex forms of human happiness is an equally pervasive feature of our discursive practice. We did not get corpuscularian physics, quantum physics, classical art, or Romantic art, either from arbitrary whim or from empirical and practical constraint. We got all of these from the interaction between our ancestors and the rest of the universe. This interaction can be described equally well as a search for ever bigger and better social norms as a means to ever bigger and better forms of human happiness, or as the desperate attempts of a species to adapt to its harsh environment. As Bruno Latour has recently argued, there is no point in trying to locate a break between nature and culture.

I see the realism-antirealism debate as futile because it is a contest between these two descriptions – descriptions between which there is no need to choose. Most of the time Brandom and Davidson rise above this obsolete debate. But at times, as in the passage I have just quoted from Brandom, and in the last paragraph of Davidson's article "On the Very Idea of a Conceptual Scheme," both briefly descend to its level. They do so by yielding to the temptation to reaffirm "our realistic intuitions," thereby distancing themselves from the sort of philosopher who is, according to realists, a creature of arbitrary whim, out of touch with reality.

I think that Brandom could avoid this temptation by saying that although there is indeed a nice clear distinction between objectivity and

---

[38] See William James, *Pragmatism*, 204.   [39] Brandom, *Making It Explicit*, 331.

intersubjectivity, and between truth and utility, at the level of statements about particular objects, as discourse becomes more general, this distinction gradually fades out. Once we start talking about natural kinds, and about our overall worldview, the distinction between objectivity and intersubjectivity becomes pointless. In the case of natural kinds, this would amount to taking seriously Davidson's point that *most* of our beliefs about what trees, rocks, witches, unicorns, and atoms are must be true, even though some reasonable number of them might turn out to be false. In the case of the world as a whole, we cannot be deeply wrong about what it is like. In particular, we cannot err in the way Kant thought his predecessors had erred: there cannot be a world-in-itself which is wildly different from the spatiotemporal one we think we live in.

Neither human subjectivity nor the intrinsic character of reality determines that the world is spread out in space and time, or that gold is a metal, or that romantic art is a great advance over classical art. One might say, in the manner of Kant, that this is because each of these is helpless without the other and that they must cooperate. But it would be better to say that neither exists. The two mutually supportive myths – the myth of arbitrary subjective whim and the myth of unmediated pressure from the Way the World Is – should be allowed to annihilate each other. But it will be impossible to get rid of this, or any other, form of the scheme-content distinction until we abandon the very idea of a nonlinguistic fact. Until we do so, Brandom's Hegelian claim that conversation is the greatest good of discursive creatures – a claim with which I heartily concur – will seem light-minded, doxophilic, and frivolous.

15

Bald Naturalism and McDowell's Hylomorphism

Here is a baldly naturalistic view of the relation between mind and world: A mind is a very large network of intentional states attributed to a very complexly behaving object – the sort of thing that produces outputs which it is profitable to translate into sentences of our language. Such a translation is profitable if the attribution of intentional states made possible by such translation turns out to be a very good, almost indispensable, help in predicting the behavior of the object in question.

These intentional states are elements in the causal interactions of the object (a machine, for example, or an organism) with its environment. We find that we can predict and control these interactions more easily by describing the object as having beliefs and desires – and thus by using the notions of "aboutness" and "truth" in addition to that of "cause" – than by attributing to it only nonmental states of, for example, organs or circuitry. But the utility of these two additional notions provides, in itself, no reason to use the notions of "representation," "intuition," "concept," "receptivity" or "spontaneity."

When, for example, we interpret the marks and noises made by a brain in a vat as about states of the environment with which it is interacting (a vat, wiring, a computer program), we need not worry whether it is *really* having beliefs about an imaginary environment (a sunny beach, for example). Nor need we worry that we ourselves may entirely misconceive either our own environment or our own intentional objects. Bald naturalism leaves no room for such skepticism. For bald naturalists do not ask questions about how, or whether, a mind "bears on" its environment, or "represents" that environment. They simply relate an object's behavior to ours in whatever way makes it easiest for us to predict what will happen next.[1]

---

[1] In contrast, McDowell thinks that Davidson's claim that we must translate a lot of the marks and noises made by anything as about the things it is interacting with "does not calm our fear that our

Here is a less baldly naturalistic view of the relation between mind and world. The mind is a device for getting the world right. This can only be done if the way the world is somehow reproduced in the mind. (By way of identity, as in Aristotle and Hegel, or by way of representation, as in Descartes and Locke.) Such reproduction will only be possible if the relation between mind and world is more complicated than the baldly naturalistic picture takes it to be. The workings of the mind must be such that the relations between the elements of its intentional states often "correspond" to or "represent" the relations between the things in its environment. So we must describe a relation between the part of the mind which outputs utterances (spontaneity) and the part which takes in inputs from the world (receptivity) which insures that the interaction between the two parts will usually preserve the desired correspondence.

The first, baldly naturalistic view (a view suggested, if not entailed, by the views of Donald Davidson and Daniel Dennett) is attractive to many contemporary philosophers. The second was first laid out clearly by Aristotle, in his hylomorphic account of the relation between mind and world. Aristotle was, however, vague about the relation between intelligible and sensible properties of substances, and about how the mind skims the intelligible cream off the sensory milk.

These questions loomed larger when Democritus turned out to have been right about our environment. Between 1600 and 1900, accounts of nature gradually abandoned form and matter in favor of atoms and void. Although Aristotle thought of himself as giving an account of knowledge which was more naturalistic than Plato's, nature turned out to be quite unlike what Aristotle had taken it to be.[2] So his hylomorphism began to

---

picture leaves our thinking possibly out of touch with the world outside us. It just gives us a dizzying sense that our grip on what it is that we believe is not as firm as we thought"; see John McDowell, *Mind and World* (Cambridge, MA: Harvard University Press, 1994), 17. Here McDowell repeats a point made against Davidson by Edward Craig in "Davidson and the Sceptic: The Thumbnail Version," *Analysis* 50, no. 4 (October 1990), 213–214. (The same point has been made against Putnam's account of how to deal with brains in vats, by Anthony Brueckner, Crispin Wright, and others.) Bald naturalists, however, are immune from the dizziness which McDowell feels. Their grip on what it is that they believe is exactly as firm as their grip on what their environment is, since they can see no way to identify an intentional object of a belief (even if that belief is their own) except by linking the behavior of the believer to the environment. (That is why Davidson says that "radical interpretation begins at home.") So they think doubts about what it is that we believe no better motivated than Cartesian doubts about what our environment is. They should dismiss the latter sort of doubt in the way sketched by Michael Williams's argument against Barry Stroud, and other Cartesians; see Michael Williams, *Unnatural Doubts* (Oxford: Blackwell, 1991).

[2] Aristotle, of course, wanted different things from science than did Galileo. Skill at prediction and control, of the sort which corpuscularian physics provides, might not have impressed Aristotle as giving the sort of understanding which physics should provide.

seem quaint. It survived only in philosophical discussions of knowledge and mind, thanks to Kant's distinction between the form and the matter of thought. Although Kant's own account of spatiotemporal objects as intuitions shaped up by concepts produced only a grandiose form of skepticism – the doctrine that the spatiotemporal world was "merely phenomenal," the subsequent rejection of transcendental idealism did not produce a rejection of Kant's hylomorphic terminology. Philosophers have, alas, continued to talk about two kinds of representations (concepts and intuitions) and two parts of the mind (spontaneity and receptivity).

Such talk is, to be sure, almost inevitable if true belief is thought of as getting something right. The picture which, for better or worse, has continued to hold philosophers captive insists that philosophy must answer Kant's question about how mind manages to get world right. The principal motive for resisting bald naturalism is the conviction that this question cannot simply be dropped – and the inference that something like what Davidson calls "the scheme-content distinction" must therefore be preserved. Davidson is thought to miss something important when, in "On the Very Idea of a Conceptual Scheme," he says that "the notion of fitting the totality of experience, like the notion of fitting the facts, or of being true to the facts, adds nothing intelligible to the simple concept of being true."[3] Those who disagree with Davidson on this point insist that causal relations are (even when supplemented by the use of Davidsonian, unanalyzed concepts of aboutness and truth) insufficient to describe the relation between mind and world. They believe that we need to describe additional, specifically *cognitive* relations, relations which will give us, if not an analysis of, at least something interesting to say about the notions of "about" and "true."

John McDowell's *Mind and World* is very helpful for getting this disagreement into clearer focus. For McDowell writes in direct, explicit response to Davidson, argues forcefully for the insufficiency of Davidson's view, and employs Kantian, hylomorphic terminology unblushingly. He thinks that naturalism in philosophy has gone much too far and hopes to replace it with what he calls "a naturalized platonism."

McDowell attributes a "bland confidence" to Davidson that "empirical content can be intelligibly in our picture even though we carefully stipulate that the world's impacts on our senses have nothing to do with

---

[3] Davidson, "On the Very Idea of a Conceptual Scheme," in *Inquiries into Truth and Interpretation* (Oxford: Oxford University Press, 1984), 193–194.

justification."[4] He thinks that when Davidson argues that most of our beliefs must be true, he simply "helps himself to the idea of a . . . body of states that have content"[5] without doing anything to explain how they *can* have content. He argues that coherence theories of truth and knowledge of the sort Davidson recommends "express precisely the unnerving idea that the spontaneity of conceptual thinking is not susceptible to rational control from the outside."[6]

McDowell's criticisms of Davidson are, as these quotations suggest, phrased in terms of notions – "empirical content," "rational control," "spontaneity" – for which bald naturalists have little use. Davidson, for example, would be baffled by finding himself saddled with the view that "experience can be nothing but an extra-conceptual impact on sensibility" and with the inference that experience must therefore be "outside the sphere of reasons."[7] For Davidson does not talk much about either experience or sensibility: given his view of the matter, he does not need to. He can simply talk about causes and effects of beliefs and desires.

Since I construe Davidson as what McDowell calls a "bald naturalist,"[8] I find it odd to think of him as holding views about "our senses" and "the spontaneity of conceptual thinking," and puzzling to be told that he has neglected the possibility that "conceptual capacities, capacities that belong to spontaneity, are already at work in experiences themselves, not just in judgments based on them."[9] This idea of judgments "based on experience" does not map easily onto Davidson's description of how minds work, and so it is hard to imagine Davidson ever envisaging the possibility he is said to have overlooked.

More generally, it is hard to see how someone who sees no need or use for Kant's hylomorphic vocabulary could be persuaded that, as McDowell believes, the key to an understanding of the relation between mind and world is to realize that "conceptual content is already borne by impressions

---

[4] McDowell, *Mind and World*, 15.   [5] Ibid., 68.   [6] Ibid., 15.   [7] Ibid., 14.

[8] See ibid., 67, where McDowell says that Davidson is not tempted by "a bald naturalism which would opt out of this area of philosophy altogether, by denying that the spontaneity of the understanding is *sui generis* in the way suggested by the link to the idea of freedom." (For more on what makes bald naturalism bald, see 108–109.) I think Davidson's view is as bald as naturalism can get. As far as I can see, all that Davidson needs to say about the sui generis character of the mind is that the holistic character of the ascription of mental states suffices to distinguish them from physical states and that such ascription enables us to make a movement-behavior distinction, as well as a Humean distinction between freedom and constraint. I do not see what this has to do with spontaneity, nor with what McDowell calls "Kantian freedom." See, however, 148–156, where McDowell argues that I misunderstand Davidson. I take up these pages briefly below.

[9] McDowell, *Mind and World*, 24.

that independent reality makes on one's senses."[10] Telling *that* to Davidson, the sworn enemy of any scheme-content distinction, seems to beg all the interesting questions. Using Kantian jargon to straighten Davidson out strikes me as like telling Galileo that he would not have become so baldly corpuscularian had he grasped Aristotle's point that the mastery of form over matter extends to local motion as well as to sub-stantial change, and that therefore motion may be natural as well as violent.[11]

To evaluate McDowell's criticisms of Davidson, one has to figure out whether we need the circle of interdefinable terms whose utility McDowell takes for granted. Besides "empirical content" and "rational control," these include "friction against something external to thinking,"[12] "thought's bearing on the world,"[13] "rational interaction between receptivity and spontaneity,"[14] "rational answerability to the world,"[15] "germaneness rela-tion" (between experiences and beliefs),[16] "appearances constituting rea-sons for judgments,"[17] and "Kantian freedom."[18] The inutility of any of these terms means, for McDowell, the inutility of all. He (rightly, I think) suspects that Davidson would question the utility of each of them.

McDowell thinks that the question "How can anything have empirical content?" is a good one. He thinks the question "How can the world exert rational control on the mind?" equally good. Trying to meet McDowell half way, Davidson might answer the first question by saying that any belief ascribed on the basis of a radical interpretation which starts from observing the causal interaction of the machine or organism with its environment has as much "empirical content" as one can reasonably ask for. He would

---

[10] Ibid., 67.

[11] It is hard for Davidson to make sense of "conceptual content" because he, I should assume, regards having a concept as being able to use a term – a nominalist view which has become increasingly popular since the appearance of *Philosophical Investigations* and which entails the claim that blind-ness from birth does not, pace Locke, prevent the acquisition of the concept "red." Despite his esteem for Sellars, McDowell seems to dissent from this view, and to agree with Locke that visual experience is required to have color-concepts (see *Mind and World*, 167, and also 172: "a concept that is made available by the presence to experience of the original sample").

This difference is important for the issue of whether the question "Do our concepts have content, or are they empty?" is a good one. On the view common to Locke and Kant, that question can be given a sense. On the nominalist view I attribute to Davidson, as well as to Wittgenstein and Sellars, it is hard to give it one. Ability to wield a certain term (e.g., "substantial form," "phlogiston," "rational constraint") may be useless, but that is not because the relevant concept is somehow *empty*. It has content in the nominalist sense – a sense in which all that is required for conceptual content is that sentences containing a term should stand in complex inferential relations to lots of other sentences. Yet it may be a term we would be better off without.

[12] McDowell, *Mind and World*, 68.   [13] Ibid., 142.   [14] Ibid., 141.   [15] Ibid., 143.

[16] Ibid., 160.   [17] Ibid., 62.   [18] Ibid., 182.

presumably answer the second question by saying that if the world exerts causal control in the familiar way – by making the mind alter its beliefs and desires in more or less predictable response to changes in its environment, that *is* rational control. But such replies would really amount to rejecting the questions being asked – rejecting the demand for further light which is built into McDowell's use of the various interdefinable terms I have quoted.

Quine got rid of a lot of bad questions – and, as Davidson says, "saved philosophy of language as a serious subject" – by segregating certain interdefinable terms ("analytic," "synonymous," "semantic rule," "conceptual," "question of language," etc.) – terms which, in Carnap's writings, propped each other up – and refusing to use any of them. My own reaction to McDowell is that we can save discussion of the relation between mind and world as a serious subject only by junking the interdefinable terms which he uses in arguing for the inadequacy of bald naturalism.

McDowell criticizes my predilection for junking terminologies and questions, in some detail. He grants that sometimes such junking is a good idea, as when he says that we can properly shrug our shoulders at such questions as "What constitutes the structure of the space of reasons?" – that such questions "should not be taken to be in order without further ado, just because it is standard for them to be asked in philosophy as we have been educated into it."[19] But he thinks that I take shoulder shrugging too far. I have, he says, deprived myself of the right to say that "philosophical problems about how thought should be in touch with the world are illusory" because my own way of thinking "makes these problems urgent" by "separating relatedness to the world from the normative surroundings that are needed to make sense of the idea of bearing – rational bearing – on anything." So my refusal to address the philosophical problems about how thought should be in touch with the world "can only be an act of will, a deliberate plugging of the ears."[20]

---

[19] Ibid., 178.
[20] Ibid., 151. See also 154–155, where McDowell says that he and I share the pragmatist's "dualism-debunking and problem-dissolving" aims, but that "Rorty's own pragmatism is half-baked, according to standards set by his own account of what pragmatism is." In a footnote to this passage, McDowell says that I am insufficiently alive to the possibility that Kant and others "aimed at having the right not to worry about its [traditional philosophy's] problems, rather than at solving these problems." I agree that Kant had this aim but claim that he created too many new problems in the course of asserting this right. Pretty much the only parts of Kant I want to appropriate are the passages where he suggests that we can switch, as with bifocals, between describing ourselves in terms of causes and in terms of reasons, without needing to mediate between these two descriptions (except by explaining how language-use, and thus reason-talk, could have emerged in the course of

What seems to one philosopher a well-justified refusal to take seriously certain questions standardly asked in the philosophy into which we have, alas, been educated often looks to another like a deliberate plugging of the ears. In the case at hand, I think of Davidson as having told us all that we need to be told about the relation between normativeness – the regularities exhibited in language use – and relatedness to the world. He has done so by describing how we infer to such regularities from observing "what episodes and situations in the world cause an agent to prefer that one rather than another sentence be true."[21] McDowell does not think that this is nearly enough, because it leaves us unable to make sense of an idea – "rational bearing" – which I see no need to make sense of. A philosopher who would like to erase a certain circle of interdefinable terms (e.g., the Carnapian terms criticized by Quine, the Aristotelian terms criticized by Galileo) will often see no problem at a place where those who find these terms indispensable will find all sorts of problems. McDowell, in short, looks as willful to me as I look to him.

The issue between McDowell and myself (and between McDowell and Davidson, if I understand Davidson right) is a straightforwardly practical one about the success of our respective therapies. He thinks that my approach "leaves the [traditional] philosophical questions still looking as if they *ought* to be good ones" so that "the result is continuing philosophical discomfort, not an exorcism of philosophy."[22] Like me, McDowell wishes to practice exorcism and seems willing to accept absence of residual discomfort as the test of successful exorcism. But he says that "exorcism requires a different kind of move, which Rorty is much less good at"[23] – the sort of move which he himself makes. So the only way to decide between bald naturalism and McDowell's "naturalized platonism" will be to observe the amounts of discomfort produced by our alternative exorcistic and therapeutic practices. We both predict that the other's cure will be more uncomfortable than the disease being treated.

More specifically, I predict that McDowell's rather hairy version of Platonism is likely to cause more discomfort than my bald naturalism. He thinks that "our philosophical anxieties are due to the intelligible grip . . . of a modern naturalism, and we can work on loosening that grip" by Platonizing naturalism.[24] I want to tighten that grip until it

---

biological evolution). But McDowell thinks my appropriation of this Kantian point simplistic and gross.

[21] Davidson, "The Structure and Content of Truth," *Journal of Philosophy* 87 (June 1960), 322.
[22] McDowell, *Mind and World*, 142n.   [23] Ibid.   [24] Ibid., 177.

produces, in the patient, exactly the result which McDowell thinks we must avoid –namely, "thinking that there is [a] problem about the idea of how things are anyway, independently of communal certification."[25] I think the idea of "how things are anyway" needs amputation rather than further rehabilitative manipulation.

Like Putnam (and, I think, Davidson) I want to make Bernard Williams's notion of an "absolute conception of reality" – a way things are anyway – look as problematic as I can. I try to minimize the discomfort caused by repudiating Williams's intuitively plausible notion by spelling out the counterintuitive consequences of retaining it. I start by construing "anyway" as "apart from any description" – a construal that seems licensed by Williams's glossing "absolute" as "apart from human needs and interests." (Descriptions are, surely, products of human needs and interests.) Then I argue that the idea of how things are anyway is the problematic, and useless, idea of a world under no description.

Analogously, my strategy for making McDowell's naturalized Platonism feel uncomfortable is to ask how he can view the world "as something whose elements are things that are the case"[26] without populating the world with what Strawson, criticizing the notion of truth as "correspondence to facts" called "non-linguistic sentence-shaped objects." As I see it, McDowell's way of getting the world to exercise rational, rather than baldly causal, constraint on us is to give the world a quasi-language of its own, a set of descriptions in which it formulates the "that"-clauses which it impresses upon our sensibility. The cash value of McDowell's claim that "conceptual content is already borne by impressions that independent reality makes on one's senses"[27] seems to be that Nature is trying to tell us something – and that its medium of communication is our faculty of receptivity.

As far as I can see, had McDowell not already Platonized and personified Nature by endowing her with such a quasi-language, it would do him no good to insist that our "perceptual sensitivity," unlike that of dumb brutes and of thermostats, is "taken up into the ambit of the faculty of spontaneity."[28] No matter how conceptualized my perceptual sensitivity may be, nothing is going to exert rational constraint on it unless the constraining force is conceptualized too. I take it this is why McDowell wants to "incorporate the world into what figures in Frege as the realm of sense."[29] For only thus can the abyss look back, show us a quasi-human face, make rational demands on us, rather than just intimidating us.

---

[25] Ibid., 175.   [26] Ibid., 179.   [27] Ibid., 67.   [28] Ibid., 64.   [29] Ibid., 179.

I agree with McDowell that there is "no ontological gap between the sort of thing one can mean, or generally, the sort of thing one can think, and the sort of thing that can be the case."[30] Indeed, I think that claim tautologous. But I do not think that eliminating this gap requires us to see the world as filled with nonlinguistic "that"-clauses, or with "that"-clauses phrased in no specific human tongue, or with all the "that"-clauses ever formulable in any human tongue. That third alternative seems to me the implication of McDowell's claim not only that "*that things are thus and so* is the content of the experience, and it can also be the content of a judgment" but that "*that things are thus and so* is also, if one is not misled, an aspect of the layout of the world; it is how things are."[31]

In order to make McDowell's Platonizing move look as hairy as possible, I round up the usual scoffing, anti-Platonic, rhetorical conundrums – the ones which trace their ancestry back to Plato's self-criticism in the *Parmenides*: When a faculty of sensibility up against a cloud chamber is rationally constrained by being impressed *that things are thus and so*, is it impressed that there are a lot of elementary particle collisions going on or that there are a lot of evanescent darker gray lines on a lighter gray background? When it hits the *Mona Lisa* is it impressed that there is a smiling woman or that there is a complicated arrangement of fading pigments? When it revisits grandmother's house, is it impressed that *Es ist etwas unheimliches* or that *C'est une ambiance tout a fait proustienne*? Does the layout of the world contain *all* these "that"-clauses, plus those which human beings have not yet gotten around to formulating, ready and waiting to be impressed on a visiting sensibility?[32]

So much for a quick stab at inducing discomfort among those who accept McDowell's prescription. I turn now to mitigating discomfort among those inclined to accept mine. McDowell says that it is an "intolerable"

---

[30] Ibid., 27.   [31] Ibid., 26.

[32] Charles Taylor once rebuked me for using the phrase "Nature's Own Language" to describe the view of those who defend Our Realistic Intuitions, thereby implying that realists were what Taylor called "Raving Platonists" (people who believe that "a vocabulary is somehow already out there in the world"). I promised never to use the phrase again. (See my "Taylor on Truth" in *Philosophy in an Age of Pluralism: The Philosophy of Charles Taylor in Question*, ed. James Tully (Cambridge: Cambridge University Press, 1994), 21–22.) But McDowell's book tempts me to renege on my promise. I agree with David Lewis that "realism that recognises a nontrivial enterprise of discovering the truth about the world needs the traditional realism that recognizes objective sameness and difference, joints in the world, discriminatory classifications not of our own making" (Lewis, "Putnam's Paradox," *Australasian Journal of Philosophy* 62, no. 3 (1984): 228.) But I regard the idea of "classifications not of our own making," and of what Lewis calls "elite" objects, as a reductio ad absurdum of the idea that truth is getting "an independent reality" right, and as confirming Davidson's view that "it is futile either to reject or to accept the slogan that the real and the true are 'independent of our beliefs'" (Davidson, "The Structure and Content of Truth," 305). I think that McDowell's view forces him to join Lewis in what seems to me absurdity.

consequence of a view like mine that "how things are ... cannot be independent of the community's ratifying the judgment that things are thus and so."[33] My view does not entail that our community cannot go astray, but it does entail that how things are cannot be independent of a language in which they are said to be that way, and that the world has to wait for us to come up with a language before there can be anything remotely like a Way the World Is.

If "how things are" signifies something other than one or another among the descriptions of the world produced by the "triangulation" between world, others, and myself which Davidson describes, then I do not understand the term. McDowell's view avoids the attempt to, in Wittgenstein's phrase, get between language and its object only by giving the world as many elements in its layout as there are linguistic responses to its various segments. This prodigality should, it seems to me, create a lot more discomfort than Davidson's claim (quoted earlier) that talk of fitting the facts (a phrase which epitomizes McDowell's notion of the happy outcome of "rational control" of mind by world) adds nothing intelligible to the simple concept of being true.

McDowell rightly says that I deny that "the whole point of the idea of norms of inquiry is that following them out improves our chances of being right about 'the way the rest of the world is'."[34] If one thinks, as antipragmatists do, that there is such a way – that the world has a layout which rationally controls thought, rather than just shoving thinkers around – then such improvement will, indeed, seem the point of norms of inquiry. But pragmatists like me (who strive to keep their naturalism as bald as possible) think that the point of those norms is to get us what we want, and that trying to discover the way the world is, apart from any linguistic description of it, is a bad thing to want. Antipragmatists approve of inquirers who want to fit the facts, get things right, figure out the way the world is, etc. Pragmatists do not. They think that these inquirers are pursuing will-of-the-wisps, just as are agents who want to obey the Will of God. Such communities should redescribe their motives and goals. They should not do so because of the way the world is but because they will, in the long run, endure less discomfort if they do.[35]

****

---

[33] McDowell, *Mind and World,* 93.

[34] Ibid., 151. I defend this denial in "Is Truth a Goal of Inquiry? Davidson vs. Wright," in my *Truth and Progress: Philosophical Papers, Vol. 3* (New York: Cambridge University Press, 1998), 19–42.

[35] For the claim that the long-run benefits of pragmatism offset the confusion and puzzlement which its doctrines initially cause, see my reply to John Searle's claim that Kuhn, Derrida, and I are doing harm to our culture by undermining what Searle calls "the Western Rationalistic Tradition": "John Searle on Reason and Relativism," in *Truth and Progress,* 63–83.

McDowell and I both want to be good Sellarsians, but he sees me as inferring from Sellars's criticism of the Myth of the Given to a crazy antirealism. He thinks that I have thereby moved from one end of a seesaw to the other, and claims that he has found a way to end the seesawing between the Myth of the Given, on the one hand, and simply ceasing to demand rational constraint of mind by world, on the other. It is to recognize that "receptivity does not make an even notionally separable contribution to the co-operation [between receptivity and spontaneity]."[36] He says, rightly, that the Myth of the Given is a response to the threat that there is insufficient "external constraint on our activity in empirical thought and judgment," but he views "the Davidsonian response" to abandoning this Myth as just one more plunge on the seesaw.[37] By contrast, I want to tie the seesaw down once and for all on the side of abandoning the very idea of rational constraint, rather than attempting any sort of balancing act.

When we disagree about whether to improve on Kant's model of the relation between mind and world or rather to junk it, what are McDowell and I disagreeing about? Not, it seems to me, about how best to reconcile our various intuitions. The disagreement is really about what intuitions to cherish and which to try to get rid of. Here I differ from Cavell, Putnam, and others who think that philosophy should, in the end, leave everything as it is – that the task of philosophy is, in words Putnam has quoted from John Wisdom, to complete a journey from "the familiar to the familiar."[38] Agreeing with McDowell that "our philosophical anxieties" in this area are due to "a modern naturalism," I want to surrender to this naturalism by junking the picture of our relation to the world offered by the scheme-content distinction, and in particular by Kant's notions of spontaneity and receptivity. This means propounding a counterintuitive view.

---

[36] McDowell, *Mind and World*, 8–9. I suspect that if you postulate two faculties whose function is to cooperate on a given job, and then deprive one of them of an even notionally separable contribution to that cooperation, you are no longer postulating *two* faculties. Hegelian monism looms. I think Hegel was right that as long as you have two faculties you will wind up with skepticism, and that the only choice is between a Hegelian version of monism and a baldly naturalistic one.

[37] Ibid., 8.

[38] See Putnam, *Words and Life* (Cambridge, MA: Harvard University Press, 1994), 300. I argue for the claim that philosophy is a response to cultural change, and that intuitions should change when such change occurs, in "Philosophy and the Future" (in *Rorty and Pragmatism*, ed. Herman Saatkamp (Nashville, TN: Vanderbilt University Press, 1995)). I view Darwin as the crucial figure in the process of cultural change to whom philosophers should accommodate, and think that their obsession with Kant is still preventing them from coming to terms with Darwin. See my "Dewey between Darwin and Hegel" in the same volume [reprinted in *Truth and Progress*. – Eds.].

McDowell says that his naturalized Platonism is the idea that "the dictates of reason are there anyway, whether or not ones' eyes are opened to them; that is what happens in a proper upbringing."[39] I think that what a proper upbringing opens us up to is the demands of one or another human community. Such communities adopt different norms of inquiry, depending on what they want to get out of inquiry. He and I differ about whether some communities' dictates are more in conformity to those of reason than others, because we differ as to the utility of the term "reason." So, predictably, we differ about whether philosophers need say anything much about the relation between reason and nature.[40]

Whereas McDowell thinks that the fact that a human being is sometimes "above the pressure of biological need" means that "there is a bit of objective reality that is within her reach,"[41] I think that it means only that we can have pleasures which pigs cannot.[42] Whereas he thinks that "our very experience, in the aspect of its nature that constitutes it as experience of the world, partakes of a salient condition of art, its freedom from the need to be useful,"[43] pragmatists like me think that cognition is still saddled with the latter need. We agree that art is freed from this need but claim that science is not. Our understanding of science is utilitarian through and through.

These are very large issues, and I have only scratched some of the surfaces of the very deep disagreement between McDowell and myself. *Mind and World* is an extraordinarily rich and subtle book, one which marks a substantial advance in the argument between those who want to discard and those who want to rehabilitate Aristotle's picture of our relation to the rest of nature.

---

[39] McDowell, *Mind and World*, 91.   [40] See ibid., 153–156.   [41] Ibid., 116.

[42] McDowell, following Gadamer, connects the pig-human distinction with that between world and environment, and contrasts Davidson invidiously with Gadamer (see ibid., 114–119, 184–187). I think he fails to appreciate the great similarity between these two philosophers – similarities brought out in the concluding chapter of Bjørn Ramberg's *Donald Davidson's Philosophy of Language* (Oxford: Blackwell, 1989). But he is right that Davidson would see a Gadamerian *Welt* as just the pig's *Umwelt*, linguistically coped with.

[43] McDowell, *Mind and World*, 119.

16

Reductionist vs. Neo-Wittgensteinian Semantics

A recent book by Kenneth Taylor titled *Truth and Meaning: An Introduction to the Philosophy of Language* starts off by asking the reader to take an interest in the question: "How can there be contingent statements of identity, given that everything is necessarily identical with itself?" Taylor identifies this as "Frege's puzzle" and treats it as an appropriate starting point for philosophical reflection on language: The puzzle is, Taylor says, "to explain how a statement of the form 'a=b' can differ in cognitive content from a statement of the form 'a=a'."[1] This is the first of his examples of strange linguistic phenomena that have called the discipline we call philosophical semantics, or philosophy of language, into existence. Other examples include the referential opacity of belief-statements, true statements about nonexistent objects, and various other familiar usual suspects.

Someone who comes to Taylor's book fresh from reading either Wittgenstein's *Philosophical Investigations*, or Wilfrid Sellars's "Some Reflections on Language-Games," or Brandom's *Making It Explicit* may balk at the idea that these are strange phenomena in need of explanation. They may feel that Taylor gets philosophy of language on a wrong, question-begging foot. The same reaction is likely to be found in someone fresh from reading Donald Davidson's later essays ("A Nice Derangement of Epitaphs" or "The Structure and Content of Truth," for example). In these papers, little is heard of the so-called Davidson program – the attempt to find extensionalist ways of paraphrasing intensional statements. Much is heard, however, of the need to stop thinking of linguistic expressions as representations and to remember Quine's strictures against the existence of entities called meanings or intensions. Anyone suspicious of those notions will be suspicious of Taylor's use of terms like "cognitive content" or "representational content" as primitive terms.

---

[1] Kenneth Taylor, *Truth and Meaning: An Introduction to the Philosophy of Language* (Malden, MA: Blackwell, 1998), 2.

Someone fresh from reading either Wittgenstein or the neo-Wittgensteinian philosophers of language I have mentioned may react to Taylor's description of "Frege's puzzle" by recalling a passage in *Philosophical Investigations* that says that there is no finer example of a useless sentence than "A thing is identical with itself."[2] Wittgenstein mockingly compares this sentence to "Every colored patch fits exactly into its surroundings." This recollection may lead her to wonder whether the only use of identity statements, at least in the language-games which are their original homes, is to make such contingent identifications as that of the morning star and the evening star, or the mind and the brain. The idea of self-identity, and a fortiori that of necessary self-identity, is one that everybody except certain philosophers seems able to do without. If we agree to abjure that notion, there will be no reason to take Frege's puzzle seriously. To a Wittgensteinian, the puzzle can hardly serve as a paradigmatic problem whose existence is used to excuse the continued existence of a discipline Wittgenstein himself came to think we could do without – the philosophy of language.

A reader of this sort is also likely to balk at Taylor's invocation of Church's translation test. Taylor explains that Church criticized Frege's solution to his puzzle by invoking two plausible principles:

(1) The Paraphrase Principle: A sentence S' is an adequate paraphrase of a sentence S if and only if what S' expresses is identical to what S expresses.

(2) The Translation Principle: If T is an adequate translation of S then T expresses what S expresses.

Church pressed these principles home by noting that if

"The morning star" denotes the same object as "the evening star"

were an adequate paraphrase of

The morning star is the evening star.

then the German translation of the latter sentence should express just what the translation of the former does. But it does not, for

"The morning star" *und* "the evening star" *bedeutet der gleichen Gegenstand.*

does not express the same thing as is expressed by

Der Morgenstern ist der Abendstern.[3]

---

[2] Ludwig Wittgenstein, *Philosophical Investigations*, trans. G. E. M. Anscombe (New York: Macmillan, 1968), §225.
[3] Taylor, *Truth and Meaning*, 4–5.

Someone steeped in Wittgenstein, Sellars, the later Davidson, or Brandom is likely to protest at this point that the notion of "expressing the same as" is no more useful than that of self-identity. She of course agrees that two different sentences can, sometimes, in certain contexts, be used interchangeably. But for reasons like those which led Quine to mock the notion of synonymy, she is dubious about the idea that one can seek out a sentence that means, tout court, regardless of context, the same thing as another sentence. She is dubious, in short, about both the notion of "finding the meaning" as opposed to finding various uses, and about the notion of something that sentences express, or that makes them true, in every possible context. Having been led by Davidson to be suspicious of the notion that truths are representations of reality, she may wonder whether noncontextual use of "expresses the same thing as" may not be as dubious and dispensable a locution as "represents the same bit of reality."

Again, having been led by Brandom to neglect the context-free question "What does this sentence represent?" in favor of the context-ridden question "What deontic score will be chalked up against an utterer of the sentence by a certain person in a certain situation?," this person may be inclined to remark that it is hard to see in which situation what sort of person could give an utterance of

(S) The morning star is the evening star

a different score than an utterance of

(S') The thing we anglophones call "the morning star" and what we call "the evening star" are the same star.

or of

(S") "The morning star" and "the evening star" denote the same object.

For the only differential scoring she can envisage is one which results from a situation in which somebody is prepared to infer something from one of these sentences that somebody else is not. That situation, she suspects, is only going to arise within a special, rather dubious, area of culture – the philosophy of language.

Only there will be some people who say that the representational contents of utterances of these sentences vary, or that they are made true by different bits of reality, for only do we find uses for terms like "denote," "object," "is made true by," and "expresses the same as." Within that area of culture, of course, no appeal to commonsense usage will be admitted, any more than in would have been in seventeenth-century discussions of whether and how to use terms like "natural motion," "violent motion," "quantity of motion," "inertia," and the like. So, once again, the question raised for Wittgensteinians, Brandomians, and the like is: Is philosophy of language an area of culture in which language has simply gone on holiday, or one in which real problems are being addressed with the help of an appropriately technical and noncommonsensical vocabulary?

This latter question boils down to: What good do we think philosophy of language is going to do us? Are there, as Taylor thinks, strange phenomena that need explanation, as there were in the days when people were debating the relative utility of the terms "natural motion" and "inertia," or are there, as Wittgensteinian therapists sneer, merely pseudoproblems created by a picture that has been holding us captive?

Putting the alternatives in this way suggests that we might view not just Wittgenstein but also Sellars, Davidson, and Brandom as therapeutic rather than systematic, constructive philosophers. This prima facie implausible suggestion has a grain of truth in it. For these four philosophers I have just mentioned do have a common target. They are all trying to help free us from the captivity of the same picture. The fact that some of them do so by offering us large structures of interconnected arguments rather than brief and bracing aphorisms should not obscure the fact that they all see certain problems as unreal which Taylor, David Lewis, Saul Kripke, David Kaplan and many others see as real.

These are the problems which notions such as "intensions" and "meanings" are intended to solve – problems created by the claim that the same objects and states of affairs can be described in many different ways. The Fregean idea is that there are things called intensions which are finer grained than the represented extensions, and that philosophy of language seeks to correlate these intensions with the use of linguistic expressions, and thereby to show how language manages to function as a representational system.

Taylor says of Davidson, in tones of puzzlement, that on his view, "meanings play no role in the theory of meaning."[4] The same remark could be made, mutatis mutandis, for Wittgenstein, Sellars, and Brandom. Insofar as these philosophers have theories of meaning, they are not the sort of theories which could be used to figure out what a given linguistic expression means. Except for Davidson, they are not in the business of paraphrasing expressions by finding equivalent and more perspicuous

---

[4] Ibid., 147.

expressions, and even in the case of Davidson, such paraphrase is incidental to his larger project of substituting a holistic for a building-block account of how linguistic expressions relate to extralinguistic entities. Davidson's semantic holism – defined by Taylor as the claim that "the meanings of the expressions of a language depend on the totality of the relations that these expressions bear one to another" – is viewed by Taylor as a way of making semantic notions "physicalistically respectable even if there can be no physicalistic reduction of the semantic primitives."[5]

Discouragement with reductionist projects is intensified by reading Wittgenstein and beginning to think that any linguistic expression has a perfectly respectable meaning merely by virtue of having a use and that any such expression has a use if you give it a use. Despite Wittgenstein's own dubiously consistent epithets like "nonsense" to characterize expressions like "A thing is identical with itself," readers of *Philosophical Investigations* find themselves reluctant to suggest that some expressions in actual use lack "a clear meaning." For without some specific reductionist program in mind, the untranslatability of those expressions into an alternative vocabulary does nothing to show lack of meaning or lack of clarity.

Although in the *Investigations* Wittgenstein still sometimes talks about detecting conceptual confusion, for the most part, he is content to let a thousand language-games be played without suggesting the need for philosophical supervision. Davidson and Brandom never talk about conceptual confusion or nonsense. This is because both philosophers follow Quine in rejecting the very idea of stable objects which are more clearly seen, better understood, when described in one set of terms, the analysandum, than in another set of terms, the analysans. The price that Quine paid for, as Davidson put it, preserving philosophy of language as a serious subject, was to cast doubt on both the reductionism which was dear to Quine's own heart and on the Carnapian idea that philosophy of language could be a tool of culture criticism.

As I see it, contemporary anglophone philosophy of language has split into two camps. In the first, or neo-Wittgensteinian, camp are the people whose favorite philosophers of language are Davidson and Brandom. In the second, or reductionist, camp are the people whose favorite philosophers of language include David Lewis, Saul Kripke, David Kaplan, and John Perry. The latter typically find congenial either the sort of physicalistic metaphysics that Lewis shares with Frank Jackson and many of the other philosophers of Australasia or the attempt to ground both semantics and epistemology in evolutionary

---

[5] Ibid., 175–176.

biology that is found in the work of Dretske, Millikan, and Gibbard, or both. Were Russell and Carnap to return from the grave, they would find the work of this second camp more intelligible than that of the first. For their work is continuous with the idea of "the philosophy of unified science" in a way that work done in the first camp is not.

The idea that philosophy can be rendered scientific by carrying through on the sort of reductionist research program that Carnap envisaged goes hand in hand with the claim that one function of philosophy is to purify culture by getting rid of "unscientific" elements. The latter claim is no longer advanced in the rather crude and sneering tones which were characteristic of Ayer and Popper. But the dissatisfaction that many philosophers in the second camp feel with the work of philosophers in the first camp has a great deal to do with the need to keep something like Carnap's and Popper's crusading zeal alive – the need to fashion weapons which will keep politically and spiritually dangerous philosophers (Hegel and Heidegger, for example) at bay.

Another source of their dissatisfaction is that it is hard to envisage a Wittgensteinian or a Brandomian research program in semantics. Neither philosopher offers a budget of unsolved problems for graduate students to tackle in their dissertations. Back in the 1980s, it did seem as if Davidson had such a research program to propose, and this illusion had a good deal to do with the enthusiastic reception of his Locke Lectures at Oxford. But in the ensuing years Davidson appears to have lost interest in beating linguistic expressions into extensional shape. His recent work seems as remote as does Brandom's from any attempt to answer the question "What now remains to be done?"

1.   Brandom as Nonreductionist Naturalist

So much for a fast overview of the split that I had in mind when I chose the title for this paper. Now I want to turn back to the topic of the respectability of modal notions and to consider Brandom's claim that there is only one good reason for this new-found respectability. This is that we have come to realize that every use of every concept presupposes the ability to wield a normative vocabulary.

When we grasp this point, Brandom thinks, we realize that we cannot even use "Red here now!" as a meaningful utterance – that is to say, as a move of what Brandom calls "the game of giving and asking for reasons" – unless we understand and acknowledge expressions which formulate norms for the use of the component words, and for the expression as a whole. Since even the strictest reductionist would agree that a normative vocabulary provides sufficient resources for "clarifying" counterfactuals and modal locutions, if you have that vocabulary, you have it all. We can, for example, define nomologicality in terms of projectibility and explicate projectibility in terms of locutions such as, "If you project that predicate, we shall either beat you with sticks or withhold your teaching credentials, and perhaps both."

The threat of Cartesian dualism which was the original incitement to worry about belief-sentences now recedes. For, as Brandom puts it, we have shifted "from a broadly Cartesian dualism of the mental and the physical to a broadly Kantian dualism of the normative and the factual."[6] But this latter dualism is perfectly compatible with Darwin's naturalistic account of how intentionality came into the world. For a norm is just a sociological fact – a regularity of behavior – viewed from the inside. The sociologist tells us that, as a matter of fact, a given group hits you with sticks or withholds your degree under certain conditions. The members of that group tell us about the norms by which they are bound, but there is, as the reductionists say, "nothing more" to being bound than the prevalence of the regularities that the sociologist reported. Analogously, a fact is just a norm viewed from the outside: the fact, for example, that members of a certain group feel bound to use the expression "Red here now!" only under certain condi-tions, on pain of being beaten with sticks or being refused degrees.

The crucial move here is to interpret "nothing more to a norm than a regularity" not as the claim that a statement formulating a norm can be replaced by one reporting a regularity but rather as the claim that the causal explanation of how the norm came to exist is the same as the causal explanation of how the regularity came to exist. The difference between the two camps in contemporary philosophy of language boils down to the question of whether this difference makes any difference: whether a simple assertion of supervenience can replace a long series of analyses of meaning and can do so without loss of philosophical insight.

This question suggests the more general question: How much backup does an assertion that something is supervenient upon the physical need? If we say that the central problem of contemporary philosophy is to avoid falling into any sort of dualism, and thereby encouraging the believers in ectoplasm to come out of hiding, it may seem contemporary philosophers are preaching to the converted. For most readers of books, including many

---

[6] Robert B. Brandom, *Making It Explicit: Reasoning, Representing, and Discursive Commitment* (Cambridge, MA: Harvard University Press, 1994), 623.

devoutly religious readers, have long been convinced of the truth of physicalism, thought of as the claim that, in Frank Jackson's formulation, "Any world which is a minimal physical duplicate of our world is a duplicate simpliciter of our world"[7] and therefore a psychological duplicate, a sociological duplicate, a world containing all and only the norms found in our world, and a world in which all and only the same states of affairs are necessary or possible. Fear of spooks, and gratitude for allaying such fears, are simply not much in evidence in the high culture of the West.

I shall come back to this question of the utility of philosophy of language for the culture as a whole later. For the moment I simply want to note that Brandom's reason for regarding modal terms as respectable cannot be a reductionist's reason, and so his explanation of why these concepts are now so widely accepted fails as a sociological account.

Reductionists like Jackson want to know what physical states of affairs make normative or modal statements true. As Jackson puts it, "serious metaphysics requires us to address when matters described in one vocabulary are made true by matters described in another."[8] Brandom's assurance that normative discourse is inevitable, in the sense that it must be deployed if any discourse is to be deployed, and that modal discourse can be boiled down to normative discourse, is of no help in addressing that question.

Brandom's own strategy can be of no help in what he calls, citing Dretske, the reductionist project of making intentional soup out of non-intentional bones. Brandom tells us what we cannot do without doing something else – what inferential moves we have to be able to make if we are to wield this or that concept. But telling us which inferences and concepts are parasitic on which others does nothing to help us single out the meanings of expressions, or delimit what a given expression expresses or what a certain true sentence is made true by.

I take it that Brandom has never doubted that a physical duplicate of our world would contain all and only the norms found in our world, but I doubt that he has ever been attracted by what Jackson calls "conceptual analysis, understood as the business of finding necessary and sufficient conditions by the method of possible cases" – that is, the method of figuring out what intuition tells us we should say in various fantastic and unforeseeable situations.[9] This method is, Jackson thinks, admirably illustrated by Putnam's discovery that the watery stuff on Twin Earth is not

---

[7] Frank Jackson, *From Metaphysics to Ethics: A Defense of Conceptual Analysis* (New York: Oxford University Press, 1998), 12.
[8] Ibid., 41.   [9] Ibid., 60.

a different kind of water, but not water at all, and by Gettier discovering that justified true belief is insufficient for knowledge.

From Brandom's point of view, if I understand it properly, nothing of any particular philosophical interest could possibly turn on whether we agree with Gettier or Putnam or instead have intuitions, as Jackson admits some people do, which lead us to use "knowledge" or "water" differently than these philosophers think we should. Only those who think that there are such things as intensions that determine the limits of extensions in the way that cookie cutters determine the limits of cookies could take an interest in the question of what intuitions should prevail. If you do not think that there are such things, then you will treat controversies about whether there is no water, or just a different kind of water, on Twin Earth as of little value for establishing the truth of physicalism as controversies about how many sacraments Christ instituted. You will think that once the two different sets of inferences from the sentence "XYZ is the common drinkable clear liquid on Twin Earth" drawn by the people with conflicting intuitions have been made explicit, and once the two different sets of inferences which Lutherans and Catholics draw from the sentence "This is the ordination of a priest" have been made equally explicit, nothing can turn on the further question of whether or how these two sentences are made true by what physically described states of affairs.

Presumably Jackson would see Brandom's book's adhesion to physicalism as what he calls an "act of faith," unless Brandom is willing to go on to the heavy lifting which consists in conceptual analysis.[10] Obviously, however, Brandom's book is not just a negligent, matter-of-course assertion of the supervenience of the normative on the physical. It is more like a tour through the sequence of events which was the coming to be of norms, intentionality, modality, and all the other things which to philosophers might be evidence of spooks having been at work. But that description, too, is misleading. For Brandom is not giving us a chronology of events but rather an explanation of how these things could not have come to be unless certain other things – anaphoric reference, singular terms, and scare quotes, for example – had also emerged. It is more like a biologist saying, "Before you could get what we call sight, you had to have tissues of this sort and that sort and the other sort," than like the same biologist saying, "First this happened and then that happened and then, for the first time in the history of the planet, at exactly 2:42 PM, an organism saw something."

---

[10] See ibid., 29.

Any biologist who said something of the latter sort would be exceeding both her competence and our degree of interest in the subject. All we really want to know is that she understands how evolution managed to bring the trick off. We only want enough details to help us grasp what sort of thing it took to get the job done. This is what Brandom gives us. He asks a question that philosophers have rarely asked: How many moves of what sort have to be made before we can say, "Hey, those organisms are giving reasons now!"

Jonathan Bennett, in his admirable little book *Rationality*, asked whether bees counted as rational. He concluded that they did not, if only because their so-called language lacked both quantifiers and a negation operator.[11] Brandom starts by going down the path that Bennett broke, but he extends it far beyond anything Bennett envisaged. His answer to the question "What does it take to be rational?" is, in one way, very familiar: to be rational you have to use logic. But his explanation of just why any species that is going to use patterns of marks and noises to glue together large groups of its members to engage in cooperative projects is going to have to be able to formulate and endorse all the inferences found in the elementary logic books is novel indeed.

Brandom describes his own enterprise as insuring that "the *advent* of intentionality not be left seeming magical or mysterious."[12] Anyone willing to regard the psychological as supervenient on the physical will have already concluded that it was neither. But to be told that the advent of logic is simultaneous with the advent of the psychological is surprising. For we tend to think of logic standing to thought as form to matter: bringing order out of chaos, constraining unruly impulses. It is startling to be told, as Brandom tells us, that it is not irrational but the common lot of mankind to have inconsistent beliefs. It is equally startling to be told that there is no such thing as irrational thinking, as opposed to thinking that defeats the reasonable expectations of a human community.

One way to describe the change in philosophical climate that Brandom wishes to bring about in our understanding of the relation between logic and psychology is to note that the Platonic tripartite division of the soul – a division that Descartes accepted without substantial alteration – inclined us to envisage a human being who acts responsibly as having had the lower and worse parts of his soul constrained by the higher and better part. In contrast, Brandom tells us that the only constraint is of the individual

[11] Jonathan Bennett, *Rationality: An Essay Towards an Analysis* (Indianapolis, IN: Hackett, 1989).
[12] Robert Brandom, "Modality, Normativity, and Intentionality," *Philosophy and Phenomenological Research* 63, no. 3 (2001): 607.

organism by the surrounding group of organisms. We have no responsibilities to either the moral law or the laws of logic which do not boil down to our responsibilities to live up to the trust reposed in us by the human beings whom we encounter. Brandom is following up on the Wittgensteinian/Rylean debunking of the Platonic/Cartesian idea of the mind as an extra ingredient added to our animal nature by saying that what makes us human is the relations of trust which bind us together with other members of our species.

This line of thought would probably have sounded to Russell, Husserl, and Carnap like a reversion to the psychologism from which Frege purportedly helped save us. But Brandom's sociologism can also be seen as a way of rescuing us from psychologism – or at least the Cartesian brand of psychologism which interprets mentality as something a human being can have all by herself. The object rescued by both philosophical initiatives is the same: it is the erring individual who needs a greater sense of responsibility. But for Brandom the source of rescue is not nonempirical and ahistorical but simply a historically contingent group of people.

Brandom can answer Wittgenstein's rhetorical question "Why did we think that logic was something sublime?" by saying "Because we thought that we could appeal from local communities to something universal, and because we confused universality with necessary existence." Logic is indeed universal, but only because it is implicit in anything we call linguistic practice. Once we follow Quine and Davidson in seeing that charity is necessary for translation, we can see that we are never going to come across anything that can be called a systematically illogical or systematically irrational use of language. The worst we can encounter is a set of conversational partners who disagree with us on a large range of topics.

The sociologism which Brandom recommends as a way of saving logic from psychologism amounts to saying that we should obey the rules of logic not because they stand augustly above the world of time and chance but because doing so enables us to cooperate with other people. Logic's constraint is not the constraint that the permanent and stable exercises on the transitory, nor the mastery that form exerts on matter, but the constraint that the group exercises on the potentially uncooperative individual.

2. Brandomian Semantics as Therapy and as Natural History

Suppose we define semantics as spelling out the meanings of various linguistic utterances, and then define Brandomian semantics as treating the meaning of an utterance as the deontic score chalked up against it. Then we shall have to say that for Brandomians there will not be just one meaning of an utterance but as many meanings as there are relevantly distinguishable deontic score-keepers. Unless there is a way of privileging some score-keepers over others, however, there will be no way of using semantics to criticize anybody's utterances.

Brandom does not, as far as I can see, give us such a way. He never intervenes in disputes between score-keepers in order to bring greater clarity. For his position requires him to leave deontic score-keeping to the relevant linguistic community, a community which may be a tiny expert culture or may be the public as a whole. The Brandomian philosopher of language agrees with Quine that we must abandon the "museum" notion of meaning – meanings considered as a set of enduring and unchanging objects labeled by linguistic expressions – but breaks with Quine over the question of whether philosophy, as opposed to the arts and the sciences, can show that some linguistic expressions are better for us to use than others. For Quine as for Carnap, the philosopher of language can still be of use to the culture critic. For Brandom as for Davidson, he cannot. Once one drops the myth of the museum, these latter philosophers say, you are not in a position to tell anybody what they are "really" talking about when they use a certain expression. Nor are you in a position to tell them that their use of language is confused. At best, you might be able to say that it is unusual or unproductive.

So what good is a philosopher of language who cannot diagnose unclarity or confusion? Well, one thing such a philosopher can do is to help the wider culture understand why no roads lead from an account of how deontic score-keeping works to a critique of contemporary score-keeping practices. This is something that needs to be done, because if you know how deontic score-keeping works, you know all that will ever be known about intentionality and therefore about such traditionally dark and deep subjects as "the nature of the mind." If the notion of culture criticism can be broadened so as to include the activity of explaining to people why philosophy will not do some of the things sometimes expected of it, then Brandom, Davidson, and Wittgenstein can count as culture critics.

To try to get from Brandomian semantics to cultural criticism in a narrower sense – the sort of culture criticism Carnap and Popper thought they were practicing – would be like trying to get from an understanding of what it takes for a social practice to count as a card game to a critique of the various games included in Hoyle. To make more explicit what Hoyle takes for granted does not help one decide whether to play poker or bridge. To make explicit why you have to have anaphora in order to have singular terms does not help you decide which singular terms to use or what inferences to make from any particular utterance containing the ones you do use.

Brandom's book can only have the desirable therapeutic effect I am imputing to it, however, for those who accept the claim that there is nothing deep and dark about the mind save the irreducibility of the intentional and the further claim that the latter boils down to the irreducibility of the normative. Nobody is going to bother reading *Making It Explicit* who is not prepared to see these claims as at least plausible suggestions. (That is why reading it would be profitless for Searle or Nagel, for example.) Persons not so prepared will not be impressed by the argument for the ineliminability of the normative that I summarized above, and modal discourse will still seem to them as requiring something like possible-world semantics before it can be made respectable.

At this point it is fair to ask: what does Brandom tell those of us who had already accepted both theses that we did not know before? What exactly does his neologism "deontic score-keeping" add to the familiar notion of language-game? Perhaps the simplest answer is: he shows us what the constraints on the use of marks and noises are that makes it possible for us to be said to be *reasoning* rather than simply sounding off in habitual and accepted ways. The reason that *Making It Explicit* is six hundred pages of heavy lifting rather than two hundred pages of debunking aphorisms is that nobody before has ever combined the virtues of *Philosophical Investigations* with those of *Tractatus Logico-Philosophicus*. Nobody has explained why languages have to be pretty much as they are if they are to serve the purposes they do, other than philosophers who think that the main purpose they serve is to represent states of elementary physical particles with the help of handy abbreviations.

For Brandom, in contrast, the main purpose languages serve is to enable us to engage in cooperative projects of a complexity significantly greater than those of the bees and the beavers. Languages are as they are because, for example, language users have to have anaphora, scare quotes, and singular terms to get that job done. It turns out that you would not be able to give and ask for reasons if you had not mastered these basic moves, just as you would not be able to construct a catapult or a computer if you had not mastered the lever, the pulley, and the other so-called simple machines. The difference between Brandom's conception of logic and those of Russell, Carnap, and Husserl is the difference between something that is owed respect – especially if we want to do what most becomes a human being, represent reality accurately – and something that we have to use in order to get a lot of things we want. This difference goes along with the difference between making representations fall out of inferences and treating inferences as a way of juggling representations.

17

Remarks on Nishida and Nishitani

My colleague Norihide Suto kindly suggested a few texts by Kitarō Nishida and Keiji Nishitani that I might read in order to get some sense of the intellectual tradition of Otani University. I am very grateful to him for doing so. Obviously, my knowledge of these authors is extremely super-ficial, and I am almost entirely unable to relate the few texts I have read to the Buddhist background of these philosophers' thought. Nevertheless, reading these texts made me think that a few remarks about the relation between pragmatism and absolute idealism might form a useful preface to the four lectures on pragmatism that I shall be giving.

Many of the arguments which Nishida and Nishitani find in Western authors such as Leibniz, Spinoza, and Hegel, and which both enthusiasti-cally endorse, are variations on the following set of inferences:

1. To know an object is not to get an accurate mental picture of it in isolation from all other things, but, on the contrary, to put it in relation to other things.
2. So to know an object completely, adequately, as it truly is, would be to put it in relation to all other things.
3. So knowledge of any object, including a human self, requires knowl-edge of all things, interrelated in one coherent system. In a sense, there is only one object to be known. Plurality is an illusion.
4. Such knowledge would be knowledge of what Spinoza called "God or Nature." To have such knowledge would be to experience what Hegel thought of as the final union of subject and object, Man and God – the Absolute Self-Consciousness of Spirit.

Call this chain of inferences the Argument from Holism to Monism. Holism, in this sense, is the doctrine that we should reject the atomism of, for example, Aristotle and Locke (who thought of intellectual or sensory intuition as sufficient to grasp the full nature of certain entities). Instead, we should think that a thing is nothing but its relations to everything else.

This argument is found in many anglophone philosophers of the late nineteenth century, such as T. H. Green, F. H. Bradley, and Josiah Royce. Of these, the adherent of absolute idealism best known to the founders of pragmatism was Royce, whose books (such as *The Religious Aspect of Philosophy* and *The World and the Individual*) were very popular in the United States at the beginning of this century. Royce believed, as Nishida also did, that there was a purely philosophical, argumentative, route to the same thought as is found in many religious writers: the thought that ultimate self-knowledge consists in the realization of the identity of the self with God. Like Nishida, Royce thought of the divine life as "an eternal now," and of self-knowledge as beginning when we realize that plural (e.g., spatiotemporal) existence is an internally inconsistent notion. Royce could easily have echoed Nishida's words: "The self is authentic only when it knows its own eternal death. Once we have grasped this fact, we find ourselves already existing in eternal life."[1]

James and Dewey were personally acquainted with Royce and thoroughly familiar with his views and his arguments. But they saw the Argument from Holism to Absolute Idealism as a *reductio ad absurdum* of the metaphysical, intellectualist, tradition. They thought absolute idealism to be a dead end.

Pragmatism is an emphatic reaction against Hegel, against absolute idealism, and against metaphysics – a reaction made possible by the need which philosophers such as James, Dewey, and Nietzsche felt to come to terms with Darwin's theory of evolution. This reaction consisted in saying that knowledge – in the sense of adequate representation of, or union with, an object – is not the aim of human life. What we call the pursuit of knowledge should be seen as the pursuit of successful action – where "successful" means "conducive to greater human happiness." This means that we should drop the idea of "complete" or "adequate" knowledge (either of the self or of anything else) as the goal, or even as one goal, of human life. Instead, we should think of ourselves as clever animals.

On this view, our goal in scientific, political, and other inquiries is simply to grasp the relations between those features of our situation which we want to change and other features which we do not, so as to acquire efficacious tools for improving that situation. We should not say, as Nishida and Spinoza both would, that "rational existence can never contain self-contradictions in itself," but rather the opposite: that rational

[1] Kitarō Nishida, "The Logic of *Topos* and the Religious Worldview: Part II," trans. Yusa Michiko, *The Eastern Buddhist* 20, no. 1 (1987): 87.

existence is precisely the process of dealing with contradictions, not in order to come to a contradiction-free state but in order to solve the practical problems which those contradictions create.

We may think of Dewey as countering the Argument from Holism to Idealism with the following Argument from Holism to Pragmatism:

1. To know an object completely would be, impossibly, to know its relations to all other objects – and thereby to know everything about everything.

2. Since this is an impossible ideal, we must abandon the very idea of "knowing an object completely" (and a fortiori of knowing the self completely or adequately or as it truly is).

3. We should stop thinking of knowledge as a union of subject with object, or of adequate representation of object by subject, and instead think of knowledge as skill in manipulating objects, including skill at redescribing them.

4. We should stop thinking of a human being's task as knowing himself or herself as he or she truly is (a conception which, in the West, goes back to the Greeks) and instead think of a human being's task as social cooperation with other human beings in building a better world – more specifically, building an egalitarian social utopia.

5. Changing our sense of the purpose of human life in this way will have the effect of secularizing culture. People will come to think of themselves as simply clever animals rather than as half-god and half-best, or half-divine and half-diabolical.

This Darwin-inspired "clever animal" line of thought was common to James and Dewey, but James left more space for religious experience than did Dewey. James believed that the kind of union between the self and the universe which mystics describe was possible and desirable, but he did not think of it as supportable by philosophical argument. He dropped the Argument from Holism to Monism and substituted a nonargumentative appreciation of the special states of consciousness which mystics and other religious persons have described. Dewey, on the other hand, had no interest in religious experience, except for a kind of vaguely pantheistic, nonecstatic sense of community with the universe (of the sort described by Wordsworth).

James and Dewey wrote before the so-called linguistic turn in philosophy. They still talked about experience rather than about language. Later pragmatists, however, were influenced by Frege, Russell, and Carnap. Such figures as Wilfrid Sellars and Donald Davidson asserted not only that the only difference between ourselves and the animals is our ability to use language but that, as Sellars put it in announcing his doctrine of "psychological nominalism": all awareness is a linguistic affair. For Sellars, Davidson, and myself, the animals and the prelinguistic infants are capable of conditioned responses to stimuli, but they do not know anything. To have knowledge of something is to place statements about that thing within the social practice of justification – of giving and asking for reasons.

Following up this line of thought, one will say, with Nelson Goodman, that there is no Way the World Is. One will also echo James's and Dewey's claim that truth is not a matter of corresponding to the intrinsic nature of reality but rather of finding efficient tools for self-improvement – where self-improvement is a matter of achieving more and better forms of happiness. From this point of view, the trouble with absolute idealism is that it does not help with the projects of social cooperation (building an egalitarian, classless, casteless society, for example), whose furtherance should be the aim of philosophy. It is no help to the poor and suffering to be told that plurality is an illusion.

Dewey thought a certain idea propounded by both Plato and Aristotle had done the West a great deal of harm: the idea that there is an activity called contemplation which is more truly human – and more important for a fulfilled human life – than such sociopolitical projects. Dewey thought that overcoming this idea was essential for revitalizing Western philosophy. (He used *Reconstruction in Philosophy* as the title of the lectures he gave in Tokyo immediately after World War I. In my opinion, these lectures make up his best book.) Although Dewey had himself been an absolute idealist in his youth (a period when he was also a fervent Christian), his turn toward Darwin led him to regard the pursuit of self-knowledge as an unfortunate distraction from more worthwhile enterprises.

For pragmatists, as for Nietzsche, the whole idea of self-knowledge – of finding out what one really is, as Socrates wanted to do – is a bad one. The ambition of self-knowledge needs to be replaced with the ambition of self-creation. The self is nothing save a constantly self-reweaving network of beliefs and desires. The point of thinking is to enlarge this network and to make it more coherent, rather than to find something which lies behind and is presupposed by this network. So Nishida and Descartes and the Greeks are wrong to think of human beings as specifically intellectual creatures, where "intellectual" is explicated as "capable of knowing how things really are, of penetrating through appearance to reality." Humans, like the other animals, are seekers after happiness, and talk of "the human intellect" is simply a way of referring to the fact that humans are able to use tools in this quest which animals incapable of language (and thus of social cooperation) lack.

Dewey would have agreed with Kierkegaard that the Western intellectualist tradition which runs from the Greeks to Hegel takes as its fundamental assumption that "self-knowledge is a knowledge of God." Kierkegaard, like Nietzsche, protested against this assumption from the individualistic perspective we have come to call existentialist. Dewey, and such later writers as Sellars and Davidson, protest against it from the social perspective of democratic humanism.

From the latter perspective, the great world religions have provided consolation to the victims of social injustice but have not done enough to change society so as to minimize such injustice. The task of a thoroughly secularized philosophy will be to contribute to efforts to make this world better, rather than deferring human hope to another world. It is useful to think of Marx and Dewey as two men who both started off as Hegelians, turned Left, and wound up keeping only as much of Hegel as was compatible with Darwin

When Deweyans like myself read Nishida or Nishitani, there is of course much that we can agree with. In particular, we can agree with their preference for Leibniz and Spinoza over the British Empiricists, and agree that the latter did not understand that the quest for knowledge is the attempt to relate things to one another. On the other hand, we are deeply suspicious of "religions of absolute dependence," a phrase Nishida uses to describe both Christianity and Buddhism.

The democratic humanism which motivated Dewey takes as its first principle that we human beings are on our own: that we can look for help to nothing save our fellow humans. As Yeats put it, "Whatever flames upon the night / Man's own resinous heart has fed." So when Nishida says that "situations of extreme misfortune . . . are bound to awake religious awareness in every one of us,"[2] Dewey would agree with Nietzsche that this is a reason to be suspicious of religious awareness. Dewey would insist that human beings should band together to minimize the possibility of situations of extreme misfortune, rather than seeking consolation in the nontemporal.

Consider the following passage from part II of Nishida's "The Logic of Topos and the Religious Worldview." He writes as follows: "Certainly there is no reason why human beings have to be religious, particularly if one

---

[2] Kitarō Nishida, "The Logic of Topos and the Religious Worldview," trans. Yusa Michiko, The Eastern Buddhist 19, no. 2 (1986), 1.

postulates social existence as the foundation of self-existence. One might also deal with the problem of life and death from the standpoint of society. But is it not human existence that lies at the ground of society?"[3] I take it that Nishida is saying that although one can attempt to replace religion with sociopolitical hope, this attempt is bound to fail. It will not work because it neglects the nature of the human self, the nature of human existence.

Dewey would rejoin that there is no such thing as the nature of human existence, or of the human self. Human beings are, apart from their merely biological attributes, what culture makes them. You can construct a new sort of human being by creating a new sort of culture (or, with Nietzsche, by bravely attempting to turn oneself into the Overman). From a Darwinian point of view, the only thing that human beings have which is not malleable by culture are those extra neurons which enable us to use language.

But there is nothing of philosophical interest to be learned by studying what all human languages have in common. So philosophy should not aim at grasping the intrinsic nature of a stable and continuing object called human existence or the human self or human language. Rather, it should aim at changing the language we use – developing new ways of speaking, ways which will enable us to become happier people. The transition from medieval to modern Europe is an example of the development of new words which enabled people to do new things.

Dewey would indeed wish, in Nishida's words, to deal with "the problem of life and death from the standpoint of society." As he saw the matter, this problem was to be solved by persuading individuals to view their lives as contributions to a utopian human future, and their deaths as redeemed by the hope that their descendants would live in a better society. Whereas for Nishida, as for Kierkegaard, "only one who knows his own eternal death truly knows that he is an individual,"[4] for Dewey there is no eternal death as long as there has been a life which has contributed to social good. In that sense, as in many others, social existence is for Dewey "the foundation of self-existence." Social hope takes the place which Nishida reserved for Compassion.

To put all this another way, Dewey would deny the claim that Nishida formulates as follows: "At the bottom of the self there is something that utterly transcends us, and this something is neither foreign to nor external to us."[5] Dewey would rejoin that in this formula Nishida succeeds in neatly

---

[3] Kitarō Nishida, "The Logic of *Topos*," Part II, 82.   [4] Kitarō Nishida, "The Logic of *Topos*," 18.
[5] Kitarō Nishida, "The Logic of *Topos*," Part II, 85.

encapsulating the central doctrine of the Western metaphysical tradition. But Dewey wants us to abandon that tradition. It should be abandoned not because it has been refuted but because the attempt to build a better world on the basis of this metaphysical doctrine has been a failed social experiment. We should simply turn our back on this experiment, rather than reappropriating it (as both Nishida and Heidegger would have had us do).

Nishitani wrote that "wherever there are finite beings – and all things are finite – there must be nihility; wherever there is life, there must be death. In the face of death and nihility, all life and experience lose their certainty and their importance as reality, and come to look unreal instead. From time immemorial man has continually expressed this fleeting transience of life and existence, likening it to a dream, a shadow, or the shimmering haze of the summer's heat."[6]

Dewey's reaction to this passage would be: It is true that this comparison has been made from time immemorial, but drawing this comparison has not produced any useful results. It has been an obstacle to social progress rather than a help. So let us stop making this comparison and throw the process into reverse. Let us instead think of the infinite, the complete, the self-contained, the perfect as "a shadow, a dream a shimmering haze." Dewey's attitude is the epitome of what Nishitani called "progress atheism."

I do not know how to resolve the issue between Nishitani and Dewey, and I shall make no attempt to do so in the lectures that follow. Instead, I shall be sharpening the differences between them, by presenting as coherent a defense of pragmatism as I can. One way to bring Eastern and Western philosophical traditions together is to emphasize their many similarities. I shall be doing the opposite and shall be trying to make the differences as striking as I can. I think of the struggle in the West between metaphysics, culminating in absolute idealism, and progress atheism, culminating in the linguistified pragmatism of Sellars and Davidson, as mirroring certain aspects of the East-West tension. I hope that this tension may be clarified by restating the case for the Western philosophical tradition which has least in common with Eastern thought.

---

[6] Keiji Nishitani, *Religion and Nothingness*, trans. Jan Van Bragt (Berkeley: University of California Press, 1982), 7.

Index of Names

247